THE WEEPING ROOM

Larry B. Hill

"This book is dedicated to the memory of my cousin, the late Robert "Butch" Shivers. Before his death at a young age, Butch revealed to me his artistic talent, which for some reason, was hidden to the world. He was on the same talent level as Vincent Van Gogh, Leonardo Da Vinci and a few others in ancient world art. A few years before his untimely and mysterious death, he destroyed all of his paintings. RIP Butch!! I will always love you, my cousin."

Peaceful is when a spider can spin its web in a quiet hallway undisturbed. Quiet is when a butterfly can flap its wings, and happily fly around down in the basement, and land on the back of a sleeping cat in order to rest for a while. Peace and quiet is when a single drop of water from the upstairs bathroom sink causes the spider to stop spinning, and go into combat mode. The butterfly becomes frightened, and leaves the comfort of the cat's fur, and lands on the doorknob of a locked room.

The cat opens its eyes, and looks around, detecting nothing out of the ordinary. All is well. The spider starts spinning its web again. The cat closes its eyes again. However, the butterfly is more frightened than ever. The doorknob that it just landed on is giving off a terrifying vibration. The butterfly can't hear anything from inside the room because the room is soundproof. However, it feels that something terrifying is going on behind this door. It starts flapping its wings again. The spider spins faster after noticing the butterfly confused and in distress. The cat starts walking around in circles. There is now total chaos and confusion in this small quiet animal kingdom.

There are millions, perhaps billions of doors on this planet. Some doors are not to be opened at all, unless opened by a professional and only then, in an absolute emergency. No one should open the emergency door of a plane while it is in flight. It is alright to open the door that leads to a college English class. Behind some doors are rooms with no people at all in them. Behind other doors we can expect to find rooms with people in them. These people could be doing something or doing nothing at all. They could be sitting quietly playing chess or they could be sitting on the floor watching television.

They could also be sitting quietly building bombs. Good things could be happening in a certain room or bad things could be happening in a certain room. A person could turn the door knob of a room, and walk into his or her surprise birthday party: "Surprise!!" Another person could turn a door knob of a room, and walk into a waiting ambush: "Oh my Lord! Please don't hurt me!" A lovely young woman could walk through the door of a tour bus. She takes a seat next a well-dressed clean shaven young man. Then, after the bus is full of passengers, the clean shaven young man stands up, and shouts out these words: "God is great!!" He then presses down on a detonator button, and blows up the bus; killing most of the passengers instantly. When it comes to walking through doors; be very careful. Behind the door that had the butterfly in so much distress, is a room of sheer terror. If you are ready, let's step right on through it.

THE CHAIR

"Praise his name!!! Jesus!!! Jesus!!! Wash me in the blood!!!"

The small gathering of homeless men and women were totally into what the preacher was preaching about. There were twelve of them, hand picked by Preacher man—representing the twelve disciples of Jesus—to follow him into a rundown vacant apartment building that was set to be torn down in about three months.

"Throw down your fishing nets, follow me, and I will make you fishers of men" is what he told the group of Long Beach drunks, prostitutes, crack heads and heroin addicts. Long Beach California was full of these kinds of run-down people. But he wanted to only preach to twelve at a time. So, he moved his version of the twelve disciples away from the main drag, and into a quiet environment, so that they can really focus on his message.

Folks along the California beach community called him: Preacher Man. And he could indeed preach!! He got his certification from his father back in Plains Iowa. His father—who is a powerful preacher himself—required that his son preach twelve trial sermons at their church before he presented him with his papers to preach.

"The angle told the Virgin Mary that she is pregnant, and she will carry the savior of the world in her belly!!

"Preach the word, preacher man!!" An old black drunk shouted out.

"When Mary told Joseph, the man she was promised to, he became angry!! He told Mary that she had committed the sin of adultery, since he had never laid down with her. He was well within his right to cancel the engagement. Also, according to the laws of Moses, Mary could be stoned to death. Do you hear me disciples? Stoned to death!!"

"I would never want that to happen to me, preacher man..." A young white woman, that was a heroin addict softly told preacher man. She was rubbing the inside of her elbow that was full of needle tracks. She needed a hit bad. However, she did not move away from the group. She—although hurting for dope—was really digging what preacher man was preaching about.

"You are right young lady; I would not want that to happen to me either...It had to be a terrible way to die. However, that was the law back then. However, guess what happened right before Joseph was about to report Mary to the elders?" Twelve sets of bulging eyeballs intensely looked to preacher man for the answer.

"An angel came to Joseph and told him that his young future bride had not committed adultery. The baby she was carrying was the prince of peace and the son of God. The angel told Joseph to marry Mary...and that is what he did."

"Alright preacher man!! Things worked out fine and dandy!!" An old white woman that was a crack addict shouted out.

"And that my friends, was the beginning of the New Testament. The old laws of Moses were about to leave the earth, because Jesus was about to bring about a new way of living. Jesus would bring about love and forgiveness. Now don't that sound good to everyone?"

"Yeah, I like the sound of that. We need more love in this world!!" A white alcoholic young man shouted out.

"My friends, you all have had a hard life. You have been kicked around and spit on by society. Are you ready to give your life to Jesus? Are you ready to turn your life around? Are you ready to walk with the man from Galilee? Are you ready for a brand-new life?"

"We ready preacher man...damn right we ready." The old black drunk shouted. All twelve of them turned their heads to each other and nodded in agreement.

"Well then, if that's the case...it's now communion time." Preacher man said, as he reached in his backpack, and pulled out a pack of saltine crackers. He then pulled out a pair of white gloves and broke a few of the crackers into small pieces, then gave everyone a piece.

"Jesus said, eat this, for it is my body." Everyone ate their small piece of cracker. He then reached into the backpack, and pulled out twelve small paper cups, and gave each one a cup. Reaching back into the backpack, he pulled out a quart bottle of Wild Irish Rose wine. "My favorite!!" The old black drunk shouted. Almost everyone laughed. Preacher man frowned at the outburst. The bottle was about half full, however, it was more than enough for twelve small paper cups.

"Jesus said, drink this, for it is my blood." Everyone eagerly turned up their cups to their waiting lips.

Preacher man turned away from the group, faced the dirty wall, and silently began to pray. After about two minutes—one by one—the twelve people slowly began dropping to the floor. The wine contained a powerful knock out ingredient. The bodies dropped in different positions. Some fell backwards, some sideways, and some forwards.

Preacher man reached into the backpack and pulled out a black towel and an icepick. After putting the almost empty wine bottle back into the backpack, he walked over to the bodies. He did not reposition any of the bodies. If all the heads were clearly visible, everything was all good. He bent over and stuck the sharp point of the icepick into the forehead of the old black drunk. He pushed it all the way into the skull until it entered the brain. Then he pulled the icepick out and put his finger to the tiny hole outside the skull and pressed hard. Then he wiped the metal part of the icepick clean with the black towel. Investigators will have a hard time trying to learn the cause of death. Next, he moved over to the young white girl that was a heroin addict. She had fallen on her side. Preacher man stuck the ice pick through her temple and quickly entered the brain. He slowly and carefully went through this procedure on all twelve victims. After finishing up, he put the towel, gloves and icepick back into the backpack. Before walking out the door, he looked back at the still bodies and said one final prayer to the lord.

"Dear Lord, take the souls of these lowly beings, and keep them safe with thee for eternity. They have been through so much; trying to exist in this cruel world. I have done as you commanded me to do. I trust that you are pleased. Amen."

As he walked back towards his apartment, he made up his mind to leave California. He had moved up and down the beach communities of Northern and Southern California for about two years now. He had killed about two hundred people in this state. If he stayed much longer, law enforcement would most likely one day find out that a preacher was killing people, and find out the identity of the preacher, whose name is Gunther Heisman.

Now is the time to see what had the butterfly so filled with distress in a different state in America, a gulf state. The West Coast was now a place of Gunther's past life.

Something terrifying is happening on the other side of the door. The butterfly was now flying into the door as if it wanted to hurt itself. It flew around in circles, then repeatedly flew into the door. Landing on the floor, it flapped it wings, and went through the same process repeatedly. Can an insect go insane? I think so.

In the room on the other side of the doorknob, a man of great physical beauty is marching back and forth in a high kicking goose step. His right arm is stretched out in front his face and his palm is faced down. His face is glistening with sweat as he kept on marching back and forth.

Now perspiration is beginning to form all over his half naked body as he had been marching this way for over sixteen minutes. The right arm that is extended began to shake from the pain of holding in place. However, the man kept on marching back and forth for another four minutes. He then stopped, and faced a lean and naked Caucasian man with brown eyes, ghostly pale skin and black hair that was cut very short. At the moment he was tightly strapped into a huge brown chair made of Oakwood.

The chair is the original Ole' Smokey; the electric chair used in prison electrocutions in South Carolina. The only thing missing from the chair was the metal headgear used to shoot the juice to the brain. All the other restraining gear was intact, and at this very moment was being put to use. The naked causation man's skinny body jerked involuntarily when the marching man moved in closer.

Thick leather straps were tightly bound around the skinny man's ankles, arms, torso, and legs.

The half-naked man—clad in only a pair of white boxer shorts— had been marching back and forth is also causation and has a deep tan on his face and body. It is obvious that he loves sunning himself in his back yard on sunny days in the summer. He also visits the local tanning booth in the fall and winter. He has a beautiful smooth face, bright blond close cut hair, sky blue eyes and a powerfully built body. He just might be the most beautiful man on the planet.

And he is also hopelessly insane.

He moved in even closer to the thin naked man.

When his beautiful blue eyes were about three inches from the thin man's watery brown eyes, the thin man began to scream even louder than before.

"Alright now, let's get this party started again. Break time is over with. Now I want you to stop acting like ah' little crying bitch!" the handsome man shouted.

The thin man continued to scream.

The handsome man stood back up, and walked over to where a red hot poker iron was laying on a bed of hot coals that he had inside a brick bowl near the furnish. The bowl was on a pit that was directly under a vent that sucked up the smoke into one of two chimneys that were built into the room.

He walked back over to the thin man, and held the hot end of the poker close to the thin man's face.

"If you don't stop all this crying and whimpering, I'm going to put this poker in your mouth. I'll shove the fuckin' thing down your miserable throat."

The man in the chair just kept right on screaming.

"Hey, I've got a better idea. I think this option will be more effective if you want to continue your stubborn ways. I have never tried this method before. I am now very anxious to try it. You will be the very first. Now this is what I have in mind: I'm going to count to six, and if you're still screaming, I'm going to stick that ice pick in your eye," he said, pointing to an ice pick he had placed on a table nearby.

He put the hot end of the poker into a bucket of water. Steam rose up from the bucket as the poker quickly cooled.

Then the handsome man picked up the ice pick from the small table next to the wooden chair. He positioned the point of the ice pick very close to the left eye.

With his left pointer and thumb he opened the man's eye lid wide, and kept it open. The man's eye lashes were now in contact with the sharp point of the pick.

The handsome man was looking at the skinny man's eyeball just as if he were an eye doctor giving the man an eye examination. He wanted to do his job precise. After all, just like an eye doctor, he too was a perfectionist.

"Alright my man, here goes nothing: One…two…three…four… five…"

Please Lord, take control of my emotions. I need to stop crying right now.

The skinny man all of a sudden stopped crying.

Thank you Lord.

"Now that's better. I knew you could do it," the handsome man said; now pulling the ice pick away from the skinny man's eye, and placing it back on the table.

"Now I want you to keep that trap of yours shut, and listen to what I am going to say to you. You need to man up. Your very life is in my hands now. You need to get in the game, and stay focused. The answer you give to my questions will determine if you live or die."

He turned around, and walked over to a portrait of Adolf Hitler hanging on the back wall. He stood in silence for about ten minutes. It was obvious that he was in *time out…*

Fifteen-year-old Gunther was in the middle of his seventh trial sermon. He was preaching up a storm. A few members of the congregation were running around the sanctuary, hands waving over their heads and screaming out testimonies. A few members sitting in the congregation had passed out… ushers were trying to revive them with wet towels. His father was standing in the pulpit behind his son with his arms raised towards the ceiling, shouting: "Praise the lord!!" The one thing everyone in the church knew for a fact: young Jesse could preach his little ass off!!

After coming out of *timeout*, he walked back over to the skinny man, and peered deeply into his eyes. The skinny man once again started screaming…

The screams caused the handsome man to go into a rage. He began punching the skinny man over and over again on his left ear with his right hand. After about ten hard punches; the skinny man finally stopped screaming.

"Now let's try this again. I've given you much longer than the twenty minute break that I intended for you to have. Your mind should be clear by now. Instead, you start screaming your fuckin' head off just as soon as I came near you. Try manning up, and quit acting like a little skinny bitch."

He then walked over to the Hitler portrait, folded his arms across his bare hairless chest, and looked intensely into the eyes of a fellow madman.

Over the years, he had become a Hitler scholar. He had studied just about everything thing there was to learn about the late German ruler. He had grown to love him.

"What I want to hear is what do you think about Hitler the man? What do you think about his plan to wipe out a whole section of the population? Although I don't agree with his method; do you think it took sheer genius and imagination to come up with his final solution to solve his Jewish problem? What say you? I want you to be honest, and don't hold anything back."

The man in the chair said nothing; he only closed his eyes, and thought about his family at home. He wondered what they were doing right about now.

The handsome man walked back over to the table, and picked up the ice pick again. Without hesitation, he walked back over to the skinny man, and stuck the point of the icepick through the man's jaw. It went all the way through, and lodged into his tongue. Surprisingly there were no loud screams this time; only a sick grunting sound.

"Peeeshh"…

The reason why there were no loud screams this time was because getting an ice pick thrust into his jaw was nothing compared to what he had already endured. An hour earlier the handsome man put the red hot poker iron to the man's dangling testicles. That made the man scream just like a women; a very frightened women. The scream reminded the handsome man about a movie he once saw. In this movie, a woman awoke from her sleep, and found a wolf man looking down at her. It was just that kind of a scream.

However, now the skinny man was feeling a different kind of pain; a much less painful kind of pain. An icepick through his jaw was no more than a pinch to him at that moment. This much lower level kind of pain allowed the skinny man to at least beg for mercy.

"Peeeshh…No mo…" "Peeeshh…No mo…"

The handsome man slowly pulled the icepick out of the man's jaw. He then stepped a few feet back from the man, and patiently waited for a response to his question.

After a few moments of silence from the two men, the handsome man started marching again. This time his legs kicked up higher, and his right outstretched arm was raised a little higher above his head.

The victim slowly raised his head; a head that looked like a ragdoll by this time.

Not only was he bleeding from the stab wound to the jaw; his eye lids were swollen from repeated blows from the handsome man's fists. His nose was broken, and his front teeth were knocked out.

The handsome man and the victim really got to know each other earlier. The handsome man really went off on the victim.

The handsome man suddenly stopped marching and looked intensely at the skinny man; anxious to finally get some answers to his questions.

The skinny man opened his mouth, and spoke as clearly as he could.

"AAAdofff HHHii Hithcceer…" He stopped to spit out a wad of blood from his mouth.

"Adoff Hithccer wasshh ah monsta' and he ishh burnen' en hell!"

Those were the last words that the banker said on planet earth.

He was going to leave this world defiant. He did not give the handsome man what he wanted. Instead, he called Hitler a monster, and said the monster was at this very moment burning in hell.

The handsome man was furious that this man would—in his last moments of his life—choose to badmouth his beloved supreme German Chancellor.

The handsome man closed his eyes, and remembered the things he had read about Hitler from books that he had mail ordered when he was a child.

In his mind he saw Hitler triumphantly standing up in the front passenger side of a huge six wheel Mercedes Benz, riding through his native Austria.

The driver, as well as the six other people riding in his car were all senior officers of the dreaded 'SS': the Secret State Police, and Hitler's personal body guards.

The car was an open top, thus he was exposed, and an easy target for a sniper hit. However, Hitler felt like he was divinely placed on earth for a heavenly purpose. Since he had already narrowly escaped numerous assassination attempts, he looked at himself to be invincible, and could not possibly be killed by a mere mortal.

There was no resistance to his invasion. The German chancellor waved his hand up and down with his elbow straight out to the side like a traffic cop. He must have felt like Alexander the Great at that moment. An entire country was too afraid of him to even try to defend itself. Thousands of people lined the streets with flowers and cheers.

"Hiel Hitler! Hiel Hitler! Hiel Hitler!" the people shouted.

"Welcome my grand leader!"

And they held up their children for him to see them.

"We stand ready to serve you my Fuhrer!"

The handsome man snapped out of his trance, and opened his eyes again.

"There is a ninety percent chance that I am going to pick up my trusty sledge hammer and bash your head down into your chest. Then I'm going to burn your body until there is nothing left of it but brittle bones. Then I will grind those bones into ashes," he said, quietly.

"I can do this because I am an undertaker."

"Then again there is always hope. There is a ten percent chance that you can convince me not to kill you. It's been done before," he said, once again doing the German goose step slowly back and forth across the room with a heavy iron sledge hammer resting on his shoulder.

"Once upon ah' time, there came a sailor from Spain. This sailor was on shore leave, and he was, like most sailors on leave, drunk. I met him on Bourbon Street while we were both enjoying the Mardi Gras parade. It was a good thing he spoke fluent English, because that lucky bastard gave me a speech that I still hear in my head, even to this day. It was just that good. He was calm, cool and collective. He totally convinced me that he would never tell the cops or anyone else as long as he lived if I would just spare his life," he said, still marching as if he were a German storm trooper in a parade, with his right arm extended, legs kicking high, and sweaty white hips pumping.

"He promised me that if I let him go, he would quickly return to his ship, and stay there. He said that when his ship leaves port, that would be the last time he would find himself in America; and he promised to never return," he said, now stopping directly in front of the man.

He bent down so that his eyes were directly in from of the skinny man's puffy eyes. He peered into the skinny man's slightly opened eye lids as if he were looking for something that he had lost. After about fifteen seconds of searching, he stood back up straight, and continued his story.

"After much thought, I loosened the sailor's straps, and off he went, like an Olympic sprinter going for the gold. He even left his clothes behind. The idea of him getting arrested for indecent exposure obviously did not cross his mind. To this day I regret not killing him. I keep getting a sick feeling in my mind that one day he is going to tell someone," he said, sticking a raised pointy finger up to his lips as to say, *don't tell anyone about what you've seen or heard.*

"So for the final time, what do you really think of the genius of Adolf Hitler? And this time I want the right response! You will not get another chance!"

With that said, the handsome man walked over to a foldout chair near the door, and sat down.

Instead of saying the right thing, the man said nothing at all. The man showed incredible bravery in this truly dire situation. He had already made his last statement, and he was sticking to it. He knew he was doomed, and made up his mind to go out like a man.

He thought about his wife and three children back in Boston. He now wished he had hugged them longer at the airport. He wished he had French kissed his wife instead of the peck on the lips as if they were two children experimenting with their first kiss.

And he thought about the first time he laid eyes on this homicidal maniac disguised as the most beautiful man he had ever seen in his life.

About five hours earlier, around nine that night, he walked into Pat O'Brian's, a very popular and world famous watering hole on Bourbon Street in the French Quarter in New Orleans. After buying a much talked about drink called 'The Hurricane', he slowly strolled around looking at all the happy faces.

Sitting at one of the back tables were two gorgeous women, one white and one black. There was a blond haired man sitting with them, however, he had his back turned talking to a waiter. Now the man skinny man, who was a banker by trade, walked over to the table, and asked the black woman for permission to join them. He had a thing for black women anyway. The woman pointed to the only empty chair at the table; he gladly sat down.

Just as he was leaning over to whisper something into the ear of the black woman, the man that had his back to him turned around…

The banker's jaw dropped…

He was nowhere near gay, but he felt something inside of him that he never felt before. He had an appreciation for beauty. The man he was looking at was beauty to the max. He wanted to reach out, and touch the blond man. However, he quickly dismissed the urge. After all, he liked pussy, especially black pussy. But he could envision this man being hit on by hundreds of weak minded men. He introduced himself to the man, and proceeded on whispering romantic words into the ear of the black woman.

But after several rounds of drinks, he found himself sitting next the man, and very close. It wasn't only the man's beauty that fascinated him; it was his knowledge of the financial world.

After shouting banking terminology across to each other over the loud music, and making the black girl more and more uncomfortable; she got up and left after a half hour of being ignored.

"I hope you two queers have a wonderful time in bed tonight," is what she said as she left. The white girl also left after she finished her last drink.

The last thing the banker remembered was leaving the club with the man. The beautiful man must have somehow drugged him. He still had his spiked drink in his hand as he followed him into the cab like a person sleepwalking. He woke up in this strange looking chair; and naked as the day he was born.

The first thing he saw as he woke up was a white fist moving in toward his face…

And then his nose was broken.

The judge, jury and executioner now looked intensely at the doomed man. He had never had a man or woman in this situation that did not beg for their life until the very end. They always told him what he wanted to hear, but not this one. This one was a curiosity for him.

He bent down again, and moved his face in close to the man's face. Their noses touched. It was as if he were looking through the man. The beautiful man was now in an almost trance like state of mind. His thoughts were now not on the man, but on his youth back in Iowa. And he closed his eyes. He could smell the blood in the man's nose. And he started smiling. He reflected on the simple, quiet and routine life that he left so long ago.

Plains Iowa was a town of about twelve families, which amounted to about a hundred people if you counted the children. There were six people in his family, two brothers, two sisters and his parents. There was Rudolph Heisman the father, Helga the mother, Gustov the brother, Greta and Ingrid the sisters. And of course also was the future judge, jury and executioner Gunther Heisman.

The Heisman family was of German extraction. Rudolph was the patriarch of the fourth generation to be born on American soil. The first generation settled in Nebraska, and worked as share croppers on host families land until they had saved enough to buy their own land. They then moved to Iowa, and settled down for good.

They dug right into their version of the American dream, which was farming. Rudolph on the other hand was a little different from the other farmers in Plains, or for that matter, different from other farmers in Iowa. He was a master of all trades instead of a Jack of all trades.

Besides growing corn and soybeans, he had a vast hog and turkey business. He also grew every type of vegetable a farmer could grow. There was no need to go to Des Moines or Ames for groceries. He raised everything his family needed for food.

They only went to the bigger Iowa cities when his wife wanted to shop for clothes for the family.

Rudolph hired seasonal Mexican workers to pick vegetables; however, he also had a small full time crew of fifteen to work the hogs and turkeys. He built these workers a huge dormitory type housing facility about a mile from his home.

Rudolph was also the town's mayor, magistrate, jailer and the town's only undertaker. But the job he loved the most was being the town's only preacher.

And preach he did.

He was a fire and brimstone preacher, screaming about the hot fire in Hell, and how nothing but the righteous shall see God. But when he went home he would move on to other business. He would not be talking about God and Satan. He kept church in the church. He held all of his positions the same way. That is why he was not a Jack of all trades, but a master. Most people that were jack of all trades were a master on none. This man was indeed a master of everything he did. If there was one word to describe this man it was, Chameleon.

Gunther snapped out of his trance and stood up looking down at the silent man. He once again picked up the heavy forty pound sledge hammer. This was the same hammer he had used over thirty times on tourists coming to New Orleans. Those people were never to be heard from again. Their disappearances hardly ever made the front page of the local Times Picayune newspaper. New Orleans had its own share of the missing. A mean hurricane named Katrina had saw to that seven years ago.

After Katrina came ashore and crashed the party in the Big Easy, the word *missing* seemed to have poured out of the mouths of every citizen of the city. Conversations right after Katrina centered on fear and confusion all across the country. Questions arose about what really happened? What was the cause?

Did the government intentionally break the levees? Why was it taking so long to get help to the people? Confusion Suspicion

Finger pointing Hunger

He's Missing She's missing Who is missing? Where's Chuck? Where's Sue? Where's Pastor Luke? Went to New Orleans Is he back yet? I'm worried? Help us!! Red beans and rice She went to The Big Easy Bad ass Katrina I want my son back! Bourbon Street Superdome Ninth Ward I got that killer dope! Fats Domino We need water!! Come with me, I know where he's at Come here bitch Open your legs We in the Superdome! Don't you scream! We hungry mama! Please help us! The lord is punishing that wicked city Most of you folks have to go to Houston I got a niece that is a student at Dillard University

Turn on the light from Heaven Lord, Shine on me We thirsty mama Lord why have you forsaken us? Da goment done blew up dim lebies We all gonna' still have church up in here! Mighty strange it ain't no flood in the French Quarter Ah finally got me ah seat in the Superdome I don't know where my family is at Lord Jesus, they are raping that women over there Just look the other way We lucky to be in this here Superdome God sent a great flood this ain't right Are we still in the United States of America? This one's dead Where is my horn? I'm hurting!! I need a shot of dope right fuckin' now!!

Gunther stood in front of the banker with the huge hammer resting on his shoulder like a railroad worker taking a pause after hours of driving new spikes into thick six inch wooden railroad ties. He stood tall and proud, and completely insane. He loved to doing this work in the name of the lord.

If Gunther had lived during Adolf Hitler's Holocaust time in the 1940's, Hitler would have made Gunther the poster man for his Arian super race dream. This near perfect human male would engulf everything a superior Anglo Saxon German man was born to be. He was tall, at least six three.

His weight was one seventy eight. His hair was blond and his eyes were as blue as the afternoon sky. And this one was powerfully built, almost like a weight lifter, but without all the ridiculous bulging muscles that made some lifters look like circus freaks. No, this one was near perfect in appearance, a sort of Arian God of Thunder. He was like Thor with an attitude.

The banker had long given up. He knew he was doomed. His last thought was the fact that he should have gone to Hawaii for his holiday instead of New Orleans, and most of all, he should have taken his wife. She really wanted to go with him. It would have been no problem at all for her parents to stay with the kids for a week, and to get them off to school every morning, and then get them to bed at night.

The parents would have loved it, especially since they also lived in Boston. However, he told her that she could not go; it was strictly a business trip, and the convention was for the country's top bankers only.

"No I won't have your parents coming here for a week doing what you should be doing. Besides, you would be bored stiff, stored away in a hotel

room all day alone. I'll be in meetings all day, and into the night. I'll tell you what I'm going to do. Next month we'll all take a cruise together."

He told his wife one fib after another fib, and those fibs was going to cost him his life. There was no convention at all. What this rich, white, powerful banker really wanted to do was, slip down to the Big Easy and creep. He wanted to hit some bars, eat some gumbo, enjoy some good ole' jazz music and wind down each night with some good ole' black pussy.

Ever since he got his first shot of ebony ass three years ago in Houston, he was hooked. After that, he couldn't even watch a pretty black woman walking down the street without getting a slight erection.

Gunther stood in front of the banker, and got into a wide stance. When the banker brought his blood soaked and puffy eyes up to him, Gunther whispered, "Hold very still, it's almost over."

He brought the hammer down so hard that the banker's left eye popped out of its socket. When it comes to bringing a forty pound sledge hammer down on the top of a person's head—with the rest of the body tightly bound to a chair—it can be a guessing game as to what the head will look like after a massive blow such as that.

You never know what you gonna' get, is what Forest Gump would say about the matter.

His victims would always be tightly bound in the same sturdy wooden chair. The head would be the only body part the victim could move.

His first kill was like trying to catch a greased pig. He had to swing down on the hammer four times to finally get that good solid and direct hit that he cherished so dearly. Both of her collar bones were crushed. The young pretty Creole's head had been moving around like a cartoon character that you would see on Saturday morning children's television.

In a cartoon, a head could move in incredible ways; and a neck could stretch like it was made of rubber; especially after one cartoon character hits the other one under the chin. Before Popeye could get his hands on a can of Spinach, his arch enemy Brutus sometimes hit him so hard on the jaw that his head would spin around like a top.

They just don't make cartoons like that anymore.
Remember the road runner and Wiley Coyote?

Wiley's head was constantly being flattened.

That was just one of the outcomes that Gunther was looking for; one good swing of the hammer, and the result being a flatten skull. He wanted to create a Wiley Coyote head just like on television, when the anvil falls from the top of the mountain, and lands right on top of ole' Wiley's head.

Another outcome Jessie liked was after a powerful crash down of the hammer on a head; the head would end up occupying the chest cavity. That outcome did not happen often; however, when it did happen, it was both exhilarating and *creepy.*

Gunther stepped back until he felt the wall to his back. He then slowly lowered his body until his buttocks rested on the cold cement floor. He sat in that spot for about half hour thinking about the corn fields back home. Then a reality check hit him.

I've got a mess to clean up.

It took him a little over thirty five minutes to clean up all the blood, slime and brain matter from the floor, and on the walls.

It was two thirty Sunday morning. He was now in the shower cleaning off all the dried blood from his head and body.

"Always look on the bright side of life
Always look on the bright side of life
Always look on the bright side of life
Always look on the bright side of life"

He was suddenly in a Monty Python kind of happy mood as he danced and sang his way back to his bedroom, drying off as he went.

"...Always look on the bright side of life..." he continued to sing.

When he got to his bed room, he tossed the wet towel to the side and extended his arms out to the side. Then he started doing the high kick made famous by the Rockets of Radio City Music Hall.

He high kicked with his left leg, kicking to the right. Then he did the same thing with his right leg, then the left, and the right, over and over.

"...Always look on the bright side of life," he sang loudly, looking up to the ceiling.

He was so happy and delighted with himself. If this murder had been a baseball game, then Gunther would have just scored a homerun to win the game with the last at bat at the bottom of the ninth. He had completely smashed in the top of the banker's skull. Not every swing he made in the past had been like this one. The top of the skull was as flat as a pancake. Pieces of brain shot out through the ears and unto the walls. The left eyeball was not the only thing that shot out from its socket; dark fluids and parts of brain also sprung out from where the eyeball was housed. Also long strings of slimy looking things that were attached to the eyeball rushed out, and hung down the man's cheek, with the eyeball still dangling on the end.

He decided to reward himself with a hot breakfast at The Ruby Slipper on Cortez Street not far from the French Quarter in his latest city of residence, New Orleans, Louisiana.

After the hot shower, he put on a white suit, white fedora, white shoes, and a sky blue shirt along with a dark blue necktie. He looked like a movie star.

…A real leading man, a blond Clark Gable.

"Frankly my dear, I don't give ah' damn," he said, looking at himself in the mirror. That scene was his favorite part of the 1939 classic: Gone with the Wind.

He hopped in his dark blue Bentley, headed up North Claiborne, took a left on St Bernard Avenue, and then headed towards Cortez Street.

A few minutes later he was greeted by the staff of the Ruby Slipper and shown to his table.

He was well liked by the staff. As a matter of fact he was well liked by all the establishments in town. Although he was not what one might call *old money,* he was very wealthy. Not top shelf New Orleans wealthy, but wealthy enough to be on the local social register. He was invited to all the best parties and social events in town.

His name was even mentioned as a future candidate for a seat in local government. Even if he was not rich, he would make a formidable candidate just on his looks alone. It would be hard for any candidate to run against a fellow with a face like Brad Pitt, sky blue eyes like Paul Newman, and a body like Conner McGregor.

As this beautiful specimen of a human being slowly took small bites of his ham and cheese omelet, he occasionally glanced up and smiled at a few of the customers that were smiling at him.

These grinning branches are in need of pruning. I think I'll go with the fat man at the counter that keeps flicking his disgusting tongue out at me, he said to himself.

He waved the fat man over to his table.

Later on that evening the fat man was chasing Gunther around the killing room trying to get hold of his penis. They were both naked. The fat man was breathing hard, and sweating profusely. He must have weighed well over four hundred pounds.

Gunther had a particular hatred for obese people. He found them to be disgusting. To him, fat people had no control over their lives.

"Seems to me that somewhere early in their pathetic lives they would notice that they were turning into the Goodyear Blimp," he says to a fellow body watcher at the State Fair in Knoxville Tennessee. At that moment they were observing a husband, wife and daughter each buying the jumbo ice cream cup at one of the many food concession stands located throughout the fair. His fellow observer was a white man that stood at least seven feet; however, he could not have weighed more than a 175. He was a walking bean pole. He and Gunther laughed at fat people so much that day that Gunther's rib area began to hurt. When the fair closed that night the bean pole followed Gunther out to his car.

"Man, I had a great time with you. It seems like we have known each other all our lives," the bean pole said while sliding into the passenger seat without getting permission. He talked Gunther into buying some cocaine. He liked shooting the drug into any vein on his body that his could find. On the way to the University area, Gunther stopped the car at a stop sign. He looked around to make sure the coast was clear. He then pulled out his handgun, and blew the bean pole's brains out.

The passenger window was a mess, as well as his dash board, console and floor.

He drove a few blocks more, and pushed bean pole out into the street. He then headed home to begin the task of cleaning up the inside of the car.

He now looked with disgust at the naked fat man. He looked like a giant bowl of white Jell-O trying to chase Gunther. His arms were outstretched in front of him, and his fat fingers were opening and closing.

"Come on sweet heart, stop running, you're gonna' kill me! My heart can't take this! Please sweetie, let me have ah' little taste," the huge man pleaded, flicking out his fat tongue like a snake.

"First I want you to get some liquids in your body before you pass out," Gunther said, walking over to the small refrigerator he keeps in the room.

"Why are you so mean to me?" the fat man said, smiling, with his hands resting on his knees, and trying to catch his breath.

"I'm not mean to you; I just don't want you to have a heart attack that's all. Now drink this, and sit down in that chair behind you. After you rest for a while, we can have us a little fun," Gunther said, handing the man a cup of lemonade, and pushing him back at the same time.

"I can't fit in this chair," the fat man complained, wiggling his gigantic balloon hips from side to side trying to fit in the chair.

"Drink the liquid first," Gunther said.

The fat man turned up the cup, and drank every drop. He then handed Gunther the cup, and resumed wiggling his hips. Gunther jumped on the man's lap to add more weight. The man's lap was not really a lap; it was a mountain of flabby belly that hid his massive thighs.

Gunther bounced up and down on the huge hanging belly, while holding on to the man's gigantic balloon breasts. The man wrapped his huge white jell- o arms around Gunther with delight.

Finally the fat man nudged his huge hips down into the chair.

After finally settling tightly into the chair, the fat man was reluctant to let Gunther go. He started kissing him on every spot that his lips could reach.

Gunther somehow managed to keep his own lips from within reach. After about thirty seconds of Sumo wrestling, the fat man became frustrated; however, he kept on trying to get that one special kiss.

"…just one little kiss…" he kept pleading.

"Alright, I give up. Let me up, and I promise to give you one kiss; then I want you to rest," Gunther said, hoping that will do the trick.

Gunther was a powerful man himself; however, he was no match for this giant *Pillsbury Dough Boy*. This one was just as strong as he was fat.

"You promise?"

"I promise," Gunther said, giving the fat man a good look into his blue eyes.

After releasing Gunther, the man sat looking like a child waiting on candy.

Gunther kept his word, and bent forward. He let the man put his tongue in his mouth. After a few seconds he pulled away, and looked at the man. The man had his eyes closed in almost a dreamlike state. He had a smile on his huge face.

"Now I want you to sit there and rest for a while. Just keep your mind on all the fun we're going to' have later on," Gunther said, backing away slowly.

"Wait just one minute. Please let me hold it ah' little bit," the fat man said, with his eyes locked in on Gunther's dangling penis. His fat fingers were reaching out while opening and closing.

"Now there you go again. Why are you so damned hardheaded? You need rest. I'm not going anywhere. If I let you grab my pecker, you know damned well you'll never let it go. Now if you don't start acting like you got some sense, I'm going to' have no choice but to ask you to leave; now do you want that?" Gunther asked him, pointing to the door.

"No sweet thing, I don't want that. I'm sorry, I'll be good," the fat man said, still looking between Gunther's legs.

"That's better, I'll be back to check on you in ten minutes or so," Gunther said, heading for the door.

"Hey sweet thing!" the fat man shouted.

"Yes," Gunther said, turning around to see what he wanted.

"I think I'm in love," the fat proclaimed, giving the inside of his huge right hand a kiss, and blowing the invisible kiss toward Gunther. Gunther caught the invisible kiss, and pulled to his heart. He then smiled, and walked out the door.

The fat man woke up two hours later. He was bound to the chair in straps.

Gunther had put a few extra drops of his knock out serum into the fat man's lemonade to account for the fat man's extra weight.

"Sweetie! Sweetie! What's going on here! Sweetie! I'm afraid Sweetie!"

Gunther was at that moment watching television. A re-run of an old Price is Right show was on the tube. The host Bob Barker's hair was jet black; not the shiny gray hair he has now.

Gunther took a bite of his ham and cheese sandwich, and tried to guess the price of a washing machine and drier.

A Puerto Rican Lance Corporal in the Marine Corp won the showcase showdown. His prize was an all-expense paid trip to Paris France for two, plus five thousand dollars spending money.

After the Price is Right re-run went off, another re-run of the Price is Right came on, so he switched channels to catch Matlock.

The fat man was now silent. His thoughts were on the possible reasons for him being bound in this chair. He tried to think positively.

It could be that this was going to be part of some kind of kinky sex act; that would be fine with him, just as long as there would be very little pain involved. He had tried pain sex before; however, he didn't like it. Whips were not his cup of tea. Maybe this beautiful man that he had foolishly followed home was into domination? That also would be fine with him, just leave out the pain part.

Gunther watched Matlock carefully lay out what really happened in his very complicated murder case. He was slowly building up to the climax. The judge was getting impatient. *Where are you going with this line of questioning Ben?*

The fat man was also getting impatient.

"Sweetie! Sweetie! I'm ready to go home now! I've got a meeting tonight! Let's get together at another time! Sweetie! Do you hear me?"

An hour later the door to the killing room slowly opened.

Gunther left the television playing. Gunsmoke had been on for about half an hour. Festus was pleading with Doc.

Matt Dillon had been shot multiple times as usual.

"Doc, you got to save him. I just ah soon die maself as ta see ma friend Mathew ah layen thar with them thar holes in his belly."

Doc says, *"Now hold your horses Festus! Matts as tough as anyone I've seen in my life. If anyone can survive three bullets in the gut, it's him. Now go on, take Miss Kitty back into the saloon; I'll do what I can for Matt."*

The door to the killing room was now opened all the way; however, no one walked through the door. Everything was quiet. There was no movement at all, not even from the fat man. He just sat there motionless watching the open door.

He finally heard a noise from outside the door. It sounded like something riding on squeaky wheels.

The squeaky rolling sound came closer and closer.

Upstairs on the television, Matt was recovering in one of Miss Kitty's upstairs rooms at the saloon. She was wiping his forehead with a wet towel. Ole' Doc had done a fine job patching up Matt's bullet holes; he was going to make it.

"Matt, you had a close call this time; I was worried sick," Miss Kitty said, smiling down at her man.

"It's a close call every time I put on that badge," he said, smiling back.

Downstairs, the noisy wheels were now in the room. Gunther pushed the metal surgical table next to the wooden chair that held a now very frightened and confused fat man.

On top of the surgical table held several instruments used in surgery. There were scalpers and knives of different sizes, pincers, large pliers, rubber gloves, masks and a black marking pencil.

"Sweetie, don't hurt me please! I can't take pain!" the fat man shouted.

"Do you ever watch National Geographic?" Gunther asked.

"Sweetie, what the fuck are you talking about? Why am I bound to this chair? Why all the knives? What the fuck is going on? I want to go home!!" he shouted, jerking his giant tree trunk size head side to side like Ray Charles singing and playing the piano: *"I got a woman, way cross town, she's good to me, oh ho yeah..."*

As the giant head rocked from side to side; its fat jaws landed on one shoulder, then the other shoulder...

"I got a woman, way cross town..."

And then he started crying. His huge belly was shaking up and down.

"Do you ever watch National Geographic?" Gunther asked again.

He waited patiently for an answer.

After about twenty seconds, the fat man—still crying—replied, "Yeah, sometimes."

"Do you have a favorite feature from the show?" he asked, picking up the black marking pencil.

"Fuck no! I want to get the fuck out of this chair!!" the fat man screamed.

"My favorite feature on the show is when they study the hunting habits of the native Alaskan Eskimos. I especially like the part when they hunt the big Sperm Whales. They make use of the entire whale; nothing is wasted. They use the bones to make all kinds of tools for hunting and building. The meat is used to feed the entire village for weeks to come. The skin is used to make many useful things including clothing. However, what fascinates me the most about whaling is the blubber. Blubber when melted, is used for heating and cooking. And that's where you come into the picture."

He started marking rectangular shapes on the fat man's body; starting with his belly and on to his thighs, arms, sides and around his two huge male breasts; breasts that were bigger and fuller than Dolly Parton's breasts.

When he was done, the fat man had ten measured rectangular drawings on his massive body that were ten by four inches.

"Ever since I laid eyes on your big fat disgusting looking ass, I have wanted to perform a special surgery on your morbidly obese body in order to find an answer to a burning question that has been in my head ever since I first saw the Eskimos on television dissect a whale. The question that came into my head was this: Is there any difference between blubber and fat?

What I really want to find out is, do morbidly obese people like you have blubber?

If you do, can it be neatly cut out in chunks like the Eskimos do when they dissect the whales?"

"You can Google the question!! Google it you fuckin' crazy ass moron!!" the fat man shouted at the top of his voice.

"Yes I know how to use a computer thank you very much. I just think it will be more fun finding out this way. However, I know it won't be much fun for you I suspect," Gunther replied, standing back to observe the drawings.

He put on the surgical gloves, and that started the fat man's head to again start rocking from side to side on his shoulders...*I got a woman...*

"I might have put you into a deep sleep with my wonderful Anesthesia before the surgery, however, because you stuck your big fat disgusting tongue in my mouth, you're going to have to deal with the pain," he said, tracing the pencil outline with his pointer finger.

"I'm so sorry I put my tongue in your mouth; please forgive me. I'm a good person, really I am. I live with my mother; I take care of her. My mother needs me; I'm her only child. Please don't take me away from my mother," he pleaded, tears flowing down his huge jelly like cheeks like water falls.

"Those Eskimos are incredible people, living on the land, killing animals not for sport, only for survival. When they cut the blubber into the chunks, they cut it evenly and neatly so that every family in the village can get the exact same amount," Gunther said, picking up one of the sharp scalpels, and turning his attention back to the drawings.

With his left pointer finger he traced the penciled outline around the fat man's huge left breast.

"The blubber that's left over after all the families have received their share is given to the chief to do with as he pleases."

"Jesus Christ Almighty God!! No!! Please don't!! I'll do anything you want, give you everything I've got!! I'm fuckin' rich!! My mother and I are billionaires!! You can have my share!! Don't do this, I beg you!!" the fat man screamed.

Gunther put down the scalpel, and walked to the door. Before opening the door he turned, and looked at the fat man for a full minute; then he opened the door, and walked out; closing the door behind him.

The fat man took in a deep breath, and let it out slowly.

Dear mother, keep me in your prayers that I may come home to you...

Ten minutes later, the door opened again. Gunther returned wearing musical head phones. He didn't want to have to listen to the fat man screaming once the surgery gets underway. He planned on doing plenty of cutting, pulling, tearing, and removing. Death, he knew, would not come quickly. The music would come in handy. The headphone itself was very expensive and guaranteed to deliver only top quality sound, with no other sound except the music itself.

Lovely…

The fat man's real name was George Hemingway. He was a distant cousin to the late great American writer Ernest Hemingway. That fact constantly poured out of the mouth of his mother Mildred Hemingway…

"Yes my dear, I'm Mildred, and Ernest Hemingway was my cousin!!" she would loudly proclaim to anyone that she greeted as they entered her mansion on the outskirts of the French Quarter at one of her many costume balls.

Mildred was most likely the richest person in New Orleans. Her billions came from centuries of shrewd investments from her ancestors. Some of these investments came from the free labor of slaves on the cotton plantations.

She married her cousin Milton Patterson who was a lawyer. When he died, she went back to her maiden name Hemingway. Together they had only one child, George.

From the time George was able to walk, it was obvious that he was a girl trapped in a boy's body. That fact most likely led to the father's early demise, victim of embarrassment and a broken spirit. He died when George was six years old. He just went to bed one night weeping and never woke up.

Mildred had always accepted George as he was, a girly boy. She allowed him to play with dolls. She even joined him for pretend tea parties. When he turned ten she started buying lavish dress's and gowns for him to wear at her parties.

The child was so beautiful that people that the two met while shopping thought he was a very pretty little girl.

That all changed when the boy fell in love with food. When he turned fifteen he was well over three hundred pounds. And the beauty vanished.

Gunther wasted no more time. He walked directly over to the table, and picked up the scalpel again. The fat man's mouth was already wide open with screams, with just the sight of the scalpel.

He plunged the blade as deep as it would go into the belly at the bottom of the black line that he had drawn earlier. Blood quickly shot out from the rear of the scalpel's trail of pain, as the front of the blade stayed precisely on the line. When the blade reached the end of the mark, it changed directions, and went up. Then it went across, and down again. The last cut was the meeting up point where the blade first went in.

Lovely

"There now, a nice neat rectangle," he quietly whispered to himself.

He then looked up at the fat man's face. The man's mouth was opened so wide, you could almost stick a whole loaf of bread in it. However, Gunther heard no screams to his delight. Instead he was listening to Freddy Mercury and Queen, one of the greatest musical groups to ever come out of Great Britain:

> **"We will we will rock you**
> **We will we will rock you**
> **We will we will rock you..."**

Gunther picked up two pairs of pliers, and stuck the jaws of each pair into opposite corners of the rectangle cut on the belly. After maneuvering the jaws into place in order to get a good grip, he closed the jaws tightly and pulled...

Upstairs on the television, a commercial was on: *"What would you do for a Klondike Bar?"*

Forty five minutes later Gunther was sitting on the concrete floor disappointed. After cutting through all the lines, and pulling up what he could, all he accomplished was to make the biggest mess he ever made in his life. What he found out was this: There was no blubber inside an obese human being. He couldn't even tell if what he was looking at was fat or flesh. All he had to show for his research was a pile of blood and solid matter that he could not identify.

The chunks didn't come up evenly as when the Eskimos did it.

Fuck...

Now he had to turn his attention to cleaning up the mess he had made. If he didn't get started right away, the blood would harden of the floor; that would not be good.

After about two hours of cleaning, the killing room looked to be fairly decent. Now the real work begins. Normally all he had to do after killing a victim was to roll the corpse over to the oven, and lay it on the rollers; then push a button, and off it went.

However, this corpse was huge. He estimated the body to be close to 450 pounds. On top of that, it was wedged tight into the chair. He would have to slowly cut the body into pieces so that he could pick up and carry the pieces one by one to the cremation oven.

He picked up his chainsaw, and started this engine.

He started with the massive flabby arms. Then he started on the legs.

He then looked at the fat man's giant head. He wondered why this man's skull was so huge. It seems to him that bone had nothing to do with being fat. This man's head should be normal size no matter how much fat was hanging from his body. However, there it was; a gigantic head that was tilted back. The mouth was still wide open as if waiting for food to be dropped into it. Its beady eyes were looking up in shock, as if he was falling from the rooftop of a high building, with his back getting ready to kiss the side walk first, and his eyes glancing at a flock of pigeons flying from one rooftop to another.

The eyes also had the look of terrified disbelief that this is really happening to him.

Gunther now realized that he was going to have another major cleanup on his hands. Blood was now gushing all over him and the floor.

The chainsaw quickly tore through the neck, making quick work of the flesh and bone. The head fell from the body and rolled about nine feet towards the oven as if it knew where it was going to end up. The beady eyes were now placed as if looking directly at the oven.

Beady eyes of disbelief.

Then he stopped to rest awhile. He was halfway there, however, he needed to shift gears, and clean up more blood. This was going to be a long afternoon. However, it had to be done. Who else was going to do it?

Gunther Heisman is a mortician by trade. He studied and learned from the best: his father. In 1991 at the age of 21 he left his family, and struck out on his own. His father did not want him to go. The young man was extremely valuable to him around the farm. On top of that he was a genius at restoring the faces of corpses that had been disfigured after violent deaths, such as in car crashes.

The father reluctantly gave him his blessing to hit the road. He was of legal age, and he did possess many trade skills including carpentry and electronic wiring. The only thing that really bothered the father was Gunther's obsession with the monster named Adolf Hitler.

Even as a young boy of six, Gunther started reading about the German dictator. Because of his prolific reading and math skills as a young child, his father allowed him to order the books of his choice, and the subject did not matter. By the age of thirteen, Gunther became a Hitler scholar of sorts.

He agreed with Hitler's Final Solution to a point. Both he and Hitler were on the same page when it came to killing off a certain percentage of the population; however, he did not like Hitler's selection of the Jewish population. He felt as though the Jewish people had suffered enough.

Gunther, after years of research and study, had come up with *an alternate solution.*

He was a firm believer that some people needed to die before their time. In his mind, the world would be a much better place if some people were no longer in it. He at first contemplated mass murder following the footsteps of his Fuhrer; however, he dismissed that idea.

Blowing up a football stadium full of people would defeat his purpose. Too many really good people would have to die. Some child that would be killed in the explosion could be the one that might have discovered the cure for cancer.

He then thought about trying to recruit others that had the same thinking as him. He could recruit maybe thirty or forty likeminded men, spread them out across the country, and put them to work; systematically killing people that needed killing. This killing had to be done without prejudice or any type of stereotype.

He would teach them that the color of a man or woman's skin does not matter. They can be black, white, yellow or brown. They can be young or old, gay or straight. They can be doctors, pimps, gangbangers, lawyers or preachers. It did not matter; his job on earth was to stop certain people from breathing.

He spent his first two years on the road in places such as Montana, Wyoming, Idaho, Nebraska and both Dakotas. He knew from his mail order studies back home that these remote areas were infested with racist groups such as skin heads, neo-Nazis and all sorts of white supremacy factions.

"How is everybody doing out there on this glorious day for white America?" A roar from a crowd of over six hundred skin heads went up into

the bright Wyoming sky. Gunther was in the middle of the crowd. In the past two years he had infiltrated several groups throughout the Midwest. So far he was not getting anywhere in finding the right kind of men to recruit. When he talked to some of these men one on one, he discovered that their hatred of all races other than their own was so great that they could not grasp his alternant solution.

Many had personal demons inside of them that tormented them into grasping hold of the race hatred idea. Family situations in their home life were the reasons most of them looked to these groups as their new family, and the leaders as their new fathers.

"There is no room in God's sweet America for Niggers, Jews, wetbacks, queers, chinks, japs and those God awful desert monkeys wearing them diapers on their heads..."

Gunther followed lockstep in giving the Nazi salute, thrusting his right arm straight before him and tilting it upward to about a forty-five degree angle.

He also made up his mind to kill at least three members of the group before he leaves the area. He knew exactly how he would do it. It was going to be so easy.

His victims were going to die after the sun goes down when many of the people would be in their tents.

One victim would be drinking when he pulled the tent opening back; one would be smoking pot and still one would be crying. The one crying would be having second thoughts about what he had gotten himself into. All three would invite him to come into the tent and sit. When the sun rose for another day of Jew bashing, the group would be horrified to find three people in three tents with their throats cut from ear to ear.

He did not kill those people because of their ideology—*he didn't care one way or another*—or their lack of understanding about his alternate solution. He killed them because he could, and felt as though the act was needed. He, at the time, really did not fully comprehend why the murders were needed; he just knew that it was of the utmost importance to get it done.

Gunther then traveled to Colorado. He pitched a tent in the woods close to a mountain range near Denver.

After a week of eating rabbits, squirrels, snakes and frogs, he decided to go on a fast. He needed his mind clear to think and receive messages;

hopefully from the Fuhrer; however, a message from God couldn't hurt either. *It worked for Jesus.*

For three solid days all he consumed was water, which he scooped up from a nearby running stream. The water was pure and good. It rushed down over rocks from the rapids high above the mountain range.

On the morning of day four he woke up laughing. It came to him at last. He had at last found a way to really put his alternate solution into action. *Th*is new solution will be called, pruning.

After realizing that he would never find the right people to work this solution with him; he decided that this mission was going to be a one man show.

He would be the star, director, producer, and his own critic. He knew that he could only handle this business in the United States because of logistics and timing. He felt as though God had smiled upon him and gave him the task of pruning right here in the good ole' USA.

The following is a few statements that Gunther made before a small group of college students in New Mexico:

"Pruning trees is the trimming a few branches to make the regrowth stronger thus helping the entire tree become more healthy, thus producing better fruit.

"Pruning people is the process by which a few people in certain sections of the population are killed for the greater good of that section of the population.

It will not change the dynamics or culture of the group being pruned; however, it will give the remaining members of the group a better chance at living a more fulfilling life."

The more Gunther spoke to the students, the more they became frightened of him. Some looked at each other in disbelief as to what they were hearing. These students were a kind of outcasts; some were nerds, dope heads, hard drinkers and anti-establishment students. They met up on weekends at the home of a retired Chemistry professor who was single and an outcast. He was never invited back to the University for social events. They often invited like-minded students to join them at their retreat—as they called the professor's home. The membership was always kept to about thirty people. As students graduated, replacements were needed. After the graduating students were replaced; students that wanted to join the group were rejected. There were also about six former students that did not graduate; however, they stayed close to the group, and were never asked to leave the group.

The group had heard many speeches by visiting nutty people. However, they had never come close to hearing someone as crazy as Gunther. It was no doubt that a few students would go out to the campus the following Monday and spill the beans as to what they had heard from Gunther. Talking to others outside of the group about what they have seen or heard was strictly forbidden. However, some could not help it… they just had to tell somebody.

Gunther took a huge chance with this group. Of the thirty plus people that listened to his speech; no one offered him a chance to join the group. And everyone wanted him to finish his speech so they can eat. At that point, Gunther realized that he could get himself in trouble before he had the chance to do God's will. At least he did not give anyone at the group his real name.

He shaved his head and face. Then on that Monday, he blended back into the student body. And for a while he took a CHILL PILL.

Back at the mountain range, Gunther was still on his knees praying.

He was now motivated once again.

When he lifted his head up after thanking God for his goodness and mercy, he spotted a nice fat rabbit looking at him about ten yards away.

Slowly he reached behind his back, and grabbed the handle of his twelve inch hunting knife. He maneuvered the knife around in his fingers until he had the blade part of the knife in his palm.

The rabbit's small red eyes seemed to say what was in its mind: *I don't feel good about this guy. I don't feel good about this situation. I think that I might be up shits creek, without a paddle…*

Just like a Ninja warrior, he quickly threw the knife into the side of the rabbit's belly.

"*Thank you Lord,*" he said, as he ate the rabbit raw.

He went back to the Nazi group in Wyoming and killed five more members, even though the place was still swarming with cops investigating the first murders.

"*My Fuhrer adores you,*" *he whispered to the last of the five dead members, before leaving the group for the last time.*

After slipping quietly away from the group in 1994, Gunther knocked around Utah and the Dakotas for another two years; killing six bird watchers during that time.

(He admired the bird watchers for their love and dedication to the preservation of all bird species. They were good, quiet, and loving people; with a burning desire to watch birds in their natural habitat. However, they had to die for the good of all bird watchers according to Gunther.)

After that he spent four years in places like New Mexico, Arizona and Nevada. In those four years he did not kill one single human being. He went back into his study of Adolf Hitler. He became fluent in German after taking a few classes in night school at the University of New Mexico.

He became a licensed embalmer and funeral home director after graduating from the Nevada school of mortuary science in Reno Nevada. He then started embalming bodies for funeral homes in Arizona.

Sometime around the fall of 2001 he left Arizona and hit the West coast. He had saved a little money in the past few years because he did not have any expensive habits. He did not drink or use drugs. He had no taste for woman or men in a sexual way. And he had no intension of acquiring that taste.

In November 2001—after two months of quiet time in Oregon—Gunther invaded California like an invisible Viking on steroids. He completely snapped mentally, and went straight medieval on anyone unlucky enough to be within his striking distance.

Eager to get back in the game; he temporary discarded his philosophy of pruning.

He started slaughtering people like they were hogs being prepped for market. He split heads open with his short handled ax. He stuck ice picks in the back of people's heads while they watched a movie at the cinema.

He found out that ice picks were great silent weapons. The pick would penetrate the skull and cleanly settle into the brain. Upon retrieving the weapon back out of the head, he found out that the blood would not rush out as it normally would as in other fatal wounds; especially if he pressed his finger on the tiny hole. All he had to do was place a finger to the entry point of the wound, and press. After a few seconds he would remove the finger, and sit back, and watch some more of the movie.

This quiet smooth type of killing spoiled Gunther for a while. He loved it. Once in a dark movie theater in Fresno California, he moved around like a snake, and killed four movie watchers, sitting behind the victims for a few minutes before plunging the sharp pointed ice pick into their skulls. He would wait a few more minutes before moving on to the next one.

In the summer of 2003 the United States Justice Department in Washington finally made the announcement everyone was dreading:

"There is a serial killer on the loose on the West Coast. We have no leads and no credible description of the killer. There seems to be no pattern in his or her selection of victims. We urge all citizens to be on the alert. Travel in groups if possible. Do not try making a citizen's arrest if you think you know who the killer is. If you think you know someone that may be the killer, please contact your local law enforcement office; do not do anything on your own. This person is extremely dangerous. Also there is a substantial reward for information leading to the arrest and conviction of this killer."

"Jim Bruce, director of the Los Angles field office of the Federal Bureau of Investigation will head up our pursuit of this killer. The Justice Department and the President of the United States wish to express our sincere condolences and heartfelt sorrow to the families of the victims of these senseless murders."

Gunther put down the Los Angeles Times newspaper after reading the announcement from the Justice Department. He was lying on the sand sunning himself at Venice Beach, a world famous tourist attraction outside Los Angeles. Gunther fit right in place. This was the place where people with beautiful bodies come out to play. In this place Gunther did not have people eyeballing him with their tongues hanging out; there were hundreds of young hunks walking around flexing their muscles and of those hundreds, many of them had blond hair. For the first time in years, Gunther did not feel out of place. He was totally relaxed.

The women at the beach were some of the most beautiful he had ever laid eyes on. Their bodies were slim, tan and very curvy. And although he had no desire to get any of them into his bed, he could appreciate their hard work and dedication in getting their bodies into the best shape possible. He knew that it took discipline to watch you eat, exercise and monitor any weight gain. On top of that there were hundreds of these walking Barbie dolls that have spent thousands of dollars getting tummy tucks, boob jobs and facial nips. Gunther appreciated that.

"The body is the temple of God," is what Gunther would always say to himself every morning when he wakes up and looks at his naked body in the mirror.

He flexed his muscles, bringing his arms up and making a fist, then pumping up the muscles up and down. His eyes burned into his reflection in the mirror. The face became sinister looking.

Jim Bruce of the FBI was turning up the heat. He had hundreds of agents searching up and down the west coast from Mexico and California to Washington and Oregon. He brought in agents from all over the country to help. They had stakeouts on street corners, movie theaters, bars, apartment buildings, parks and camping areas. But what they did not concentrate on was the beaches.

California had over 450 sunny beaches, and since Gunther blended in so well at beaches, he decided to try once again to implement his pruning method.

His solution would certainly work in this environment. First of all the beach goers were a large segment of the overall population. They were indeed a culture apart from normal society. They went by their own rules. They went against the norms of regular Americans. They are different. They were bold, provocative, and comfortable in their own skin.

Gunther decided that some of them must die for the greater good of the group, even if some of the victims were good decent human beings.

His new pruning solution could be a bit confusing to a person hearing it for the first time. They could not understand it at all. His plan was not much different from his initial thought about blowing up thousands of people in a football stadium; good decent human beings would die there also. What was the difference? There was only a slight difference.

Because this new solution involved victims from a select group, instead of a random crowd, it made all the difference to Gunther.

When he tried to explain it to a few people in the past, they looked at him as if he were crazy; *and he was.*

If only they had taken the time to truly analyze the plan, to look ahead to a much better future for America, they would be alive today, Gunther thought to himself.

He got up off the sand and headed for the boardwalk. Once there he ordered a chocolate ice cream cone, and started slowly walking towards the north end of the beach. He stopped, and sat down on a bench to watch roller skaters, bikers and skateboarders zoom by.

He observed a black man on roller skates playing a guitar and singing a strange song. The man wore a strange looking turban on his head that made him look like a cartoon character that Gunter had seen on television long ago.

He remembered seeing this particular man on television during a documentary about life on Venice Beach. He smiled and waved at the man as he zoomed by, singing something about life in the rain forests.

He walked a little further and stopped to watch body builders lifting weights. People were gathered around a huge cage gawking at the men as if looking at animals in a zoo.

Gunther finished his ice cream, and continued walking. His one bedroom flat was just up ahead about a quarter of a mile. He stopped at a food stall and ordered a slice of pizza and a coke.

A group of African drummers were performing up ahead. He stopped to watch some of the show. As he sat on one of the benches observing the show, his mind went forward to the task at hand.

In order to put this new solution to work, he would need to obtain a few items. First he needed a steady stream of money. That would be no problem at all. There were many funeral homes in Orange, Los Angeles and San Diego counties. Most of them could always use a brilliant embalmer such as Gunther to come in to get a body ready for viewing. He could also be on call to assist in funerals as time permits. He could have a nice chunk of money steady coming in. He had already found a small clean flat right here on the beach to live in. He paid six months in advance on his rent with the money he had already saved. He also rented a little Kia convertible for getting around in.

What he needed now was a boat. The reason being is that after killing his new victims, there must be a perfect way to dispose of the bodies without any chance of discovery. The ocean would be the final resting place. It would take quite some time before panic would set in around the beach community. And since there were so many beaches in California, he could possibly kill 50 or maybe even 75 people in a year's time before Jim Bruce could get a whiff of what was going on. If ever the attention starts drifting towards the beaches, he would just disappear again like a puff of smoke that the wind snatched up.

In the morning he planned to go over to Marina Del Rey—which was about three miles away—to check on the rental price for a boat. He also needed ropes…lots of ropes. However, his biggest concern was how was he going to get the cement blacks he needed to weigh the bodies down when he dumped them overboard. He certainly did not want bodies floating back up to the surface. He would later solve his cement problem. The problem would be simplified down to the basic elements. He would go to the company that sells cement blocks, and buy four or five blocks every day, and load them in the trunk of his Kia. He would do this every single day if needed. After parking his car near the beach area; he would take two of the block out of the trunk, and simply carry them across the sand, and load them on the boat. No one was going to be staring him down. Who cares about a guy carrying two cement blocks across the sand? Answer: No one.

After opening the door to his flat, he immediately got down on the floor and did a hundred pushups. Then he did a hundred sit-ups. He did this every day. Late at night he ran six miles along the beach, three miles one way and three miles on the return. He liked to work out alone with as small amount of people glancing at him as possible. If he ran in the daytime, he would have too many eyes on him.

Even with all the other great bodies on the beach, he still was a curiosity for most observers. Even the body builders in the cage took a long look at him when he stood outside the cage.

He was perfect in appearance from head to toe. That is why he stayed away from women. He did not want offspring, because his children would never be as perfect as him. And he knew that for sure. Adolf Hitler knew it also.

Hitler did not possess the physical beauty that Gunther had, but he had an incredible positive view about himself. He felt as though he was divinely placed on earth to carry out a great mission, and he knew that he was God like. Therefore he never had children. After all, they would only be mere mortals.

He opened the small refrigerator door and got a bottle of water. Sitting on the side of the bed, he picked up his favorite book and began to read it again from the beginning. He had read it over 20 times already. The name of the book was *Mein Kampf.*

The book was an autobiography of Adolf Hitler.

Mein Kampf in English means *My Struggle.*

He would often weep when reading about the hardships that his beloved Fuehrer had to endure.

He could not understand why he was not born during Hitler's time on earth. He would have loved to have been able to help and protect him.

Gunther shook his head in sorrow after reading that Hitler first had to deal with a dominating father that wanted his son to become a civil servant like him. He also had to deal with the rejection and laughter of students when the frail bodied young Adolf tried to be a leader and a spokesman.

He defied his father and did not continue his studies to become a civil servant; instead, he went back to his birth place Austria, to study art.

After being rejected twice for admission into the Vienna Academy of Fine Arts, he sunk into a deep depression. He lived for a while on the money he got for his art work and sketches. He did not get the amount of money that he thought he deserved for his work. He felt like he was being cheated. To make him feel even lower, most of his work was sold to Jews whom he despised.

After the money ran out, and he did not have any more sketches to sell, he became a homeless beggar. He was too depressed to sketch again or to look for a job. Many nights were spent in shelters for the poor. There he often quietly wept.

All that changed when "The Great War" came along in 1914. World War I was the greatest thing that had ever come into his life. He volunteered for the German Army, and his life changed forever.

One rainy morning after going to the front of the brutal war as a messenger, he got down on his knees in the muddy trenches and thanked God for being alive. He said these words to his comrades beside him as the mustard gas was making its way towards their position:

"For me, as for every German, there now begins the greatest and most unforgettable time of my earthly existence. Compared to the events of this gigantic struggle, everything past receded to shallow nothingness."

Hitler received numerous combat bravery awards including the Iron Cross during the first three years of the war. As 1918 rolled around he was badly wounded, and had to recover in a hospital.

When he was well enough to return to the front, Germany had surrendered; the Great War was over. Hitler was crushed. He blamed the Jews for being behind the negotiations to end his beloved war.

Gunther put the book down. He had been reading for over three hours. He drifted off to sleep. He was tired.

He slept until four in the morning. When he opened his eyes, Adolf Hitler was standing in his room looking down on him.

He closed his eyes again, convinced that this is nothing but a dream. When he reopened his eyes, the Fuehrer was still standing before him with his arms crossed over his chest.

Hitler came closer to Gunther, and said to him, *"Whoever feels that he is the carrier of the best blood…and knowingly uses it to attain leadership will never relinquish it! Today we must examine ourselves and remove from our midst's the elements that have become bad!"*

Before Gunther had a chance to speak, Hitler vanished.

He got up off the bed, and waved his arms around the room as if trying to touch something invisible.

"Come back my Fuehrer," he whispered into the quiet room.

"I have a brand new solution; this solution is perfect," he said, hoping for a response. He went on like this for over an hour.

It was obvious that Gunther Heisman was completely insane, and extremely dangerous. Although he had the face of an angel, his mind was twisted like a fox with rabies.

It would take another month before he could get everything in place. However, by the end of July 2003 he was again ready to get his pruning solution in motion. Armed with a visit from Adolf Hitler himself, he felt invincible and untouchable. He would keep what Hitler had told him in his memory. That would be easy to do since he had read it before in the book *Mein Kampf.*

DECEMBER 23, 2009
NEW ORLEANS CONVENTION
CENTER CHAMBER OF COMMERCE
AND VISITORS BUREAU
MAN OF THE YEAR AWARDS BANQUET

"…and as your mayor for the past six years, I have seen this city rise up from the most devastating natural disaster in history of the United States of America. We banded together, rolled up our sleeves and went to work. No one worked harder than the person we honor here tonight. It would take me all night to list all the humanitarian and heroic ventures that he dove into after Katrina hit us.

What is most important here is the fact that he wasn't even living here when the hurricane hit. He came to help, and never left. So it gives me great pleasure to present to you, our man of the year, Gunther Heisman!"

A standing ovation followed the introduction. People started looking around. Then a 39 year old man with short cut golden hair stood up from one of the tables in the back.

This man was beyond handsome; he was simply beautiful.

He waved to both sides of the room as he made his way toward the podium, and he stopped three times to shake hands with a few power people.

He was tired. He hadn't been to sleep. This was the reason why:

Friday night around 10:00pm he was riding around downtown listening to the Beetles on his CD player. He turned off Canal Street and headed down Convention Blvd. He decided to park in the parking lot at the Ernest N. Morial Convention Center just as the song 'Hey Jude' began. He would be receiving an award in this building the next night and wanted to soak up some personal glow. He had come a long way in this city. He slid his seat back to get more comfortable.

He listened to four straight Beetles songs. By the time the fifth song 'Yellow Submarine' came on, his eye lids began to get heavy.

A police officer tapped on the windshield, and woke him up after he had dozed off. The officer recognized him, offered his congratulations, and told him he was welcomed to sit there in his car for as long as he wanted to.

After listening to a few more songs including 'Sargent Pepper's Lonely Hearts Club Band', he decided to go for a walk. His car would be safe from theft because the cop would be patrolling the parking lot all through the night.

He headed up Convention Center Blvd and made a left on Poydras Street. As he slowly walked on, he passed by several groups of intoxicated party goers.

Every one or group he passed by seemed to be having a good time. When one comes to New Orleans, one leaves all troubles behind; the city demands it.

When he came to Magazine Street, an alarm in his head went off. The theme of the alarm was: 'Watch your back; you could really get yourself fucked up here'.

He really wanted to continue walking up Poydras, but his feet turned right anyway. Before he realized what he was doing, he found himself in the middle of what looked to be 'the mother of all' subcultures.

People were wandering around in the cold like zombies. Old men and women, as well as young men and women were sitting on the curbs, leaning on the side of buildings or just moving about like slow moving turtles.

He saw something up ahead that he would never forget for the rest of his life. He saw two dirty, intoxicated young men having sex with each other. One of the men was white, and he was sitting on a stoop in front of a store that was closed. The other man was black, and he was sitting on the white man's lap rolling his hips around and singing 'You are the sunshine of my life'.

It was a very cold night; however, they both had their pants and underwear down. No one except Gunther was paying any attention to the two men.

He turned his head away in disgust and moved on up the street. An old man in a wheelchair wearing a Santa Claus hat rolled in front of him. He held up a half empty bottle of Wild Irish Rose wine to him and said, "Merry Christmas friend". Gunther sidestepped Ole' St Nick and proceeded on up the street.

He had taken about six or seven steps when a very well dressed white woman that looked to be in her late thirties came up behind him and tapped him on his shoulder from behind. He turned around and looked at the woman, and just stood there in silence. After a few seconds the woman took her hands out of the pockets of her full length white mink coat, and stretched out her arms like a traffic cop. They both stood in silence for another fifteen seconds, and then the woman began to speak.

46

"Some of these beings walking around here are not human at all. They make themselves look human; however, they are from a planet called Axom which is located in another galaxy. They have the ability to transport their bodies anywhere in the universe instantly. They then morph those alien bodies into the physical form of the host planet. They have been on this planet for about six hundred years. They have sex and have offspring just like humans do. Do you want to know how I know so much about them?"

"Yes, how do you know so much about them?" Gunther replied now looking around to what's waiting up ahead. He was surprised at himself for standing there listening to the woman.

"It's because I am one of them!!" she screamed.

Gunther quickly turned away from the woman, and moved quickly on down the street.

He stopped to witness a standoff between two old ragged looking white men that had to be in their late seventies. Both had knives drawn.

They were just standing there like statues staring at each other. Once every thirty or forty seconds, one would make a slight swinging motion with the knife.

"Come own ya' som' bitch! I'll fuckin' gut ya!" one of the men shouted.

After ten minutes of watching the two senior citizen gladiators stare and trade wolf tickets at each other, he moved on.

He stepped over a black woman that looked to be in her early sixties lying on her back on the cold pavement. She had on a red mini dress, and a dirty overcoat that her body was resting on. She wore no panties, and had her legs spread wide open to the cold night air. She was holding a glass crack pipe between her fingers, and wiggling her tongue around the outside of her mouth in a sexual manner. It was obvious that she was high as a Georgia Pine, and was opened for business. Crack Cocaine will make a person do the strangest things. Gunther had heard that some people will sell their own kids for a few hours of sex in exchange for a few rocks.

A few yards away were the tail end of a rather long line of homeless people. They were waiting for the window to open for sandwiches and coffee from the Sacred Heart Catholic Mission. The window would always open at 11:30 sharp every night; 365 days a year.

The ones standing in line were the ones that could not bear the rules and regulations of this mission or any of the other missions in the city. When

47

one is a drug addict or alcoholic, you don't want to hear the words, 'Lights out at 9:00!' These homeless men and women would rather battle the harsh elements rather than sleep on a warm cot with no access to crack or Wild Irish Rose wine.

As Gunther turned to make a step towards the other end of the street, a hand stopped him with a hard push to the chest. A tall very light skinned man had stopped him in his tracks. After the man got Gunther's attention, he put a large rock of crack on his glass shooter, and slowly lit it. As the rock melted, and the smoke slowly made its way down the pipe, he slowly brought the pipe down while still taking in smoke. He continued taking in more smoke as he worked the cigarette lighter from the end to the middle of the pipe.

He then took the lighter away from the pipe, and just stood there very still, holding the smoke in. He kept the smoke in his lungs for another fifteen seconds before slowly blowing it into the face of Gunther.

"What the fuck is you doin' out here honky?" the man asked Gunther.

"I'm just walking around looking at all the people. This is my first time being on this street," Gunther replied.

"This might be your last time on this street. Better yet, this might be your last time above ground motherfucker!!" the man said, reaching behind his back, and producing a pistol.

"Hey man, I don't want any trouble," Gunther said, stepping back two steps.

"Get yo' punk ass on down the street before I bust a cap in yo' head!!" the man loudly said. He was so high that saliva was running out of his mouth in heavy streams. When he closed his mouth, you could hear his teeth grinding together.

Gunther wasted no time getting away from the man. He moved on down towards the end of the street in a much quicker pace.

He then noticed movement across the street in a small dark archway. People went up to the archway, stepped inside for a few seconds, then rushed back out. He crossed the street to investigate. He had completely let his guard down when it came to his safety; this place had almost hypnotized him.

"What you want niggah?" said the voice inside the archway.

Gunther had heard the word nigger being used before when he visited white supremacy camps; however, he had never been called one himself.

He found it rather amusing that someone had called him a nigger. He could not help himself, he started laughing.

A large dark skinned man with a full beard and an afro haircut stepped out from the archway. He turned his head to the left and then to the right.

"Are you deaf or what? What the fuck you want niggah?" he said, while at the same time popping a switch blade knife open, and putting the point of the blade against Gunther's neck.

"I don't want anything; I was just curious, that's all."

"You could get yo' motherfuckin' head cut off being curious around here niggah!" he said, and at the same time closing the blade and quickly putting it back in his pocket.

He was a fairly well-dressed man. He wore nice looking badge slakes with a black buttoned up black shirt, a full length black leather coat, and matching black Stacy Adams shoes. Gunther was a little relieved that he was not the only one over dressed in this hellish environment.

The man quickly made a sale to a young white girl. The girl quickly stuck the small piece of crack, inside her bra, and moved on.

A very short and very old white man with a long tobacco stained beard stepped into the archway. To Gunther the man reminded him of 'Popa Smurf' from the hit cartoon show, The Smurfs.

Popa Smurf or as he was called in the streets, 'Pops', handed the large black man a worn out ten dollar bill. He looked up at the man with a comical bitter beer looking grin on his weather beaten face.

"Pops, this is your lucky night. You win the grand prize. You have officially made the last buy of the night. You win the shake and bake, as well as the last rock, which as you can clearly see is the mother of all rocks".

He handed Popa Smurf a plastic bag containing a large crack rock with the street value of 40.00. The bag also contained the powder and crumbs which had a street value of 60.00.

Popa Smurf jumped up and down landing on one foot followed by the other like a hillbilly mountaineer that just found out his sister was pregnant, and he was the father.

He kept on leaping for joy and never saying a word. Gunther wandered if he could talk at all.

He kept watching the little man moving on down the street, clicking his heels together in the air like a leprechaun finding his stolen pot of gold.

Crack sometimes makes people act like cartoon characters, and they sometimes go against the laws of nature and physics. Gunther once saw a man in Hollywood that was high on heroin; lean at an incredible angle without falling down. He remained that way for a half hour before changing positions. Gunther watched him for over two hours defy the law of physics before moving on.

"Come on niggah, lets walk; I need to get your dumb white ass off this street before you wind up dead," the black man told Gunther, and at the same time grabbing his arm, and leading him towards Canal Street.

They walked in silence; moving past the zombie like drifters, whores, robbers and a few late night doped up crack head street preachers. Everyone is an authority on the bible when they are drunk or high.

And most of the late night doped up crack head preachers always shouts out the same message:

"We are living in the last days! Jesus is coming back my brothers and sisters! You better get yourself right with God! Jesus is the way, and he is the truth and the light! Repent while there is still time! It won't be long now! Yes sir my brothers and sisters, I'm high on Jesus..."

They made a right turn on Canal Street. Now they were back on Planet Earth, sort of. The two of them now passed by a group of people that were singing, kissing, hugging, drinking, dancing and having a grand ole' time.

The difference between those people and the Magazine Street people were like night and day. These dancers, singers and kissers showered and changed clothes every day. These people had nice hotels and warm beds to crawl into every night. These people had good jobs and homes to return to once their vacations ended. These people were going to be eating steak and eggs in the morning or country ham and fried potatoes. Some would be having hot pancakes and maple syrup, along with four or five strips of crispy Arkansas cured pork bacon. All of them will be having fresh ground coffee, freshly squeezed orange juice or fresh milk.

The Magazine Street crowd that was sleeping in the Missions would be having one strip of fried fatback, powdered egg and black coffee. The ones that will be waking up outdoors will be having a Pimento cheese sandwich served from the mission window at 7:00am sharp.

The huge black man led Gunther into the famous Canal Street Bar. They sat on bar stools at the counter. Gunther looked around at the late night faces.

Some were laughing and talking; some were drunk and trying to talk. Most were just silently listening to Johnny Cash singing, 'I walk the line' on the juke box.

"What you drinking my niggah? My treat", the man asked Gunther.

Gunther had never tried alcohol but did not want to insult his new acquaintance, so he replied, "I'll have what you're having."

"Two Rum and Cokes please," he told the bartender.

Two hours later Gunther was having a real good time with his new buddy. He found out that he had a lot in common with 'Big Nine', as he was called in the street.

They both came from large farming families. Big Nine grew up on a farm In Mississippi. His father and mother were both Baptist ministers, and they had six children, four boys and two girls. Big nine was the oldest.

He got a full scholarship to Grambling State University to play left guard on the football team.

During his junior year he blew his knee out, and went into a depression after rehabbing another year trying to get back on the field.

He starting drinking and doing drugs his senior year and sinking further into depression. He got arrested for selling heroin five months before graduation.

He never got his degree. He moved to the New Orleans area after serving his full four year sentence, then started selling dope full time. He could have got out early on parole but chose to do all of his time; he did not want to have to report to a probation officer after he got out.

Gunther had never felt comfortable with any other human being until he met 'Big Nine'. He told him about his childhood and his family. He even told him that he had never had sex with a woman or a man. That did not faze 'Big Nine' one bit. All he said after hearing that was, "We all just ah couple of squirrels trying to get a nut. Jerking off is the same as fucking, and much less costly my niggah. So keep jerking off."

Gunther smiled, and then he laughed.

Big nine told his new friend something he had never told another person. "I'm six feet seven inches tall and three hundred fifteen pounds. Before I went to prison, I thought that only small girly looking guys got raped. I was so very wrong. On my first night in prison, my cell mate who was about six feet tall and weighed only one hundred sixty eight pounds, tried to pull down my pants and fuck me. I beat the living shit out of him. I put him in the hospital for three days," he said, turning up his glass to his waiting lips.

"However, my heroics cost me eleven days in solitary confinement. When I got out they put me back in the same cell with the guy that I beat up. Instead of being afraid of another ass whipping he tried to rape me again. This time I only punched him around a little bit just to keep him at bay; I did not want to wind up in solitary again. Three days later when I was in the shower, my cellmate showed up; and this time he had four sex hungry inmates with him. I did not stand a chance," he said, now lowering his head.

"After they beat me up, they put me down on the cold wet floor, and took turns raping me. My cellmate was the first to take me. After he finished, the other guys took their turns," he said, wiping the tears from his eyes.

"Six days later I was in the shower, and the same group showed up again. This time I willingly got down on my knees and gave them all blow jobs, and I enjoyed doing it. Then I started having sex with my cellmate on a regular basis. I guess now I am what you call bi-sexual. I like men just as much as I like women."

"Being a good switch hitter works in baseball," was Gunther's only reply.

The folk duo Seals and Croft was singing a beautiful Ballard on the juke box. Everyone that was still conscious was bobbing their heads up and down to the words of the song: "We may never pass this way again; we may never pass this way again..."

Gunther wished this night would never end. He was having so much fun with his new friend. As a matter of fact he considered Big Nine to be his first and only real friend. He had no real friends back home in Plains. He had a few close business associates here in town; however, none of which he would call a friend. Although there were endless dinner parties, banquets, social gatherings he attended, nothing compared to these last few hours he had spent with Big Nine.

In this relatively short span of time, he had come to love his friend. This love was in no way sexual; this was a love that one human being had for another. He planned to offer Big Nine a job at the funeral home to get him off the streets, and away from the hard life of selling drugs.

He knew that there were only two endings for a drug dealer, prison or a violent death on the mean streets of America.

He did not want either of those situations for Big Nine. He would patiently teach him the trade of Mortuary Science, and make him a master of embalming, makeup, facial restoration and cremation.

"What time is it?" Big Nine slurred, taking another gulp from his glass.

"It's time for you to buy a watch my niggah!" replied Gunther.

Big nine looked at him and smiled.

"If I didn't love you so much, you would be one dead mother fuckin' cracker right about now, calling me a niggah' and shit," he replied while almost falling off the stool laughing.

Gunther asked, "Why is it alright for black people to call each other niggah', but it's not alright for white people to call a black person niggah'?"

Big nine raised his head again and opened his drunk eyes and replied, "Niggah', suck my left nut!"

This time they both lost their balance on the stools, and fell to the floor laughing.

"Hey fellows, you gonna' hafta' leave if you can't stay put on the stools," the bartender said, pointing his finger at the front door.

"We're getting ready to leave anyway", Gunther said, while helping his friend up off the floor.

"Are you going to be able to get home alright? Where do you live anyway?" he asked Big Nine.

"I live in Algiers," replied Big Nine, almost falling down again.

"Algiers!" shouted Gunther.

"What's wrong with Algiers?" ask Bine Nine, reaching in his coat pocket for a cigarette.

"You don't understand; there's nothing wrong with Algiers; it's a beautiful little town, it's just way across the Mississippi River, that's all I meant. The bus service going across the bridge won't run again until seven, and it's only two thirty now."

"Call me ah' cab," Big Nine uttered, trying to walk to the door.

"It's hard enough for a sober and clean cut black man to get a cab in this city; you're a three hundred pound drunk black man; I think you should let me call a cab for the both of us. I'm white so it should be no problem with the cab driver allowing me to push your big black drunk ass in the cab with me," Gunther said, while helping him over to one of the empty cushion sitting booths.

They came to an agreement that going to Algiers by taxi cab would be too expensive. Money was no problem for Gunther, but it still made no sense to him to just give away money foolishly. They decided to get off at Gunther's house, which was only a mile away, and then in the morning he could drive big nine home in his car. Besides he did not want to just drop him off at his place in his condition this time of night; anything could happen to him. He wanted his new friend safe.

Gunther put the key in the front door. Big nine threw up on the front porch. Gunther just smiled, 'the cleaning lady is going to be pissed', he thought to himself.

He gently laid Big Nine on the first couch he came to. He looked up at Gunther, and said, "I need a drink."

Gunther saw no harm in giving him a drink; he could not get much drunker anyway. He always kept fine liquors on hand to entertain guests; however, tonight was the very first night that he had tried the stuff himself.

He was feeling somewhat intoxicated himself, however he was not nearly as drunk as his friend. He made a vow to himself that his first night of drinking would be his last.

He was serious in his belief that the body is the temple of God.

He brought a double shot of Absolute Vodka back to his friend and watched him gulp it down. Then he went to the downstairs linen closet and pulled down a heavy blanket. When he returned, Big Nine was already sleeping.

He gently and quietly placed the blanket over his friend as not to wake him; however, that did not work.

Big Nine looked up as he was tiptoeing away and said, "You better not try to fuck me tonight."

Gunther replied, "Niggah', if I ever took a notion to put my penis into a man's asshole, it would not be the ass hole of a three hundred pound queer like you that could be an offensive left guard for the New Orleans Saints football team."

"You know you want some of this ass," Big Nine said, smiling.

"No my friend, you are definatly not my cup of tea. Like I told you before, I've never had sex with a man or a woman. However, if I ever do get an urge to have sex with ah' man, I definatly would want someone much younger than your old dried up ass," he replied.

"I knew it; you're a mother fuckin' pedophile. You know what cons do to child molesters in prison?" he asked, starting to laugh.

"I can imagine it wouldn't be pleasant."

"Fuckin' right it won't be pleasant; so get that sick shit out your fuckin' filthy ass mind niggah'," Big Nine replied, obviously only kidding with Gunther.

"Man, all I'm saying is, I'm not the kind of guy that likes fucking the Incredible Hulk that's all. I'm sure they had plenty of pretty boys in prison, how in the hell did those cons get a hard on for your big black ugly ass, I'll never know."

"I guess it takes all kinds to make the world go round," Big Nine said, and with that, he closed his eyes.

Before he fell into a deep sleep he smiled as he reflected on his nights in the cell with his roommate. Before he got out of prison they had fallen deeply in love with each other. They cried in each other's arms when the time came for him to walk out the prison's doors.

Before Gunther left the room, he heard Big Nine shout out, "I love you my niggah!"

Gunther didn't know if he was talking to him or someone in a dream he was having. He replied back to him anyway, just in case, "Love you back my niggah."

He pulled off his clothes, and got into bed. He thought of the busy day that lay ahead of him. First he had to take Big Nine home. Then he had to do two cremations before he could get ready for his big awards night. After the awards, he would look up Big Nine to tell him about the job he had in mind for him. But first and most important, he needed sleep. He glanced over at the clock before he turned off the lights; it was 5:00am.

In the Canal Street Bar, the people that were conscious were bobbing their heads up and down to Simon and Garfunkel's classic The Sound of Silence:

Hello darkness, my old friend....I've come to talk with you again

Because a vision softly creeping....Left its seed while I was sleeping....

Two hours later, around 7:00am Big Nine woke up firmly strapped to a strange looking wooden chair. At first he thought he was having a horrible dream.

However, as the seconds turned into a full minute, he realized that this was no dream at all. He was in deep shit, and that was the bottom line.

He was as strong as an Ox; however, his strength was no match for the thick leather straps that bound his hands, torso and feet to this strange looking chair; a chair that looks so much like the electric chair that he sometimes saw in gangster movies.

The chair itself was bolted into a concrete slab in the middle of a cement floor. Everything about this chair was solid. It made no noise if you pushed, pulled or shook it. Even the straps made no noise when you tried to pry them loose from your body. There was no visible roadmap to freedom from this hellish contraption.

However, Big Nine was giving it all he had...

He was now in panic mode. The feeling of total helplessness was all over him. He was realized that he was truly trapped in this contraption.

"How could this happen? What the fuck? This can't be happening to me," he said to himself.

The room was quiet, too quiet. The only sounds were of him grunting and breathing hard. He turned his head from side to side, and even more panic set in.

He pulled and pulled and pulled and wiggled and tugged and farted and pissed and screamed and cried and jerked and tugged and screamed and pulled...

Then he finally noticed that he was naked.

"Help!! Help!! Lord in heaven, please help me!!"

"Help!! Help!! Help!! Somebody please help me!!"

No one could hear him. He had no idea that it was impossible for any sound to escape from this room.

This was a very special room. It was built to be totally sound proof. Located on the basement floor that housed the crematorium; it was specially built to be a room for murder.

When it's cleaned up for viewing, it becomes a place of great historical significance. If one has money, and is willing to part with some of it, then that person will be in for a special treat. This room will give any historian lucky enough to be invited in—for a price—a chance to sit in a real electric chair.

And not just any electric chair. This was the original South Carolina electric chair, better known as ole' Smoky.

Not only does one get to see this chair and sit in it, they get to look at all the death records, pictures before and after the sparks fly, and the actual recorded sounds of volts popping, and the burning of human flesh.

All of this information is stored in a safe in the back room.

How did Gunther get his hands on such as prize that should only belong to the State of South Carolina? The answer is: Money talks and bullshit walks. Gunther had five funeral homes in the greater Orleans Parish, thus he had plenty of the green stuff.

This gruesome chair had electrocuted 251 doomed individuals at the Central Correctional Intuition in Columbia South Carolina from 1912–1962. From 1962 on, a drastic drop off of electrocutions occurred due to the introduction of the lethal injection technique. The prisoners had a choice, and almost all chose the needle. Only six inmates chose the chair over the needle since 1962.

In September of 2007 Gunter quietly eased into Columbia South Carolina and purchased the chair for an undisclosed amount of money. The state purchased a working replica of the chair soon after; however, Gunther had the original.

He intended for the chair to be the main attraction for viewing for a select few from time to time; and they had to pay a hefty viewing price; however, he soon discovered that the chair gave him much greater pleasure in another way.

He did not intend to introduce Big Nine to the chair. He really wanted to get up early, wake him up, and take him home. He wanted the train him in his craft; after all, he really did need another assistant at this location. Business was going through the roof, and although he had plenty of workers, he needed another person—besides the one he already had—that he could train until that person would know the business as well as him. Most important was this: he needed a person close to him that he liked; and he really liked Big Nine.

So he went to bed with good thoughts on his mind, and looking forward to wonderful things in the future for himself and his friend.

Then a half hour later he heard a noise down stairs. Big Nine had awakened, and was trying to move towards the bar for another drink.

He had fallen over the coffee table.

Gunther ran down the steps, and helped his friend back to the couch.

"Fix me ah' drink," Big Nine commanded, settling back on the couch.

Gunther walked over to the bar, and did something that he had done countless times before; he put a few drops of liquid into the drink. This liquid was very powerful; it completely knocks the person out after five minutes. That person will remain unconscious for about an hour or two.

Gunther dragged Big Nine's limp body over to the elevator after taking off all of his clothes. He pushed the down button. After arriving on the basement floor, he dragged Big Nine into the death room.

"Somebody please help me! Heeeeeeelp! Heeeeeeeeelp! Heeeeeeeeelp!"

Big Nine screamed out his plea with a new determination that someone will hear him.

His heart started racing, pounding faster and faster...

The feeling of total helplessness was all over him. He thought about all the things a person could do to him, and he could not defend himself at all.

"I should have stayed home on the fuckin' farm!!" he screamed out.

Then he started thinking about his grandmother singing in the church choir.

He began to sing out loud her favorite hymn. In a time like this, he was willing to try anything; maybe God will bless him with a miracle, a miracle of freedom.

"I'm gonna' trust in the Lord
I'm gonna' trust in the Lord
I'm gonna' trust in the Lord Till I die"

The door to the death room slowly opened, and a man entered wearing a Nazi uniform, cap and spit shinned boots.

"I'm gonna' stay on the battle field
I'm gonna' stay on the battle field
I'm gonna' stay on the battle field
Till I die..."

He defiantly kept on singing. He rationalized that if his grandparents could continue singing while baking in the sun picking cotton, he could keep on singing.

The man in the uniform slowly walked into the room until he was about three feet from the singing Big Nine. He had the dreaded skull and crossbones on his black cap. He had the Swastika insignia on the sleeves of his black coat.

Gunther was no longer himself. He was now 'SS', which was the Secret State Police. However, most importantly, the 'SS' was Hitler's personal body guards.

"I'm gonna' treat everybody right
I'm gonna' treat everybody right
I'm gonna' treat everybody right
Till I die"

He snapped to a sharp attention that made him look like a giant toy soldier. He remained in that stone like position for three solid minutes. Big nine had stopped singing; instead he just silently eyeballed the man in uniform.

He was not quite sure who this man was. He looked somewhat like Gunther, but he wasn't sure.

Gunther snapped out of his trance. God only knew where his mind had wandered off to. He took three steps back, and did a precise military about face. He now was looking at a portrait of Adolf Hitler that was hanging on the back wall. Big Nine was too busy crying and struggling with the straps to notice the portrait before.

Hitler was intensely looking out into the world like a man studying the movement of ants. He looked God like, and bored with what he was looking at. He had on civilian clothes, a brown suit with a black neck tie, and the swastika on the sleeve. His arms were folded as if to say, 'get on with it, I have very little patience with petty non-sense'

Gunther opened his mouth, and these German words came rushing out:

"Mein Fuhrer, genau wie in Fruheren wir unseren Dienst und un sere Pflicht getan haben warden wir auch Kunftig Nur auf Ihre Befehle Warten.

Und wir. Kamerdan Kennen nichts anderes dab wir alten geblieben sind. Unser Fuhrer. Adolf Hitler! Seig Heil!"

Gunther had memorized the introduction speech by a party official in 1934. The introduction speech was given before an audience of over one million people in Nuremberg Germany. In was the final day for the week long Third Reich's Party Rally. On this final day, the headliner was an appearance and speech by the leader of the Third Reich, the National Socialist German Workers Party (NAZI), and Supreme Chancellor of Germany, Adolf Hitler.

Hitler waited a full hour before appearing before the anxious crowd, a crowd that was now in a state of frenzy with anticipation.

When he finally appeared to the crowd, the roar was thunderous. Hitler took another ten minutes to shake hands, and slowly make his way unto the podium.

Standing in front of the microphone, he decided to stand silently for another two minutes. He was a master in the art of speaking, and building up a crowd's anticipation. After the two minutes of silence, he moved closer to the microphone and began to speak to the crowd, a crowd that had patiently waited for him.

Hitler's speech that day would come to be known as the Triumph of the Will speech. In that speech—in which Gunther chose not to memorize—Hitler let it be known that he was the only ruler that mattered; everyone one else in the party were mere subordinates. He told of his many struggles and obstacles that he had to overcome. He also addressed the Jewish problem—which was really his problem, in his sick mind—and what he was going to do about it. However, what he wanted most to get over to the audience was this: 'I am a God'.

Gunther gave the Hitler portrait the full salute, thrusting his right arm out about forty five degrees upward from his head. He then reached into his right pant pocket, pulled out a pair of thin round rimmed glasses, and put them on. He quickly did another about face, and walked straight towards Big Nine. This time he got real close. He bent his body down to get eyeball to eyeball with Big Nine.

When he put those glasses on he had turned himself into the murderous number two man in Hitler's hierarchy. His name was Heinrich Himmler, leader of the 'SS', and head of all the concentration camps in Europe. With Hitler's blessing, he ordered the deaths of over twelve million innocent people, over six million of those people were Jews. (Also murdered were Gypsies, the mentally ill, and the physically deformed)

Big Nine did not know who Himmler was; however, he did know madness when he saw it. What he saw behind the eyes of this man made him scream. The scream was high pitched like that of a very frightened little boy.

The NAZI butcher just kept on intensely looking into the eyes of Big Nine, and Big Nine just kept right on screaming.

After four minutes of starring into the eyes of Big Nine, Himmler stood straight up, did another about face, walked over to the door, opened it, and left the room.

Big Nine cried softly for another ten minutes.

He did not look like a man sixty two years of age; however, that was his true age. As a matter of fact he had just received his first Social Security check this month. His neighbor tried to talk him into waiting until he reached sixty five before filing; however, Big Nine would have none of that.

Big Nine was smart enough to work as well as hustle no matter where he moved to. It did not matter what kind of work was available, he jumped right on it. He did longshoreman's work. He worked on a drilling rig out in the Gulf of Mexico. He did hotel work, mopping floors and cleaning rooms. He even worked ten years as a short order cook in a road side grill in Galveston Texas. And he sold dope on the side, no matter what job he had. He kept his eyes on the prize.

He knew that one day he would need his Social Security check. However, he also knew that if you don't put anything in it, you won't get anything out of it. Also he wanted to waste no time getting it. (ASAP)

He told his neighbor, "Shit, as fast as niggahs' are dying, the government should let us get our Social Security at twenty nine!!"

He stopped crying, and thought about the cotton fields back home in his native Mississippi. He was about eight years old when they finally allowed him to come to the fields to practice his cotton picking. He was told by his father to watch and learn from his grandparents.

At this moment in time, and in the situation he now found himself in, he wished he could do what Captain Kirk and Spock did on the 60's TV show, Star Trek. They could say the word, "Energize", and they would disappear, and reappear anywhere in the universe. He wished he could say, "Energize", and reappear in those cotton fields back home. Not only did he *want to "Energize" himself back home, he wanted to reappear as a little boy again, learning to pick cotton by watching the skillful thorn ravished hands of his grandparents.*

He thought about the Negro spirituals he had heard the workers sing as they picked the cotton. Those songs kept them going, and gave them the motivation and the will to block out the pain. Those sacks of cotton got heavy on their backs, and those pointy thorns that guarded the cotton tore into their hands like razor blades.

And the sun was so hot. There was no heat in America like Mississippi cotton field hot; unless you are talking about Death Valley. The workers would be wet from head to toe when they finally left the fields for the day.

As he began to sing those songs, he hoped that maybe God in heaven will forgive him for dealing drugs. Maybe God will perform a miracle, and loose the straps that bind him. After all, didn't God free Moses and his people?

Anything could happen at this point. He had to keep a positive mind. In this horrible moment in time, he had nothing to lose by trying.

Again he began to sing:

> **"We are climbing Jacob's ladder**
> **We are climbing Jacob's ladder**
> **We are climbing Jacob's ladder**
> **Soldiers of the cross..."**

After about three songs he started thinking about his grandmother's deep dish Blackberry pie. The pie was taller than a cake. It had four layers of dough in it, plus a crusty final layer on top. Sweet black berries and juice were trapped in between the layers of dough. The pie was so good that his grandmother had to get one of the adults to stand guard over it until dinner was ready to be served.

He now decided to sing one of his grandfather's favorites:

> **"...Swing low, sweet chariot, coming for the carry me home..."**

As he sang, he began to cry again. He closed his watery eyes, and kept them closed. In his mind, he was now home again. He was now living the simple life. He was now running between the cotton stalks, playing with his friends.

After four more Negro Spirituals, Big Nine opened his weary eyes to discover that God did not grant him a miracle. He was still bound as tight as ever in the strange looking chair. He started once again to pull at the straps. He strained and jerked harder than ever. He even closed his eyes again, and shouted out that one magical word that Captain Kirk would call out when he and his crew was ready to depart some strange planet, and return to the Enterprise, "Energize."

All of a sudden the door began to slowly open…

The head of a man poked out from the other side. The head was very low, and close to the floor. The man must have been lying on his belly for his head to be that low.

The head belonged to Gunther, and it was grinning.

Big nine felt just a little better seeing a happy and familiar face. His spirits were lifted, and hope replaced doom. The grin on Gunther's face made his heart race with the anticipation that maybe, just maybe, freedom from this nightmare is close at hand.

However, as the seconds turned to minutes, and the minutes turned to a half an hour, Big Nine realized that what he was looking at was frozen insanity. The grin had not changed at all, and that was the problem, it was frozen.

Gunther's grin looked like Jack Nicholson's Joker in the Batman movie, sinister, psychotic, demonic…

It was a big wide grin. And the eyes…the eyes looked lost…distant

"Hey man, let me out of this fuckin' chair!" Big nine finally shouted out to the grinning face.

The grinning face slowly pulled back, and the door slammed shut. Big Nine returned to his struggles with the straps to no avail.

It was now daybreak; however, Big Nine couldn't tell; he was trapped in a room that no sound could escape. And no sound could enter. He could not hear the baby birds outside crying for food, nor could he breathe the fresh morning air.

He wondered to himself, how could this happen to him? How could a mild mannered all American handsome looking white man turn out to be the craziest motherfucker in the whole wide world?

"If only I had left this crazy ass white man alone," he said out load.

But how could he? He looked so innocent walking around looking like a handsome politician trying to get votes from bottom feeders. He looked totally out of place, and very much in danger.

The door opened again.

Big Nine closed his eyes. He heard the door shut. Then he heard what sounded like bare feet walking towards him. When the sound stopped, he opened his eyes, and there standing before him was a very naked Gunther with a large sledge hammer resting on his shoulder.

"Oh no! Oh God no! Please man, don't do this shit!" Big Nine pleaded.

Gunther put the hammer down, and walked over to the side wall where a military footlocker was located. He pushed the footlocker over in front of Big Nine, and stepped up onto it. The footlocker was about twelve inches in height, which would make up for Big Nine's height. Being about six foot nine inches, he was the tallest person to ever sit in this chair since he acquired it. He needed to make the adjustment so that the swing of the hammer would result in a perfect connection. He made a few practice swings, pretending that he had the hammer in his hands...

"Perfect," he said in a low pitched voice.

Satisfied now that the swing would be perfect, he got down off the footlocker, and instead of picking up the hammer, he sat down on the footlocker, and looked up to face a weeping Big Nine.

"Hey man, what's this shit all about? I thought we're friends. I tried to help your ass. I could have let them lowlifes on Magazine Street fuck you up. I saved you man! Don't do this sick shit! You can let me go man. I won't tell ah soul about this shit," Big Nine pleaded.

Gunther smiled and said, "Do you know the Hollywood actor Forest Whitaker?"

"What?" Big Nine replied, confused by the question; a question that seemed very much out of placed given the situation at hand.

"Forest Whitaker, the actor, do you know him?"

"Yeah man, I know him," replied Big Nine, closing his eyes again in disgust.

"Man, he is my favorite actor; I've seen every one of his movies," Gunther replied proudly.

"That's nice," replied Big Nine, opening his eyes again.

"My favorite movie that he played in just happens to be one the best movies of all time; can you guess the title of the movie?" Gunther asked, wide eyed with excitement.

"Man, fuck this bullshit, loose these fucking straps!" Big Nine shouted.

"Can you guess the title of the movie?" Gunther asked again.

Big Nine looked at Gunther like he never looked at him before. He realized that what he was looking at was not human; instead he was looking at some sort of machine with no feelings, and programed for God knows what.

He decided to play along, and see what happens.

"A Rage in Harlem?" he answered, lowering his head; fearful that his response will cause Gunther to kill him.

"Are you fucking with me or what?" Gunther asked in a shouting voice; while at the same time grabbing the hammer.

"No sir my friend; I would never do that. I just said the first thing that came into my head, that's all, my friend, that's all, I swear to God!" he said, starting to cry again.

"That flick was a long way from being one of the greatest movies of all time. I went to see the flick, and was greatly disappointed," Gunther replied, while at the same time setting the hammer down next to his feet. He then sat back down on the foot locker, and continued looking up, and into Big Nine's watery eyes; waiting for the answer to his question.

"Good Morning Vietnam?" Big Nine tried again, attempting to recall some of the many movies that he had seen the actor in.

"No." replied Gunther, shaking his head from side to side.

"What about The Last King of Scotland?"

"No, try again."

"It's got to be The Last King of Scotland; he was fucking brilliant in that movie!" Big Nine replied eagerly. He was starting to get that hopeful feeling again. As a matter of fact, he was starting to feel damned good. After all, Gunther was smiling, they were playing a game called, 'Name that movie', and most of all Gunther didn't have that God awful looking sledge hammer in his hands.

"No my niggah', that's not it; but I'm glad to know that you are a Forest Whitaker fan!" Gunther replied, raising his voice in jubilation.

"He is number one on my favorite list of actors; following closely behind at number two is Robert Deniro, then Samuel L Jackson, then Morgan Freeman, then Denzel Washington, then Robert Redford, then…"

Gunther went on to give his top twenty five lists of favorite actors. When he was finished, Big Nine started to ask him why there were no women on his list.

He changed his mind for two reasons. One, the subject of the game was favorite actors not actresses. Two, he did not want to fuck this up. Things were starting to look good.

"Drum roll please!" Gunther beat on the side of the footlocker as if it were drums beating.

"…And the winner is…"

There was a slight ten second pause.

"One of the greatest movies ever made, staring Forest Whitaker…"

…Another pause, this time twenty five seconds.

"The Crying Game!" he screamed, and at the same time jumping up off the footlocker, and raising both clinched fists towards the ceiling.

"Big Nine, did you see that movie?" he asked, wide eyed with jubilation.

Big Nine was slow and carful with his answer; he did not want to get caught up in a lie.

"No, I missed that one," he said closing his eyes again.

"Well my niggah', you missed a great performance by Whitaker."

"Yeah, I heard he was really good, worthy of an Oscar kind of good."

"You got that shit right," Gunther replied.

"Hey man, let me tell you the part I liked best. You see, it went like this; Forest Whitaker played a soldier in the Army of Great Britain. He was walking around a small country amusement park enjoying the day; however, he wore his British Army uniform, thus became a target for kidnapping by the IRA which stands for the Irish Republican Army," he said, sitting back down on the footlocker.

"A pretty female IRA member lures him away from the crowd and into the woods where he is kidnapped by other IRA armed group members. He is blindfolded, tied up, and hauled away to a secret IRA location," he continued, while wiping the sweat off the man's forehead with a small face cloth.

"While still blindfolded he befriends one of the members that seemed to treat him more kindly than the others. This friendly IRA member constantly

*tries to reassure him that everything was going to turn out alright in the end;
the British will grant them their demands, primary among the demands is
the release of all IRA prisoners. However, the reassuring talk did no good."*

"The prisoner tells his friend that he knows he is going to be killed..."

"He then told him a story called the Scorpion and the Frog. This is how
the story went," he said, while getting up, and walking slowly around the
room, still eyeballing the man.

"A scorpion asks a frog to ferry it across a lake to the other side. The frog
at first refuses, saying that it fears the scorpion will fatally sting it halfway to
the other side of the lake. The scorpion assures the frog it will do no such thing."

"Then the scorpion looked into the frog's confused eyes and said, 'we will
both die if I sting you. You will die of the venom, and I will die of drowning.
That would not make any sense at all; I don't want to die, and I'm sure you
don't either.'"

"Finally the frog gives in, and off they went, with the scorpion riding
piggyback on the frog. However, halfway across the lake, the scorpion gives the
frog the sting of death," he said, shaking his head in sorrow.

"Why did you do that? Now we're both going to die," the frog asks,
seconds before both of the vanished beneath the surface."

"The scorpion replied, 'I did it because it's in my nature.'"

Big Nine started to feel uneasy again after the story.

"That's ah' great story. Now I really wished I had caught that movie
when it was in theaters. If you let me go, I swear on my grandmother's grave
that I'll go out and buy the video of the movie; it's called The Crying Game
right?"

He was falling apart and he knew it. He needed to get it together quick.

"That's correct," replied Gunther, smiling slightly.

"The crying game, I'm excited about seeing it. Didn't Forest Whitaker
won an Oscar for his role?"

He was trying to hold back tears at this point.

"Now that escapes my memory. I didn't watch the Academy Awards that
year; all I know is this; he certainly deserved one."

"I'm sorry man," Big Nine said.

He could not hold back the tears anymore.

"Sorry about what?"

"I'm sorry that I didn't see The Crying Game when I had the chance."

"Don't worry about it man."

"Thanks, I don't want to disappoint you in any way."

"You can never disappoint me; we're friends. Tell you what. Since I told you a little bit about the movie, do you mind if I ask you a few questions to see if you were paying attention?" Gunther asked, while smiling so cheerfully and wide eyed, that the face now reminded Big Nine of a movie he once saw called, Fargo. In this movie, the smiling cheerful face of the pregnant police chief was to him the highlight of the movie. He really liked the part when she cheerfully had an Indian named Proud Foot's balls nailed to the wall with her evidence against him:

"So Mr. Proud Foot, think you can remember anything now?" she said with a million dollar cheerful smile, and eyes as wide as silver dollars.

"Sure my niggah', ask away," he replied, getting that good feeling again. He was now comfortable enough to resume calling him "niggah".

"Alright, this is the first question; why did the Forest Whitaker character tell the frog and scorpion story to his IRA friend?"

Big Nine thought carefully. After fifteen seconds, he replied, "He wanted to show that it's in the nature for natural born killers to kill; it's a built in kind of thing for certain animals and people to kill."

"That's very good my friend, excellent answer."

"Thank you very much," Big Nine replied, breathing a sigh of relief.

"Do you think the soldier's friend developed a true loving friendship towards the soldier or do you think he was just trying to keep the soldier calm?"

"I think the friend really developed a loving friendship with the soldier."

"Very good," replied Gunther, slowly clapping his hands together.

"I didn't tell you this before, but the friend's IRA comrades had already made a decision to kill the soldier. When they came into the room to take him out for execution, the friend volunteered to do it himself instead of them. Why do you think he volunteered for that gruesome job?"

"Because the friend planned on letting the soldier escape once they got far enough away?"

"No silly, he volunteered for the job because he truly loved the soldier, and didn't want his comrades to do something that personal to him. He felt as though it was his responsibility as a friend to do the job himself. He wanted to be there for him at that final moment. No one deserved to die without

family or at least a friend present. It's all about love, caring, friendship and compassion."

"That's heavy my brother; I can see clearly now where you are coming from", Big Nine replied, his body now starting to shake. His heart began to beat faster, and he began to slowly urinate again, being very careful as to not get any of the fluid on Gunther.

"Now this last question is in two parts. And this is the first part; what does the story about the frog and the scorpion have to do with you? Second part, what do the soldier and you have in common?"

Big nine thought carefully…

After about thirty seconds he figured out the answers; however, he didn't want to reply. Tears started flowing from his eyes again.

"Answer the questions Big Nine," Gunther said, still smiling wide eyed like the woman in Fargo.

"I can't."

"You can't or you won't?"

"I can't."

"I think you can; however, for your information and convenience, I'll do the honors," he said, no longer smiling.

"In the frog and the scorpion story, the scorpion shows us the mentality of an animal that is truly a natural born killer. It was placed on this earth by God for the purpose of killing. Many lower forms of animals must die in violent ways. Many in the highest form of animal—which is human—must die in violent ways. That is why there have always been wars within the lower animal kingdoms such as Ants, Crabs, and Chimps. There have always been wars within the highest animal kingdom which is human. God is a warring and killing God. God sent me to earth to kill. I call it pruning."

Big nine was now crying and cursing God for putting him in this horrible situation.

"God, I hate your mother fuckin' crazy ass for putting me in this horrible position. Fuck you and all the angels in heaven!!" Big Nine screamed.

"Don't be cursing my God; he gave your big black ass the ability to use common sense; however, you chose not to use it. You are the one that agreed to come to a stranger's house at night. God did not pull me into The Canal Street Bar for drinks, you did. Why did you do it my niggah? I'll tell you why, because I was handsome and well dressed. If I was ugly, smelly, hungry, and

filthy looking, you would have never taken me out for drinks. Looks can be deceiving."

"Please..." was the only word Big Nine could come up with. He kept saying the word over and over again; in a very low voice.

"I know you remember that hit record that the Mighty Temptations made called: Beauty is only skin deep. Instead of dancing your big black sweaty ass off to the music—as I'm sure you did back in the day—you should have taken a seat at the bar by yourself, to listen to the words of that song. The words of that song are true; and those words have been true since the beginning of mankind; and those words are still true today. Guess what? Those words will be true tomorrow."

"Beauty is only skin deep yeah yeah yeah
Beauty is only skin deep yeah yeah"
Big Nine suddenly stopped crying and pleading.

His mind flashed back to the 1960s, sweating on the dance floor, grooving on the Temptations and the Four Tops; and not really listening to the words.

"As for the second part of the question; the soldier was well aware of his impending doom, and accepted it like a man. He knew the mentality of the IRA because he was very well trained on that subject. A recruit must pass a written test on IRA behavior before that recruit graduates from any British armed forces basic training depot. He knew that he was not going to get out of this situation alive. He was in an impossible situation. That is where you come in. You are also in an impossible situation. There is no way for you to escape. I am not going to have a sudden change of heart, and set you free. You are just a small branch in a large tree of drug dealing hustlers that will be pruned."

Incredibly, Big Nine seemed to be calming down just a little bit after finally accepting this news from Gunther. He now realized that he is going to really die.

"I have nothing personal against drug dealers. Drug dealers are just one segment of the population that keeps cops and prisons in business. You are just part of the big economical circle of life. Society needs drug dealers, robbers, preachers, teachers, fireman, killers, prostitutes, politicians, doctors, gangs and bankers to keep the capitalistic engine running. It's my job to prune as many branches as possible from each of those trees."

"So you are really going to kill me?"

"Yes I am."

"But I don't want to die; I just started receiving my Social Security check."

"Everybody wants to go to heaven, but nobody wants to die," Gunther said, getting up, and walking around to room. He stopped for a moment to once again admire the portrait of Hitler. He turned back around, and walked back to Big Nine, who was now lowering his head again. He could not help himself; he began to cry once again; this time very quietly.

"Listen to me Big Nine, you have got to pull yourself together, and man up. This punk ass on again, off again crying is not going to do you any good. You are not a fuckin' baby; you are a grown ass man for Christ sakes. Man the fuck up!"

"I thought you liked me," Big Nine whispered.

"I not only like you, I love you man," Gunther replied, looking deeply into the man's eyes.

"If you love me, then why are you doing this to me?" Big nine asked.

"Love has absolutely nothing to do with this situation; this shit is strictly business. And I am definatly about my father's business. My God is a warring God. I am his hammer. I am his sword. I am his shield. And like a fire tipped arrow, I will penetrate the hearts of man, woman or child to do his work on Planet Earth."

"Are you going to use that big sledge hammer on me?"

"You are asking too many questions. Now I have been very patient with you, mainly because I have grown more closely with you than I have with any other person than I have met in my life. I have never had so much fun in my life as when we spent those few hours together in that bar. I have told you things that I have never told another person. I even had plans for you in my funeral business. However, when you woke me up, stumbling around for another drink, my Adolf whispered words into my ear. This is what he whispered to me in German, 'What is wrong with your thinking soldier? Put that stinking nigger out of his pathetic misery.'"

"After he said that to me, I knew you had to die."

"Why do you listen to Adolf Hitler? Hitler was insane!"

"Was he? It's a very fine line between insanity and genius."

"I just think you are doing the wrong thing."

"*You have a God given right to your opinion. All I know is this; I am through with all of this chit chat,*" *he said, turning his head, and looking at his hammer.*

He then slowly walked towards the door, then turned around and said, "*I'm going to leave the room for ten minutes in order to give you enough time to get your soul right with God. I do believe that there is a place somewhere called Heaven; and in that place is someone that we all call God. If you want to see him, and once again see your loved ones that have passed on, I suggest that you pray. I don't give this opportunity to everyone that I have placed in that chair. As a matter of fact, this is the very first time that I have gone this far in allowing someone a chance to get right with God. I do this because I truly love you, and want you to live forever in Christ Jesus.*"

With that said, Gunther walked out of the room, leaving a very calm, however, stunned Big Nine to process his horrible situation. He has never been much of a praying man; however, since he now knew his fate, he decided to pray with some sort of conviction.

He closed his eyes, and turned his attention to God. If there was really a place called heaven, he wanted to go there. So he asked God to forgive him for every sin that he has committed in his life. He asked God to allow him to enter the pearly gates. At this point he really didn't have anything to lose. It would be foolish of him not to pray at this point.

He has met many people since he moved to the New Orleans area that looks at the idea of a heaven and hell as silly, childlike, and simply foolish. His favorite barber once told him while giving him a shave, "*Santa Claus, tooth fairy, mermaids, God, Satan, heaven and hell, it's all nothing but wishful thinking fantasy.*"

He wandered what that barber would do if he was in this situation. He wandered what if the barber knew that he only had a few minutes to live; would he think the idea of God, heaven and hell was foolish?

Most likely, he figured that barber would start praying up a storm, just like he was prepared to do. A person can say they don't believe God exists; however, if they are wrong in their thinking, it might result in an everlasting and costly mistake.

And so, after eight minutes of hard praying, he paused for about ten seconds, and then he closed the prayer with three final words. It just so happened that these three words were uttered by one of the two crucified thieves that hung on each side of a dying Jesus. The thief on the right of Jesus slowly turned his battered head toward Jesus who was in tremendous pain after a brutal beating from the Roman guards. After beating, they nailed him to the middle cross. It is believed that those three words uttered to Jesus by the thief immediately thrust his soul to a place called Heaven after he took his last breath. These are the three words uttered by the thief: "Lord Remember Me…"

To believers, these are the most powerful combination of words to ever be uttered by human beings on Earth. These words are believed to be spiritual and supernatural. With those words, a person might be able to truly 'Energize' and be transported to another world; a world with no pain and sorrow.

Jesus slowly looked to the thief, and said to him, "This day, you will be with me in paradise."

He heard the door open; then close back again. Bare feet were now softly walking towards him…

"Did you get yourself right with God my friend?"

Big Nine did not respond to the question; he just kept on silently praying with his eyes tightly shut.

Gunther picked up the sledge hammer, and stepped up on the footlocker. He then gently placed the heavy hammer head on Big Nine's head to get into the right stance; with his feet wide apart.

Before he raised the hammer he said, "You ready Big Nine?"

Incredibly Big Nine responded this time in a loud voice, "Yes!!"

"See you later alligator," Gunther said, raising the hammer up high over his head…

"Wait!!" Big Nine shouted out, and at the same time opening his eyes.

Gunther froze with the hammer still up above his head.

"What's the matter now my niggah?" Gunther asked, while at the same time lowering the hammer down, and resting the hammer's head down by his feet.

"Would you please kiss me?" Big Nine asked, looking up into his eyes.

"Come on man, don't do this to yourself; it's man up time."

"Please my niggah', just one goodbye kiss."

Gunther reluctantly stepped down from the footlocker, and planted a wet one right on the lips. Big Nine tried to get his tongue in Gunther's mouth with no luck. Gunther's teeth were clamped down too tight; there was no opening for Big Nine's tongue to enter his mouth. He gave up trying and concentrated on prolonging the lip kiss as long as possible. After a few more seconds of lip on lip action, Gunther pulled away.

"Thank you," the big man said, partly closing his eyes, trying to savor the last kiss he would ever receive on planet earth."

"You are very welcome; it's the least I could do under the circumstances."

"I love you," Big Nine told him, smiling for the first time since he woke up in the chair.

"I love you too."

Gunther stepped back on the footlocker, and raised the hammer high above his head.

"You ready Big Nine?"

"See you in heaven my niggah!!" Big nine shouted, closing his eyes all the way.

Gunther brought the hammer down hard on the top of Big Nine's head.

After the tremendous swing of the hammer, all that was visible was Big Nine's eyes and forehead. His chin, mouth and nose were inside the chest cavity.

His spine must have somehow shattered, and closed in like a deck of cards coming together.

Gunther had seen this kind of result before, and thought nothing of it; however, he could not stand to see his only friend's blood soaked eyes partly hanging out from its sockets.

He brought the hammer up high again, and came down even harder this time. Now the entire head vanished into the chest. Blood shot up like a volcano erupting. The top of Big Nine's afro was bright red like a strange looking plant growing out of flower pot, however; this flower pot was a human chest.

It was now 10:15am Tuesday morning December 29th. On this very night, Gunther will be receiving the 'Man of the Year' award. However, at this moment he had a ton of work to do. He had conducted two funerals last Sunday at different times, and both families had requested that their loved one be cremated, and have the ashes delivered to them no later than today. It would take a little over an hour to burn up a body and another hour to grind up the charred bones into a fine powder to be placed in the urn for presentation. With Big Nine's body added to the mix, that's six hours of work right there.

He had decided that Big Nine would have a proper send off. Tomorrow after bible study, he planned to catch the Gretna ferry, and sprinkle his ashes into the mighty Mississippi River, after a brief prayer.

On top of all of that, he had a massive cleanup to do in the killing room. There was blood everywhere; blood on the walls, the chair, the floor, and on him, including in his hair.

The first thing he decided to do was to take a long hot shower. He did not want the blood to dry in his beautiful golden blond Arian hair.

He left the room to shower; then returned a half hour later with a mop, bucket of hot water, scrub brush, towels, and a ladder. As he got busy cleaning, his mind flashed back to his first murder...

He was swimming in a muddy pond with a girl from a neighboring farm. They were both fifteen years old. In his hometown, it was very unusual for a boy and a girl to be alone together in a secluded area. As a matter of fact, it was frowned upon and forbidden in this small religious community. However, on this particular hot June afternoon, Gunther did find himself alone with this girl.

They began splashing water on each other; that graduated to wrestling. After a while Gunther suggested that they practice baptizing. The girl agreed and suggested that she practice first on Gunther.

After practicing on Gunther for about five minutes, it was time to switch roles. Gunther grabbed the girl's hair, and pulled her head back into the water...

He then brought the girls head back up.

"Do you believe in the Lord God almighty?"

"Yes."

Again he dipped her head in the water a few seconds, and then he brought her head back up.

"Are you ready to be washed in the blood of Jesus?"

"Yes."

Again he pulled the girl's head back under the water; this time he did not bring the girl's head back up until she had stopped jerking and splashing in agony.

He held her under for an additional minute just to be sure she was dead. He then pulled her limp body out of the water, and went screaming for help. The incident was ruled as an accidental drowning. Everyone was satisfied with the ruling.

He killed no more in his community. However, several farm animals throughout the community died from sudden and mysterious circumstances.

It was now 12:45 and the room was spotless. He turned and looked at the Hitler portrait. He knew that Hitler was a person that detested any kind of filth. Filth leads to disease.

Hitler, he imagined became obsessed with cleanliness after seeing so much filth, decay and diseased soldiers in the trenches during the First World War. He had witnessed rats feasting on dead soldiers, men eating rations after brushing away the flies and rats.

Things got even worse with the introduction of Mustard gas.

When a soldier takes in even one short intake of this gas, his insides start to roast, just like a pig would roast when placed on hot rocks and buried in the ground Hawaiian style.

This type of warfare, although condemned, became one of the deadliest tools in warfare. Bloated bodies became a common sight during that period.

Hitler would calmly step over this filth on his way to deliver a critical message to the leadership several miles away. When he saw the opportunity to run, and not step on any decaying bodies, he ran.

Gunther spoke to the portrait using the German language, "My Fuhrer, I hope this extermination room is clean to your liking. I have worked diligently on this.

There should be no place in this room for disease to hide."

The Hitler portrait came to life...

He unfolded his arms, and looked at Gunther with anger.

"Why do you insult me? I should have you shot! I can smell the germs in this room. You call this clean? I want this room clean. I'm giving you exactly one half hour to clean this filth. If the task is not done in the proper time allowed, I will get Himmler to boil the flesh from your bones," Hitler said, now returning back to his position in the portrait.

Gunther started back scrubbing at a frantic pace.

Thirty minutes later Hitler approved the cleaning of the room to the delight of a now relieved Gunther.

It was now 1:30pm, and Gunther had placed the first body on the conveyer leading to the oven door. This body was that of a young white woman of twenty two. She died as a result of a heroin overdose.

The oven was heated to 1900 degrees. He pushed a button, and off the girl went. The flames hungrily started consuming her flesh. Smoke rushed up the long chimney, and into the afternoon air.

This chimney was especially built for this purpose. It had to be one of the tallest chimneys in all of New Orleans. Gunther had it built to run from the basement floor, through both floors, and ten feet from the base of the roof.

There were two other funeral homes on historic Claiborne Avenue; However, Gunther's Funeral home was the largest, and most popular. It was the crown jewel of the Gunther Funeral home empire. Although his other funeral homes located in different parts of Orleans Parrish were equipped for full service, including chapel and viewing areas, the Claiborne location was where all the embalming, cremation and casket selections took place.

He had two huge rooms with over forty caskets to choose from. There was never any need for a family to place a casket on order; they always found what they were looking for at the Claiborne location, including steel vaults.

Gunther Funeral home was the new kid on the block; however, as it turned out, his funeral home was the grandest in design, construction and appearance.

The design took in the historical significance of the community. It looked like a grand old plantation mansion from the Antebellum Period.

At 2:35pm Gunther was grinding the black charred bones of the woman into a fine powder. This was done painstakingly with a round headed mallet. He pounded the bones for another hour; then he poured the ashes into an urn.

At 2:50 he went upstairs to make some calls to the families as the second body burned. This body was that of an old black man that died of a heart attack.

At 5:00 he pressed the button, and Big Nine was off the meet the flames.

The first family arrived at 5:15 to pick up the urn containing the remains of the young white girl. After prayer and comfort, in which Gunther was very good at; the family left at 5:45.

The second family arrived at 6:00, and left at 6:45.

Gunther pulled the conveyer back from the oven that contained Big Nine's charred bones. He immediately went to work beating the bones into a power. When he finished, he placed the remains of his friend in an urn, and placed it on a table in his bedroom.

It was now 8:15; time for him to grab another quick shower, get dressed, and get to the ceremony before nine. Already there were singers, speakers and other dignitaries taking turns stepping up to the mike; however, Gunther was the main attraction; and he was not scheduled to receive his award until 9:00pm.

At 8:50 Gunther stepped through the front door of the Ernest N. Morial Convention Center. He stood in the back ground until he heard his introduction by the Mayor.

Slowly he moved towards the stage, shaking hands all along the way.

"Thank you Mayor Richardson. I am humbled and honored to receive this most coveted award. I accept it on behalf of all the people that lost their lives when Katrina hit this area. That storm as you all know was the most devastating natural disaster to ever hit this country. Thousands of people lost everything. Homes and lives were lost; hundreds more are still unaccounted for, most likely washed out into the Gulf. Yes I did what I could in providing proper funerals for the families that could not afford to pay; and yes I gave a whole lot of money to the local relief efforts here in town."

"However, it was no great sacrifice on my part mainly because I'm wealthy. Wealthy men brought great gifts to Jesus, and they were upset when he praised a woman for giving to him what amounted to was a few pennies. Jesus told the wealthy men that they made no great contribution because they were wealthy. He went on to say that the poor woman gave more than they gave because she had given all she had."

"The point I'm trying to make here is that I have witnessed people in this city that had almost nothing share what little they had with others. I could never match what the people of this city did for each other. Everyone reached out to everyone else. If a man had a piece of bread he broke it apart to feed others. If a child was wandering around alone, other families would take the child into their arms."

"Families from different parts of the country came here to pick up their loved ones, if they could find them; and take them back home with them. They are the ones that should be standing here, not me. I would also like to thank our president during that horrible period, George Bush. I know sometimes it seemed to people that he did not know what he was doing; however, in my heart I felt as though he was overwhelmed with the magnitude of that situation. In truth, nobody really knew what they were doing. The people in power were in shock as a dear staring down on coming headlights."

"I would like to send out a special message of thanks to retired Lt. General Russell Honore for stepping in and regaining control of a chaotic situation. He boldly stepped in between the National Guard and a people that had already gone through a devastating and horrific trauma; and was now facing down the National Guard, that was pointing their rifles at them. The General boldly and bravely ordered the guard to put down their weapons."

As his speech went on, he started having short periods of speechlessness. The longest period of his blank time was ten seconds. He had given many speeches since coming to New Orleans; however, this was the first time he had ever found himself in this situation. He started to just walk off the stage; however, he pressed on.

The reason for this unusual behavior in this speech was due to images rushing into his head of his rampage in California.

An attendant brought him a glass of water. He really needed it, and asked to audience to excuse him for a second. After he drank about half of the glass of water, he gave the glass back to the attendant, and proceeded on…

Now this was what was consuming his mind and thoughts… California…

Let's go back in time a few years…

He was killing at very fast pace and trying to fulfill his pruning solution for all it's worth.

FBI Los Angles field director Jim Bruce now had the cooperation of every law enforcement agency on the west coast. They were processing murders from Mexico and San Diego all the way up to San Francisco and beyond. Jim had a few major problems with this case:

One, there was absolutely no description of the killer. Two, the killings seemed to be random. Children, adults, blacks, whites, Hispanics, Orientals, men, women, and gays were all victims. Three, there were no pattern in the locations of the murders. There might be three murders on one beach, and the next day they will find four more dead bodies on another beach seventy miles away. Still the next day they would find seven bodies in Seattle. The only thing they had to go on was the knowledge that all the killings were done by the same person. How did they know? Because of the crime scenes, which were absolutely clean of anything that could by analyzed in a lab. Sometimes they did find shell casings; however, even those items were untraceable.

Law enforcement was patiently waiting on the killer's first mistake; however, at this rate they could be waiting forever…

Gunther had it all worked out. When he got a call from a funeral home located in one of the west coast beach communities to work on a body, he would arrive with his suit case.

Along with his agreed upon fee, most of the funeral homes provided him a place to sleep. He would always stay until the funeral was over. Then he would move on to the next funeral home. There was always plenty of work. Some of the bodies he worked on were of people he had murdered. Those were the ones that were found on the beach or in their hotel rooms. However, many of the murdered victims of this killing spree will never be found, because they were at the bottom of the sea. Gunther kept a rental boat tied up at the boat dock in Marina Del Rey, and he used it quite often.

One bright Saturday morning he was sitting in a beach chair on the beach in Santa Monica. A gorgeous redhead young white woman walked by him and smiled in his direction. She took a few more steps, and turned around. She stood there for a few seconds then walked back to where he was sitting.

"Do you mind if I take a picture of you?" the woman asked, still smiling and revealing her pearly white teeth. She was wearing a string bikini that showed off a near perfect body. She was tall for a woman, at least six foot tall; however, her weight was a no more than 110 pounds.

Her blazing red head hair seemed to burst into life with the morning sun light. She was indeed a beauty.

"Sure, go right ahead", replied Gunther, brushing his short golden hair back with his fingers.

She took several pictures of him sitting in the chair.

"Do you mind standing up for me?"

"You are getting a lot, and I don't even know your name," he said, while getting up and flexing his arms and legs.

"Karen is my name, what's yours?" the woman answered while taking as many snap shots as she could.

"Are you a professional photographer? If you are, I want to be paid."

"No, I'm not a pro; I just like taking pictures of beautiful objects, and you are one of the most beautiful objects that I have ever seen."

"So I've been told."

"You have to be some sort of actor; if you're not, then you need to be."

"No I'm not an actor, and I have no intension of becoming one."

"That's ah' shame. Even the great George Clooney would have to take a back seat to you on the looks department."

"I've heard of Clooney, however, I haven't seen him on screen."

"He's wonderful; I just know he's going to win an Oscar someday."

"Well Karen, you are indeed easy on the eyes yourself; are you in show business of some sort?" he asked while sitting back down, and patting the seat of the empty chair next to him, inviting her to sit down beside him.

"No not yet, however, it's only a matter of time. I've been doing some photo shoots for a magazine here on the beach all this week. I'm off Saturday and Sunday; then Monday morning I have my first screen test for a movie. I'm so excited," she said sitting down, and wondering whose chair she is sitting in…

"That sounds great, what's the name of the movie, and who's the director?"

"It's called, A Walk at Midnight; it's about a woman that goes out at midnight just about every night and kills people at random with a high powered rifle. She does not remember doing it the next day. The director is Clint Eastwood."

"I've seen a lot of his work, both as an actor and director," he replied.

"I've only seen him in two movies. I watched both of them at home on my video player. My boyfriend is a big time Eastwood fan, and he bought both movies over to my apartment for us to watch. One is called, A Fist Full of Dollars, and the other is called, The Good, The Bad and The Ugly."

"I've seen both, plus the one called, Play Misty for me; and all the Dirty Harry movies, and a good portion of the Rawhide episodes," Gunther said, while taking two soft drinks out of his cooler and offering Karen one.

She eagerly took a drink of the bottled Pepsi and said, *"You should come to the audition with me on Monday. It's going to be held at Glendale High School. I'm sure the casting director could find a place for you in the film with your good looks. You need to take advantage of what God has given you,"* she said, rubbing her fingers through his golden hair.

"Yeah, I might just do that. Maybe fame and fortune is in my future," he replied while taking another sip of his soda.

"Has anyone ever told you that you have beautiful blue Paul Newman eyes?"

"Many times, although the statement gets old after a while."

"I've never met anyone like you. You don't seem to understand just what you have going for yourself," she stated, looking at him slightly puzzled.

"Don't get bewildered, I am well aware of my looks. I just don't let it go to my head. I do allow my looks to serve me on certain situations."

"Well that's better. Now promise me you will attend the audition with me," she said, looking at him intensely. She really wanted him to go. She was a smart young woman; and always looking for an ace in the hole.

Karan laid out the plan in her mind…

After the casting director takes one look at Gunther it would be a rap, lights out, ball game over. They would find a place for him, even maybe a leading role. On the way over to the casting on Monday she would make a deal with him; whichever one got a part in the movie has to insist that the other one gets a part or no deal.

"I promise to go with you Karen; the more I think about this opportunity, the more I like it."

"Super!" she shouted, putting her arm around his neck, and kissing him on the cheek.

"I have a good feeling about this. It must be written in the stars that you and I should meet. Do you believe that you and I were destined for each other?"

"I sure do, as a matter of fact, I believe God puts us in certain situations to serve him better," he said, looking out at the vast blue ocean.

"Oh I'm sorry to be getting all philosophical; I'm just excited that's all."

"That's quite alright Karen; I'm a little excited myself."

Gunther looked at this as a chance to give his father the gift of a lifetime. If he did get a part in the movie, he would bring his father in to meet the great Clint Eastwood in person.

He had only returned home twice since he left. On his second trip home on Christmas last year he found out that his father had been diagnosed with prostate cancer.

The cancer was in an advanced stage; there was nothing more to be done but wait on death. He loved his father dearly. And he always knew he was a huge fan of Clint Eastwood. He had seen every movie that he had ever played in; including the earlier spaghetti westerns he stared in when he was just starting out.

Maybe, he thought, this chance at a movie career was God's gift to him for being so faithful to his word. To top it all off, his father would meet the man that he most admired in the whole world, before death finally shows up.

Karen looked away from him. She was now looking at a pleasure boat going by with people on board having a good time. They held up Bud Light beer cans, pulled up bikini tops, men pulled down short. Some of the people were kissing…

"Looks like they're having a ball," Karen said, waving back at the people on the boat.

"Sure looks that way to me. Do you like boats?"

"I love boats; it's just been a long time since I rode on one."

"Would you like a boat ride?" He asked, putting his hand on her shoulder.

"I sure would, today is Saturday, so I don't have any shoots today anyway, super!" she shouted, jumping off her chair; clapping her hands like a little girl.

"It's such a beautiful morning. I have a boat, and we need to celebrate our budding movie careers. So let's hit the water!"

After Gunther stood up, she jumped in his arms.

As they slowly started walking the two miles to get to the boat dock, she told him about herself and where she came from.

She told him she was from South Bend Indiana, home of the Notre Dame fighting Irish. She loved football, and went to Notre Dame University to study biology, and attended the Irish football games on Saturday. When she found out that students get free tickets to the home games, she was all in.

In her second year she tried out for the cheer leader squad, and made the team; mainly because of her looks. She quit the team before the start of her junior year, mainly because although being a cheer leader gets a person closer to the team, your back was turned from the game most of the time.

She was not interested in looking at fans; she wanted to watch the game, the entire game.

Her grades were very high. She maintained a 4.0 in her Biology, chemistry, math and computer science courses. She also took two elective courses; one was French II and the other was drama.

It was doing her two semesters in that drama class that she developed a serious case of the acting bug. It was not just some pipe dream that she had; her drama professor told her that she had a real shot at becoming a professional actress. She managed to win the leading role in all the plays put on by the drama club. She seemed to have a natural ability to loose herself in her character.

Although her home was only twelve miles from campus, she lived in the dorm. She did so mainly because it was free, along with her tuition, books, meals and supplies. She was on a full academic scholarship.

At the end of her third year she came home for the summer as usual; only this time she informed her parents that she would be taking a year off from school to go to California, and give acting a try.

As she expected her parents were furious with her.

Both her parents were farmers. They got up early every morning, and shared all the household duties such as, cooking the breakfast, getting the two younger children ready for school, and going into the wheat fields to work. They also had to feed the hogs and chickens, as well as milk the cows before they got to the wheat fields. Although they were proud farmers, they wanted their eldest daughter to be a doctor.

After Karen was born they waited ten years before trying to have another. They were blessed with twin boys. They had hopes that when the boys became men, they would take over the farm if they showed an interest.

However, for Karan their first born, they wanted her to go into medicine. When she graduated 1st in her class at Notre Dame high school, the parents knew that their dreams were about to come true. Then came the full scholarship offer from Stanford university, and they were on cloud nine.

One can only imagine the shock parents felt after being told by their near genius daughter that she was quitting school to become an actress. Although Karan said she was taking a year's break from school, they knew the odds were against that. They knew that chances were that she would never return; students almost never do when they take a break like that.

Reluctantly they gave in to her dreams.

They had saved money for her education. Since she had a full scholarship they still had the money. They had intended to give it to her as a graduation gift.

However, they still gave it to her early. They knew that she would need the money in California. They did not want her to be dependent on anyone. They had watched too many television shows that revealed how young naïve girls go to Hollywood with the goal of becoming big movie stars, only to wind up on the streets, selling their bodies, and giving the money to a pimp. They didn't want their only daughter to wind up like that.

They made her promise to them that when the money ran out, she was to return home and prepare herself for her final year in college, and then move on to medical school. She agreed, received the money and set out for Hollywood.

It did not take long for her to find a good agent.

She got steady work doing commercials while waiting for her big break. She found a nice affordable apartment in the Hermosa Beach community, and was lucky enough to find a real gentlemen boyfriend. His name is Tony, and he lived in the same apartment village. He works as a set designer in Hollywood. They enjoy each other's company, and he does not pressure her for sex. He respects her wishes not to have sex until marriage. Everything seemed to be moving in the right direction for her. Meeting Gunther put the icing on the cake.

They arrived at the boat dock, and after checking out everything on board, they took off. The look on Karen's face was priceless as she breathed in the morning air from the fast moving boat. Her smile said it all. She was in Heaven.

They rode through Malibu, Venice Beach, Manhattan Beach and Hermosa Beach. They always stayed close enough to the shore to give Karen the chance to wave at the people relaxing on the sand or playing in the water. Most of the people waved back. A few drunken guys at Venice Beach pulled down their swim pants and gave her the moon. She wasn't offended by it; it was all in fun.

"Let's go out further," she shouted."

"Alright but not too far, I've only been boating for a couple of weeks; I don't want to get us stranded out in the deep."

"Oh you'll do fine; I have faith in you," She replied, stepping to the front of the boat and sitting in a fishing chair.

"Here go's," shouted Gunther, putting the two huge engines to full throttle. They were now bouncing off the waves, and having the time of their lives.

"Don't you think were out far enough?" Gunther shouted.

"If you say so, I can barely see land," she said smiling at him.

He shut off the engines.

"Hey, I didn't want you to stop; let's keep riding, just don't go out any deeper that's all," she said standing up and stretching.

"Ok, I'll start the engines back up; but first I have to do something."

"Do what?"

"Kill you."

"What did you say?"

"I said, kill you."

"Come on now, don't fuck with my mind here man. I don't find this the least bit funny. Start the fuckin' engines, and get me back to shore; you're freaking me out pal."

"I assure you, I'm not trying to be funny; as a matter of fact I am dead serious. I am going to kill you."

"Hey asshole, get me the fuck off this boat you freak!!"

"Oh yes, you are going to leave this boat, but you are not going to shore," he said, while reaching into a small chest and retrieving a German Luger hand gun with a silencer attached at the end of the barrel.

"Do you have any idea how many people I have killed? Come on, take a wild guess."

"Please Gunther don't…"

"I have killed well over fifty, and counting; however, I have never killed one with a gun; you are the first, doesn't that make you feel special?" he said aiming the gun at her head.

She put her hands across her face and pleaded with him…

"Come on now; let's make this easy for everyone. If you don't bring your hands down, and allow me to put a bullet between your eyes, I'm going to have to shoot you between your legs, right into the holiest of private places. Now that would be both painful and unnecessary. Or maybe I'll shoot you in your knees; now that would also be extremely painful. Then after that, since you had to be a horse's ass about the whole thing, I'll most likely let you suffer

for a few hours. Now which is it going to be? Will it be a quick pop between the eyes and it's over or will it be a long drawn out affair?"

"Why do you have to do this?"

"It's a long story. All I'm going to tell you is this; you picked the wrong Saturday morning to relax on Malibu Beach. Now move your fuckin' hands!!"

"Can I pray first?"

"Sure, I'm not that heartless; get yourself right with God," he said, still pointing the gun at her forehead.

She brought her fingers together under her chin to pray…

"Dear God, I –"

Gunther put a bullet right between her eyes, and dead center, an inch above the bridge of her nose. It took out a small portion of the back of her head.

After the shooting he sat down in the pilot's chair, and looked over the pistol again.

He was well pleased with his Luger. It had performed very well in its first audition. He now knew that the Luger will play a big part in his life.

This pistol had cost him a hefty price. This was not one of the newer models that were now being made on a limited basis. This was an original German Luger, used in WWI and WWII. Adolf Hitler himself had one his side when in uniform.

This pistol had cost Gunther fifteen thousand dollars at auction. On top of that, an additional five thousand dollars went to the machining of the barrel in order to be able to screw in a silencer when needed. The cost of the silencer and one hundred rounds of 9mm luger cartridges were included in the five thousand dollars.

He had to sell some of his stock in order to gather up the money. He was not rich during those early years; however, he knew how to maneuver shares of stock, and make quick money.

He finally snapped out of his trance, and put the pistol away.

He quickly wrapped her body in an old worn out tent, then tied a chain around her. He attached one end of the chain to an eight inch cinder construction block.

After he lowered her body into the water, he quickly picked up the block and threw it in behind the body. Both body and cinder block disappeared rapidly.

After cleaning the blood and brain matter from the side and floor of the boat, he headed back towards the shore.

He managed to prune two more budding actresses the exact same way before the day was done.

9:15 pm Tuesday Dec 29 2009
Ernest N. Morial Convention Center
New Orleans, Louisiana.
The ending of the Gunther Heisman Man of The Year Speech

"…I would also like to thank the firefighters and rescue personnel for their heroic efforts to save as many lives as they did. Without their tireless efforts, hundreds more would have lost their lives. I would also like to thank the National Guard for their help in restoring order. And a special thanks to the mayor at that time, Mayor Nagle. You did the best job you could do giving the horrific situation this city was in."

"In closing I would just like to say that the job is still a long way to being complete. The heart and soul of this city is still missing. I am speaking of the black people, who are still scattered out throughout this country. We need them back; New Orleans will never be the same without them. Let's bring them all back!"

With that said, the room erupted. The standing ovation lasted a full minute. Gunther had a hard time getting to his table; everyone wanted to shake his hand.

"Our next governor! Our next governor! Our next governor…"

Gunther had heard this chant before during other city functions. He was starting to hear it more and more lately. He appreciated the endorsement from the masses; however, he knew what he would be facing in a tough campaign in any election that he would try to get into.

He had three things against him that would make a successful campaign extremely difficult. First of all he had only been a citizen of Louisiana for six years. Secondly, he was not married. Thirdly, he didn't have a college degree. All he really had going for him was his good looks and expertise in trading and investments.

He was indeed a multimillionaire; however, money and good looks alone were not enough to be taken seriously as a candidate for governor.

So as usual, he locked his fingers together as if praying, and turned his head from side to side; begging the people to stop, because was not interested in running for Governor.

He returned home around midnight; the after party started at 11:00. He slipped out at 11:45. The night went very well; however, he was tired.

By 12:45am Sunday morning, he had showered, eaten a bowl of hot oatmeal, and gone to bed.

By 3:00am he was in a bar on Bourbon Street having a conversation with a young white homeless man. Sometimes a person can be too tired to sleep.

"Why aren't you drinking?" the skinny long haired man asked Gunther. "I'm drinking my coffee, if that's alright with you," replied Gunther stirring a little more cream in his cup.

"No that's fine with me man; since you're paying for everything, you can drink anything you want. I'll just keep ordering Jack Daniels," the man said, sticking his finger in the air to get the bartender's attention.

"Now what was you saying about your life, and how you ended up sleeping in the streets?" Gunther asked, taking a sip of the hot coffee.

"Like I said man, I had ah fucked up childhood. I'm from fuckin' Chalmette Louisiana; just up the road apiece. My daddy worked for ah' pipe cleaning outfit. They cleaned the pipes for the oil drilling companies. He was one mean ass motherfucker; I'm glad his ass is dead!!" the man shouted.

"Keep it down man, you're way too loud, you don't want the bartender to put us out now do you?"

"Fuck no man," he whispered. His breath smelled like horse shit. Gunther put a napkin up to his nose.

"That fucker beat me almost every damned night. He beat my mama too. He was always mad at the fuckin' world, and took it out on us. That's the reason my mama started smoking crack; she needed something to deal with the pain. One day I found her stash and took me ah good ole' hit. That's why I'm sleeping in the streets man; I'm still looking for that first hit," he said with a wide grin, exposing his yellow teeth.

"How would you like some good hot food, a nice hot shower, and a warm bed to sleep in tonight?"

"Hey man, I ain't into no goddamn fuckin' homo shit!"

"No my friend, I'm not gay; I'm straight. All I want to do is get you cleaned up, fed, and get you into a nice warm bed. When was the last time you slept in a nice clean bed?"

"Hell, I don't even fuckin' remember. I could sleep in the mission but I don't like their fucked up rules man."

"You ready to go my friend?"

"Hell fuckin' no, I can't leave all this booze. You did say I could drink all I want, remember? Come on man, be ah' good Christian brother, and keep your fuckin' word man!!" he shouted again; only this time he stood up and clinched his fists.

"If you don't hold your voice down you won't be getting shit. Now I'm not going to tell you again, keep it down," Gunther said, looking around.

"Sorry man, it won't happen again," the man said, sitting back down. He quickly downed his drink, and ordered another.

"Now you listen to me good, I've got plenty booze at my home. After you get yourself cleaned up and fed, you can drink all you want before you go to sleep. Now how does that sound to you?"

"Sounds fuckin' Jim Dandy to me," he said, turning his glass up to his lips.

After drinking two more shots in silence, he looked at Gunther and smiled.

He was finally getting drunk. It takes much more booze to get an alcoholic drunk as it would for a normal person to get drunk.

"Why are you so fuckin' nice to me? Nobody is ever nice to me? Why you?" the man asked, looking at Gunther through half closed eye lids.

"You are a child of God; being nice to you is the Godly thing to do. There are no anterior motives, other than my love for you as your brother in Christ," Gunther replied, while waving the bartender over to pay the tab.

The men then got up, and headed for the door.

Gunther helped the man get into the car.

He would have to take his car to the body shop to get the inside completely sanitized to get rid of that nauseating smell from the man's body odor.

Once they entered the front door, Gunther asked, "What's it going to be first? Do you want to start with a hot shower, maybe some food?"

"Let's start with a fuckin' drink first, and maybe some crack rocks." the man replied.

"I don't have any dope; however, I'll be happy to bring you a drink."

"Make it happen captain!" the man shouted.

Gunther helped the man over to a metal folding chair that he had in the corner. He wasn't about to let the man sit his filthy ass down on his expensive couch.

He walked over to the bar, and put one drop of the knock out liquid in the glass before pouring a double shot of Grey Goose Vodka in it. He mixed it with a stirrer then added two ice cubes. The man eagerly drank the booze then asked for a cigarette. Gunther always kept smokes in the house for this very situation. He gave the man a cigarette, and also gave him a light.

"What about bringing that bottle over here? No since in you walking back and forth to the bar," the man said, looking around the room.

"Will there be anything else?" Gunther asked the man after bringing over a small table containing a quart of the very expensive Grey Goose, a glass, a bowl of ice cubes, a pack of Newport cigarettes, and an ash tray.

"No that will be all my good man," he replied, while at the same time pouring a drink.

About ten minutes later, he was knocked out cold.

Gunther gathered up the man, and put him in a wheel barrow for transportation down to the killing room. He didn't bother to take off the man's clothes; he did not want to see or smell the man's filthy underclothes, dealing with his nasty outer clothes was bad enough.

Twenty minutes later, the homeless man was sitting in ole' Smoky, and shackled down good and tight.

Gunther went back upstairs; it would be another hour before the homeless man wakes back up.

He went into the kitchen, and looked into the refrigerator for a snack. He saw that the cook had made him a cold chicken sandwich, and wrapped it nicely in foil. Now eating the sandwich, and washing it down with milk, his mind starting thinking about things he had to do when the sun rises. First on his list was to get to bible study at Saint John's Catholic Church at 9:00am. Then give Big Nine a proper sendoff via the river. Then he had to go to Bay St Louis, and work on a body for another funeral home. A young black woman died as a result of a car accident. Her body was torn up. The family would like her face to look just as pretty as it had been when she was alive. Gunther was the only man in these parts that had the skill to make that happen.

When he finished his sandwich, he headed for the computer room to check on his investments. He had no idea what he was going to do with all the money he had made over the years. He certainly didn't need it. The funeral home business's brought in quite enough money for him to live a lavish lifestyle—which he did. Maybe God or Hitler would tell him what to do with the money.

Maybe he would die single and rich just like his hero Adolf Hitler.

He acquired most of his millions investing in the Silicon Valley Internet craze; and he did it without much effort or time.

It started out as a means of killing time between murders. It wound up becoming a cash cow. He tried to slow down the flow of cash last year by investing in risky stocks. He found that making tremendous amounts of money was taking up too much of his time. He needed to crash this money making machine that he was so good at running. However; the problem was, even the risky stocks he had invested in took off like the space shuttle. If you invest into risky stocks, and the stock crashes, you lose big. However, if the stock rises, you win big.

Thus, Gunther got even richer.

Frustrated with this new influx of money, he decided to only check his investments twice a month.

After digging into cyberspace for thirty minutes, he got up from the computer angry. He had made another twenty million dollars since he had last checked two weeks ago.

He got down on his knees to pray:

"My dear Jesus. I hope my work so far has been to your liking. I have pruned many people as to your instructions. I will continue to do your will my father. I am so grateful that you choose me for this mission. So far, the pruning has gone along with out any complications. Adolf Hitler came to me, as you know. He comes to me often these days. I will not be bullied by him. He wants me to kill Jewish people. I will not do that. Those people have historically been through enough. I will not bring down anymore hardship and pain on them. You, my father is Jewish; and I am sure that you can appreciate my decision on the matter. Thank you, my father. Now I must get back to your work.

He put his mind back to pruning. It was time to check on the killing room's quest of honor.

He went to the bedroom to take off most his clothes. He stood in front of the mirror, and admired his muscular body for a while. He turned his body around from the mirror, and looked back at the refection of his back. He then smiled.

Then Adolf Hitler appeared in the mirror just as he turned around to bring the front of his body back facing the mirror.

Hitler, standing behind him said in German, "You think you're hot shit don't you."

"No my fuhrer, I was just admiring my body. I work out a lot, and from time to time I like to see the results."

"I must admit, you are a fine specimen of Arian supremacy indeed. Your golden hair, sky blue eyes, and perfectly proportioned body make me proud to have you in my inner circle. On top of that, you came up with your own version of my Final Solution; you call it a pruning solution."

"Yes my fuhrer, I am most proud of it, and I hope you are pleased with the results it had produced," Gunther replied standing rigidly at attention. He looked like a marble stone statue that the great painter and sculptor Michelangelo might have created many centuries ago.

"Yes I am very pleased with the amount of deaths this pruning Solution of yours has resulted in; however, I am very disappointed in your progress with solving my Jewish problem. You have not pruned from the Jewish tree!!"

He shouted and pounded his right fist into his left palm.

"My fuhrer, you have already killed enough Jews. My solution is not based on race; it is based on pruning. That being said, I want to terminate as many lives as I can from every segment of the population. Race has nothing to do with my solution," he defiantly replied, knowing full well that Hitler might give the order for him to commit suicide.

He waited for what seemed like hours; however, it had only been twenty five seconds before Hitler collected himself enough to respond. He was not used to someone going against his wishes and commands.

"Very well then, carry on with your work," Hitler said before vanishing from view.

Gunther slowly breathed relief...

He took in some deep breaths, slowly exhaling, and getting a dizzy feeling in his head. He had taken a huge risk in defying the great Adolf

Hitler in whom he loved so dearly; however, he needed to make it clear to him that this particular solution was his and his only. Hitler had his Final Solution, and now it was his turn. His was a much better solution in every way, and he wanted to see it through.

However, if Hitler had ordered him to end his life right then and there, he would have no choice but to fire a bullet into his own brain. After all, if Hitler was bold enough to shoot himself, so was he.

And so he comes to Gunther from time to time; looking like he did when he was the supreme Chancellor of Germany; young, strong, brave, and most of all, God like.

Gunther heard the shouts just as soon as he opened the sound proof door.

"Hey motherfucker, come set me free from this fuckin' chair!"

The homeless man wasn't crying like most of the other victims that found themselves bound to the wooden chair. He was just pissed off.

"Hey you son-of ah bitch; free me; and I mean right fuckin' now!" the man shouted upon seeing Gunther's naked body walk through the door.

"You are in no position to give commands my friend," Gunther said, while slowly moving in closer to the man.

"Why are you almost naked you freak! I told you before that I ain't into no fuckin' homo shit!"

Gunther laughed…

"Sir forgive me, but I never asked you what your name was; would you please tell me now," Gunther asked, stopping about two feet from the chair.

"I'm not telling you ah' fuckin' thing you yellow headed freak! Now get me the fuck outta' this chair before I stick ma' foot so far up yo' ass, we both would have to go to the fuckin' hospital to have it pulled the fuck out!!" the homeless man loudly shouted, while looking Gunther straight in the eyes.

Gunther could not believe what he was hearing.

He laughed again. Then he said, "You're putting the cart before the horse. How are you going to put your foot up my ass when I've got your smelly carcass tied down from top to bottom?"

"You better be glad I'm tied down motherfucker!!"

"You really are one frisky rug rat aren't you?" Gunther said, now slowly walking around the room in a circle."

Then the homeless man said, "Allow me to lay ah good word of advice on you. If it's one person in this whole wide world you don't wanna' fuck with, it's a Chalmette man; cause a Chalmette man will fuck you up in ah' heartbeat motherfucker!"

Gunther looked somewhat totally confused by the man's bravery.

"And another thing, put on some goddam' clothes. Ain't no man gonna' fuck me, and I ain't fucking no man."

"My friend, settle down. I have no intension of engaging in sexual activities with you. The only reason why I am only in my shorts is because I do not want to get blood on my clothes."

"What do you mean by that?" the homeless man asked in a lower tone of voice.

"What I mean by that is; I'm going to bash your head in with that sledge hammer that's stationed over there in the corner."

The man glanced over at the corner of the front of the room; he saw the hammer, and winced.

"Now why do you wanna' to haul off and do a fool thing like that for?" the man asked, looking into Gunther's eyes for any sign of sanity.

"Furthermore, not only am I not interested in having sex with you, I am not interested in having sex with anyone; period."

The homeless man replied, "Fuck all that right now. I don't give ah' fat baby's ass if you never have sex in your entire freaky ass life. Let's get to the real question on the table. Why is it so important for you to hit me in the head with that big fuckin' hammer over there?"

Gunther stopped pacing around in circles. He then walked directly in front of the man, and stopped. He then took a couple of long breathes and began to answer the man's question in full detail.

"You are an important part of my perfect solution, because you are a member of the homeless population in this country. It is my intension to prune as many of you as possible from the vast homeless tree. I also will try to implement this system for every segment of the population; so don't for once think I personally have anything against homeless people. I don't. As a matter of fact homeless people are very important to the economy in this country. Your kind of human being provides jobs for other people. Your kind of human being is a very intricate, important and needed piece of the economic circle of life in this country."

"Mister, you are one crazy motherfucker," the man said looking up toward the ceiling.

"Would you like to take a few minutes to get yourself right with God?"

"No thanks man. What I really would like is a drink if you don't mind," the man replied calmly.

"No problem, I'll be right back," Gunther said, heading for the door.

"Bring some fuckin' smokes too!" the man shouted before Gunther closed the door behind him.

Ten minutes later Gunther returned with the bottle of Grey Goose, two cups, a bowl of ice, a Sprite, an ash tray, and a pack of Newport cigarettes.

He undid the leather restraints on the man's right arm in order for him to hold his drink. He then lit a cigarette for him and placed it on the ash tray.

The man gulped down his vodka straight with no chaser; then he put the cigarette in his mouth. He then took a long hard drag, and slowly blew out the smoke. After that he poured himself another drink, and started talking. This time his talk was more toned down. He knew at this point that his number was up, and he accepted that.

"You know something mister; I knew there was something very strange about you when I first met you. I put that feeling out of my mind because I never in my life had the chance to sit in a bar, and drink all the finest booze I wanted."

He didn't say anything for about a minute; then he continued.

"I felt like I was a normal person for a while. I felt good about myself. Every man should have that feeling just once in his life," he said, taking another drag from the cigarette.

"Life has really shit on me. After my no good father died from a heart attack, my mother starting having sex in our trailer for money. She was bad hooked on Heroin. I couldn't stand to watch her like that anymore so I left. I came to New Orleans to find work."

He took another sip of his drink, and continued.

"Things were good at first. I got me a good job working for the sanitation department, picking up trash. I lived in a rooming house over in Algiers, and rode the city bus to work every day. Things were good. Then one night I got with a few of my buddies in the rooming house, and shot up some heroin for the first time."

"At first I handled the smack fairly well; getting to work on time, and paying my rent. However, things got out of hand after about two months. I lost my job, got kicked out of my room, and ended up on Magazine Street begging for money."

Gunther imagined the man standing on the corner of Magazine and Canal Streets, asking anyone passing by, for a cigarette or some change.

"Help out one of the lord's children. Just some spare change please. I will take anything!! Please friend…Do not walk away from me. I'm a human being, just like you friend…"

"You've had a tough life," Gunther said, taking another drink of his soda

"You got that right. Life is hard for a man with no home to live in. People fuck with you for no reason other than pure meanness," the man said, while pouring another drink in his cup with his free hand. He then put the cup to his waiting lips, and drank every drop. After sticking another cigarette in his mouth, and lighting it, he continued his reflections on his past life.

"One morning I was sleeping on a bench in Jackson Square. I love that place; it's peaceful most of the time, although at times there is a few disturbances; young folks raising hell that don't know how to handle their alcohol. However, for the most part, it's a nice place to sleep."

"That particular morning while sleeping on the bench I woke up screaming. A group of dumb ass white kids had carefully placed stick matches between my toes. I like to sleep with my shoes and socks off even in the winter time. I had been drinking wine all night, and it was going to be hard to wake me. I was sleeping real sound that morning. If I had not been disturbed, I would have slept till noon at least. However, after those bastards managed to carefully stick four of them stick matches between my toes on my right foot, do you know what they did next?" he shouted.

"I imagined they lit them," Gunther replied, shaking his head in sorrow.

"You damned right they lit those fuckin' matches, every last one of them. And do you know what they did when I woke up screaming and jumping around like a chicken with its head cut off? Those bastards started laughing at me. I felt like a monkey in a zoo. Young people are cruel. My life sucks."

He lowered his head for about thirty second; then he said, "This is a fucked up world."

"It's nothing wrong with the world; it's just that many of the people in it are assholes," Gunther said, peering into the man's eyes like a cat would often peer into its owner's eyes.

The room was quiet for the next fifteen minutes. The homeless man kept on sipping vodka and Gunther kept look at the portrait of Hitler hanging on the wall. He then turned, and looked at the homeless man, until the man finally broke the silence in the room:

"This solution of yours, where did it come from?" the man asked in a slightly slurred voice. The alcohol was really starting to kick in.

"I get inspiration from my Fuhrer. He had his final solution, and I developed mine."

"What's ah' Fuhrer?" the man asked.

"The Fuhrer is the title we give our leader."

"Who is your leader?" the man asked, raising his head up again.

"His glorious name is Adolf Hitler, Supreme Canceler of all of Germany, and of all the lands conquered."

"Do you see him? Do you talk with him or what? What I mean is, you do know the man is dead right?"

"Yes I see him; he comes to me often. We do have conversations from time to time."

"I didn't get much education; I think I made it to the fifth or sixth grade; however, I did learn ah' few things in school. One thang I learned was that Hitler was a crazy motherfucker; even crazier than you. Hell man, he killed six million Jews; what the fucks up with that shit!"

The man then beat his free right hand on the table, and knocked over the booze.

Gunther quickly recovered the bottle before much of the contents spilled on the floor.

The man didn't apologize for the accident; he only looked intensely into Gunther's eyes for an answer to his question.

"I'm not going to try getting you to understand the entire situation. The important thing is that the Fuhrer was dealing with a problem, a Jewish problem. He dealt with this problem the best that he knew how. His solution to his problem was the attempted extermination of all the Jews in Europe."

He started again to slowly pace around the room in circles.

"Heads of government have been dealing with severe social problems for centuries. Genocide has been tried long before my Fuhrer tried it. The head of the White South African government came up with a solution to their native black African problem without genocide; they called it Apartheid. The early white settlers in America dealt with their Native Indian problem with a solution called forced resettlement; however, unfortunately they almost killed off the entire native Indian race in the process."

He stopped again directly in front of the man, and continued his speech.

"I am not the head of any government; however, I am charged by God to do his will. My Solution is my testament to his will. As long as I am living, I will take as many lives as possible from every sector of the population as possible, without discrimination on the basis of race, religion or sexual orientation," he said, then paused in silence for about thirty seconds.

"For example, when I get the chance—hopefully in the near future—to kill a holy man or holy women, who are also called ministers of God; I am not going to kill him or her because of their religion; I am going to do it because they are religious. The religious tree needs pruning the most. God is good; however religion needs a lot of work."

"So you see my friend, you are very important. You are going to make a difference in this so called fucked up world," he said proudly.

"Man that was some deep shit," the homeless man slurred.

"Tell me something, a little while back, I gave you an opportunity to get yourself right with God, and you refused, why?"

"Because I don't believe in God, that's why."

He poured another drink. This time he drank more slowly. After about a minute of silence, he continued emptying out his built up rage and hurt.

"If there is a God; how could he let my daddy turn into a mean drunk? He beat up his family anytime he got the notion to."

"Me and mama caught him screwing my twin sister Evett. Mama pretended that she didn't see anything. She made me keep quiet about it; she said I didn't see anything either. My sister died from AIDS after she run off with a black pimp. Daddy messed up her mind, slipping in her room at night, and screwing her. The bastard got his heart attack while he was between her legs."

He reached for the bottle again.

Gunther got down on his knees, and began to pray:

"God please forgive him; for he knows not what he speaks of. He is just in a lot of mental pain right now. Deep down inside, he knows that you exist. Remember him in paradise. Open your loving arms to receive him. Let him live in a place where there will be no more suffering and humiliation for him. Forgive him dear God; he has suffered so much in this world; let him enjoy peace in the heavenly world."

After his plea to God, Gunther got up off his knees, bent down, and kissed the man on the forehead.

Gunther's heart softened toward the man. In his mind, the man had suffered enough in life. He had the power to make life better for him.

He got down on his knees again, and prayed to God for further guidance.

The man looked at Gunther on his knees praying, and smiled.

"No one's ever saw fit to kiss me on the forehead that I can remember; not even mama. She might have done it when I was a baby; at least I hope she did," the man said, turning the cup up to his waiting lips once again. He was getting closer and closer to being shitfaced drunk.

After three minutes of prayer, Gunther stood back up, and slowly walked back towards the Hitler portrait.

"What if I were to untie you, and set you free? Would you keep your mouth shut about me?" Gunther asked, now standing at attention, and facing the Hitler portrait. He was quite sure that his Fuhrer was going to call for his death after pulling a stunt like this. However, he was ready for his own death if it came to that.

The homeless man sat quietly for about a full minute before he spoke.

Then he replied, "I'm fuckin' ready to die!"

"No you're not; you're still a young man. What are you, twenty five?"

"I'm twenty seven," the man replied, lighting a cigarette.

"I have already killed about fifteen homeless men and women since I have been in New Orleans; I think that's enough pruning from the homeless tree. I'm setting you free, and I really don't give ah' rats ass if you tell the cops or not," Gunther said, while reaching down to attempt to free the man's left hand.

"Wait!!" the man shouted, and at the same time blocking Gunther's hand from freeing his own left hand.

This was new territory for Gunther. He walked over to a metal folding chair next to the door, and sat down. He wanted to take his time in processing what was taking place. He thought to himself: *Is life really so terrible that a person is unwilling to go free from captivity? Is this the United States of America or what?*

America is not supposed to be like some third world country that has very few options for success. A person living in America is supposed at least have hope that things were going to be better. Is this man really telling him that he wants to die or is it the booze talking?

In America, the possibilities are supposed to be endless. A person can really become all they can be. The only thing they would need is opportunity and desire. How can a person turn down the chance to go free, and get back into the business of living?

He is about to find out; because this homeless man, living in the United States of America, was going to blow his mind with what is going to come out of his mouth.

"Don't put me back out there man! Please, don't put me back into that hell. Why would you lead me to peace, and the end of my suffering, only to snatch it all back from me? I believe in your Solution; I think it's great. I want to be a part of this. I want to make a difference in this world. This is my chance to be a part of something that will slowly change the world for the better. All my life I have been liven' like a tree or ah fuckin' river. I don't know what it feels like to really live like a normal person."

The homeless man lit another smoke and pored himself another drink. He then had a moment of relaxation, before resuming his speech.

"I have never had the chance to enjoy a trip to the beach or go to a concert. I only get sex when I manage to scraped up a few bucks for a whore. I never held a woman's hand or took a woman some flowers. I have never been dressed up in nice clothes to go on a date, and I never will."

He poured another drink, and quickly downed it; cowboy style.

"All I want to do is stop breathing; for good. My life was over the day I was born. I've been kicked and beat on growing up, and I've been kicked and beat on living in these streets. Please don't send me back to that," he said, reaching for the cigarette pack again.

Gunther locked his fingers behind his head, and looked at the man intensely. He was having a hard time trying to understand what was going on. God had clearly instructed him to free the man; however, the man did not want to be set free. He thought of a new angle...

"Would you like a job working for me? I could always use another handyman around here. I could put you up in one of the rooms upstairs; this is a huge house."

The homeless man looked at Gunther with a confused look on his face. Then he looked down at the floor for at least three minutes before speaking again. He wanted to get his words in order first.

"Mister, that won't work. I'm an alcoholic and a drug addict. I will steal you blind. No matter how good you treat me, I will still fuck you over," the homeless man calmly replied.

"I can get you into a good rehabilitation center. This city has excellent drug and alcohol treatment facilities. When you get yourself clean and sober, you can start your life over again with a good job, and a nice place to live," Gunther replied, now getting frustrated with the man's unwillingness to take his offer.

The homeless man was now crying...

After about two minutes of Gunther watching the man crying, he asked, "How about it? Are you ready to begin your new life?"

The man wiped his eyes with his free right hand, and said, "Mister if you don't put me out of my misery, I'm going straight to the cops, and tell them everything I know about you; I fuckin' mean it man. I know you said you don't care if I tell; but I know you do care. You don't really want this shit to get out"

Gunther was almost in shock with the man's response…

"Are you really telling me that you don't want to live another day?" he asked, looking very somber.

"That's what I'm telling you man, I am ready to die. My time is up. No one will care or look for me. No one is concerned about me. It is as if I wasn't even born into this world."

"I still say you should give life another try," Gunther said, while again standing up, and walking toward the Hitler portrait.

"I want to do my part for your perfect solution. I believe in it. I even believe that you sometimes talk to Hitler. I thought you were crazy at first, but I believe now in the things that you told me."

In reality, the man still believed that Gunther was insane. However, he needed him to end his miserable life.

"So you think my plan is good?"

"Oh yes, the perfect solution is a very good plan."

Hitler suddenly appeared.

He looked intensely into Gunther's eyes. Gunther stepped back frightened.

"What's taking you so long soldier? The subhuman waste sitting in that chair should have been disposed of hours ago!" Hitler screamed, pounding his fists together.

"I will do it right away my Fuhrer," Gunther said, snapping his naked heels together.

"Another thing, you wanted to free that awful excuse for a human being; that would have cost you your life, do you know that?"

"Yes my Fuhrer."

"Well then, why did you attempt to free that sewer rat?"

"I had already disposed of plenty of homeless men and women, and thought that it would do no harm to let this one go."

"Well you thought wrong. Do you want to die Heisman?"

"No my Fuhrer, I don't want to die; my solution is not complete yet."

"Well the way you have been acting lately leaves me to believe that you are ready to meet your maker."

Gunther said nothing for over a minute. Hitler's last statement hit home. He had never felt comfortable with his life ever since he really took a hard look at his appearance. He was so handsome that it sometimes shocks him when he looks in the mirror. People are always staring at him; the men seemed even more attracted to him than the women. Both males and females were constantly trying to be near him, to touch him. He feels more like a freak than God's perfect creation.

Lately he did have thoughts of suicide; not just because of his looks. He had a feeling that things were closing in on him. He knew that Jim Bruce was frantically looking for him. He and his agents, he was sure, were on the wrong tract; but still, he felt like they were getting close. He could stop the killing right now, and live a carefree millionaire's life, and run for political office, to the delight of the New Orleans's powerful political machine. However, that was not possible; Hitler would have him shot or hanged if he stopped the killing, and attempted to change his life. Hitler did want him to go into politics; however, he wanted him to get into it on when he told him to, and not before.

Gunther knew that Hitler really didn't like his solution; he was just playing along for now. On top of that he was furious with him for not killing any Jews so far. However, what Hitler did not know was the fact that he had no intention of killing any Jews. In his opinion the Jews had suffered enough. There will be no Jew killing on his watch.

"I want to live in order to complete this very important work my Fuhrer," Gunther said, just before he clicked his naked heels together once again, and bowed his head.

"Well get to it then. Dispose of this filthy varmint, and get your mind into killing some Jews," Hitler stated, before vanishing.

The Gunther did a military about face, and marched back to his prisoner. He stood silently in front of the homeless man for over three minutes. He wasn't just looking at the man; he was looking through him. His mind was not on the man, but on himself. And at that moment his mind was on suicide.

How was he going to do it? He had many options: hanging, pistol to the head, jumping off a tall building, poison…

He wondered what heaven would be like. The thought of him walking with Jesus brought a huge smile to his face. He would be able to sing with the angels and hug his grandparents once again.

He felt the same as the homeless man; he was ready to leave this fucked up world. He didn't need Hitler to order him to shoot himself in the head; he would do that on his own, and on his own time and terms. *Fuck Adolf and the horse he rode in on. Fuck Adolf and his fucked up Final Solution. Kiss my white ass Adolf.*

"That's it, pistol to the head," he quietly whispered.

With the pistol to the head, he would check himself out of this world just the same as Hitler had checked out. He was ready.

"Hey man, are you going to prune me or what?" the homeless man asked.

Gunther snapped out of his trance, and replied, "Indeed I am, with no more delays."

He walked over, and picked up his sledge hammer. When he returned, he looked down at the man with contempt. Hitler had fired him up again. It was now back to business time. It was now Showtime!!

"Hey man, just one more favor I need from you—"

"No more delays," Gunther interrupted him, firmly gripping the hammer.

"What about taking one drink with me? That's my last request."

"My body is the temple of the Lord; I will not put alcohol in the Lord's temple," he said, raising the hammer high above his head.

"My name is Walter Manning of the…"

"So long Walter!" Gunther interrupted again; shouting at the top of his voice. His two beautiful eyes stared down at the man like the eyes of a demon.

The hammer came down hard; both the man's eyes popped out.

Gunther was well experienced in the art of eyeball replacement. Even as a young boy in his father's funeral parlor; he would sometimes look down at empty eye sockets and decide which course of action he should take. People lose their eyes in many ways. And young Gunther had seen most of those ways: A boulder falling down a cliff in West Virginia, crashing through the roof of a car, and striking the driver…eyes pop out. A shotgun blast to the back of the head…eyes pop out. Gunther and his father would sometimes travel to other states to work on a body that has been damaged or disfigured by murder or an accident. Their expertise in restoring dead bodies to their former appearance was well known. As far as missing eyeballs were concerned, they often put large marbles in the empty eye sockets and superglued the eye lids shut.

Gunther looked at the homeless man's eyeballs hanging down by the slimy optic nerves and muscles. The two dangling eyeballs made the homeless man look like a sort of cartoon character.

Gunther started laughing…loudly!!

After about a minute of laughter, he started crying. He was sorry that the homeless man had to die. He again started thinking of ways to kill himself. He went over all his options. A bullet through the brain was his best way to go…

He then walked over to the corner and sat on the floor. He couldn't kill himself today anyway; he had too much to do.

The most important he had to do was to give his friend Big Nine a proper send off. He had to get his only friend's ashes into the Mississippi river even if it was to be the last thing he would do on earth.

Time was flying; it was already 8:15am. He had taken entirely too much time with Walter. He was not that close to the homeless man; he just felt sorry for him, and wanted to set him free. I any event, he had to get a move on.

He would burn Walter's body when he got back; he didn't have time at the moment. Before he could take the ashes of Big Nine to the river, he had to go to bible study.

He got up, walked to the door, and looked back at Walter and his dark sockets where his eyes had been. Looking around at the blood that had erupted, he started to change his plans, and clean up the room. The blood and brain matter is going to be very hard to clean once it hardened. However, he decided to move on; there was not enough time, and church was too important for him to miss. He would just have to work extra hard on the scrubbing when he got back.

The cook would be in at ten to prepare enough food for him to eat for the next three days. She always had each meal wrapped up tightly in foil, and placed in the refrigerator. She would return on Saturday to prepare food for that day and the next two days. She didn't have to prepare breakfast; he always had breakfast in the local eateries in town.

The cleaning lady always arrives at three. She would always clean his bedroom, change the sheets, clean his office, the bathrooms and do his laundry. She would also bring in his suits, shirts and other garments that she had put in the cleaners.

In any event Gunther would be long gone before any of them arrives; including the groundskeeper that sometimes comes on weekends to finish up work that he did not complete throughout the week.

All of his employees were very efficient in their duties; and they all had keys to the house. There was only one rule that was etched in stone; a rule that no one broke. This rule was posted in the elevator and at the stairs:

ABSOLUTELY NO ONE IS ALLOWED IN THE BASEMENT.

The hot shower felt good. He lathered up from head to toe. Walter would have loved this; or maybe not.

The St. Louis Cathedral was his destination this cool crisp morning. This church in Jackson Square located in the heart of the French Quarter was an architectural masterpiece. He loved the French inspired design of the outside. The inside made you feel as though you have stepped back in time; it is simply breathtaking.

"...and Moses was confused at that point. He wandered why God would give him such an important task, being that he was a stutterer. God told Moses to go forth, open his mouth and he would speak for him."

Gunther raised both hands up and shouted: "Amen!!"

"My brothers and sisters, we must be strong in our faith. When God calls us to do his will, we cannot make excuses. We must cast aside our fishing nets, and follow him. It does not matter about your past, your disabilities, your financial situation or your education; it's all about stepping out on faith."

On the drive to the Crescent City Connection, the ferry that took passengers and cars across the Mississippi River into Algiers, Gunther reflected on the bible school message given by the teacher of the day, Brother John. Faith was at the center of the message. His own faith in God's word had carried him through so far, and this faith would see him through to the end.

The message re-enforced his faith; a faith that was already very strong. He always knew that God was real; the message just gave him that much more energy to do God's will.

He felt sorry for the fools that get caught up in science, evolution, planetary exploration and mathematics. They are all missing a very important point: God made everything, including the solar system, evolution, and math. God even made thoughts and dreams...

After driving his car unto the ferry, he reached back, and picked up the urn containing the ashes of his friend Big Nine. As the ferry slowly moved away from the New Orleans side of the river, he got out of the car and walked over to the rail. As he began to pray, other passengers that were standing nearby joined him. A man and a woman put their arms around him, and prayed with him; they saw the urn, and knew what was taking place. An old black woman seated on the bench behind them started singing:

"Jesus, keep me near the cross
There's a precious fountain
Free to all a healing strength
Flows from Calvary's mountain..."

Gunther began to cry as the old black woman sang. He cried for his friend; and a few cried with him. Maybe they were crying for their friends or their family.

As the woman sang, Gunther opened the top of the urn, and slowly poured what was left of Big Nine into the waters of the mighty Mississippi.

Most of the people remained silent, holding on to each other for comfort until the ferry reached the other side.

After riding around historic Algiers for about twenty minutes; he decided to ride into Gretna. He was very familiar with this area; having lived in a rooming house there for a while when he first got to New Orleans. It was predominantly inhabited by black and creole people. It was a somewhat quiet and peaceful area; although it had its share of drugs and gangs just like any other city in America.

He also saw young boys and girls standing on the corner laughing and talking. The children still had a few days left on their Christmas break, and wouldn't be returning to school until after New Year's. They were trying to get in their last few days of freedom before hitting the books again.

He stopped at Joe's Corner, a restaurant and bar that he used to frequent when he lived on this side of the river. The eatery specializes in such dishes as Red Beans and Rice, Chitterlings, Collards Greens and Cornbread, Fried Chicken, Cornbread Stuffing and Peach Cobbler. In other words, if you're weight conscious, you don't want to come in Joe's Corner in Gretna. The food is great! Gunther was very much weight conscious; however, he had discipline. He never over ate; he knows how much to eat, and he counts his calorie intake.

He walked in, and took a seat at one of the tables. The place was about half full at the moment. In another hour, it will be so many people waiting on tables that you would have to take a number.

He ordered from the kid's menu. It didn't matter what a person eats, as long as the food is in small portions.

When the waitress returned with his food, he looked down at it and smiled. On his plate was one piece of boiled pig tail, small piece of baked fish, collard greens, a small baked potato, and slice of corn bread. He had also ordered a tall glass of ice water.

As he was slowly enjoying his meal, a large black man walked in with a white minister's collar around his neck. He had on a grey suit with a purple shirt, with a large crucifix hanging from his neck. He greeted everyone before sitting at the bar to order his meal.

Gunther's mind started racing…

He wandered how he could get the man alone.

This was his chance. He had to kill a preacher sooner or later; why not now?

The minister's tree was vast, and ever growing. This tree must be pruned. The Solution demands it. But how will he do it?

He finished his meal, paid the check, and left the waitress a twenty dollar tip. She gleamed with joy, and asked him to please come back again. He said that he would, and then he walked out to door.

Sitting now in his car, his mind was still racing. He needed to stop the minister before he got to his car, and somehow convince him to get in the car with him. This was going to be tough. Even if he did get the minister in his car, there were plenty of witness's standing around to inform the police about a white man with blond hair seen unlocking his car door, and allowing the minister to get in.

…and after a few minutes of talking to each other they drove off. We got a description of the car, and I wrote down the tag number. Don't we get a reward or something?

He decided to put the minister out of his mind. He started up the car, and rode around for a while. He rode a few blocks then stopped to watch some kids practicing their tap dancing moves. Once they get good enough, they will go over on Bourbon Street in the French Quarter, and tap for tips. He made a U turn in the street, and gave the two boys five dollars each; they were delighted.

As he slowly drove back toward Joe's Corner to get a slice of sweet potato pie to take home, he suddenly stopped the car in jubilation. He could not believe his luck. There was the minister, walking in his direction with his food wrapped in a paper plate. No one else was on the street at that moment. He quickly reached under his seat, and pulled out his old faithful comrade, the German Luger pistol. He then quickly screwed on the silencer. He held the gun down between his legs.

He stopped the minister, waving his hand.

"Excuse me sir, is there a baptist camp meeting going on somewhere in Gretna? I was told that it would be one, but I can't find the tent," he said looking around like he was confused. He needed the man to come closer in order to get a good clean shot in the middle of the forehead.

The minister came up to the driver's side window, and peered in cautiously.

"No sir, I haven't heard of any camp meeting that's supposed to be going on today. Maybe it's taking place over across the river somewhere," the minister said, looking around himself. He wasn't used to a white man driving around in a luxury car, and looking for a tent revival on this side of the river. He felt uncomfortable. Something wasn't quite right with this scene.

Gunther started slowly bringing up the gun; everything was perfect.

"You look troubled my brother what's wrong?" the preacher asked.

Gunther lowered the gun, and replied, "Nothing is wrong, I just got a lot on my mind that's all."

"Do you want to talk about it?" the preacher asked.

"Can I give you a lift somewhere? We can talk on the way" Gunther replied, now starting to sweat just a little.

"I just live two blocks down the road; let me put my food in the house, and we can talk," the preacher said, walking around to the other side to get in the car.

Gunther quickly put the gun back under the seat and unlocked the passenger door.

They rode in silence for the entire two blocks. The blocks were long, with small wooden houses on both sides of the street.

"That's my house right there; the one with all the flowers around the porch," the preacher said, as they approached a wood framed white home with no car in the driveway.

"Be right back, I am single so I either have to cook for myself or catch me a meal at Joe's Corner," he said getting out of the car, and running up the steps.

"What in the fuck is wrong with you Heisman? Why didn't you kill that nigger?" Adolf Hitler screamed from the back seat.

"I don't know; I just froze up," Gunther replied, feeling a little ashamed.

"You said you wanted to start killing ministers for your fucking solution. Then you get the golden opportunity to kill a minister and a jungle bunny at the same time, and you fucking blew it! Put the gun to your head. Put the fucking gun to your head now!! That's an order!! Do it now!!"

Gunther grabbed the gun just as the preacher came running down the stairs.

"I hope I wasn't too long; I had to put some dog food out for my puppies," the preacher shouted, reaching for the car door handle.

"No you're fine; everything is fine," he replied, grateful that he didn't get the chance to pull out the gun again.

"I would invite you in but the place is a mess; I didn't have time to clean up; I've been busy all week long; we've been in conference all week; today is the last day. Starting tomorrow, I'm going to take my time, and straighten the place up."

"I know how it is man; I'm single myself," Gunther replied.

"Hey, let's go inside anyway; we'll just step over the junk," the minister said, opening the door to get out.

"Tell you what, I'll come back another time; I just remembered, I have something very important to do," Gunther said, cranking up the car.

"Well if you're ever in this neck of the woods again, you know where I live. God be with you my brother, till we meet again," the minister replied, standing outside of the car, and extending his hand inside the car for a handshake.

After the handshake Gunther headed back to Algiers to catch the ferry. He wasn't lying when he told the minister that he had something important to do. He remembered that he had a 5:00pm dinner and meeting at the Mayor's house.

Several prominent business leaders in the community will be meeting with the Mayor to discuss funding for the revitalization of the 9th Ward district that was hit hard by Katrina. This particular district is still in the same deplorable condition it was in after the hurricane hit. Something desperately needed to be done.

It was already 3:30. He had an hour and a half to get home, put on a tux, and get over to the Mayor's home.

On the drive up Canal Street, the traffic stalled to almost a halt. There was an accident up ahead. A tour bus had rear ended a taxi cab. Gunther's car was stalled at the corner of Canal and Basin Street. He turned right unto Basin; this street would wind around and run back into I-10 leading to N. Claiborne Ave.

After entering Basin, he decided to make a left on Conti Street; that route would get him home even quicker.

As soon as he turned on Conti, a young black man that may or may not have been homeless jumped in front of his car. He was holding a bucket of water in one hand and a squeegee in the other hand. The man had towels hanging out of all of his pockets. There were no cars behind Gunther's car, so he reluctantly stopped so that the man can wash his windows.

He wandered why the man would set up shop on a street that does not have much traffic. Or maybe the man was heading to a more heavily traveled street when a saw Gunther's luxury car come toward him. Had he been on Canal, he could have already made some nice money since the traffic was stalled.

The young man was fast; he finished the front windshield in less than 45 seconds. When he came around to driver's side to get whatever money he would receive; Gunther shot the young man through the right eye. The bullet went through the brain, and exploded out the back of his head. The young man dropped to the ground like a rag doll.

The street was still quiet; there were still no cars behind him. If anyone showed up at the crime scene at that moment; he would have no choice but to kill that person. And he really did not want to do that. He was relieved and satisfied now that he had his kill for that day. Fortunately there were no witness's that would have to die because of their curiosity.

Dead folks can't talk

The neighborhood was quiet. The silencer on the pistol came in very handy in times such as this. Had he not had the silencer; the loud noise from the gun would have surly caused concerned people to raise their windows, and look outside; to see what was going on.

He slowly drove off. He now felt energized. He needed that kill; especially since he wasted some much time trying to kill the minister.

After thinking about his botched attempt in killing the minister, he concluded that God does not want ministers to be part of the solution plan after all.

Hitler returned.

He was again sitting in the back seat of the car, and he was pissed as usual. He wanted Gunther to fully explain to him why it was so difficult for him to kill ministers. He was already having a hard time getting him to kill Jews.

Gunther gathered himself; this is a very important moment for him. Although he didn't mind dying, he still wanted to finish his project first. He responded to Hitler's concerns boldly.

"My Fuhrer, ministers are representatives of God. Some representatives of God are shady, greedy, crooked, lustful and manipulative. Some are good, kind, honest, and God fearing," he looked into the rearview mirror; Hitler still seemed to be steaming mad.

"What all ministers; no matter what their religion is have in common, is their commitment to spread the word of God. God wants his name spread all over the world. It does not matter if a preacher has a congregation believing that he has just healed a lame person; when in fact that person was not lame in the first place. It does not matter. Even if a minister has affairs with several women in his church, and gets one of them pregnant; it does not matter."

"These men and women are telling their audience that God is real. Some ministers have their own television shows; and they are as wrong as two left shoes; it does not matter. The bottom line is this: those television ministers are telling millions of people worldwide that God is love. God's latest message to me was very clear. Just like the Jews, ministers and all representatives of God, will not be slain. The Perfect Solution will continue in full affect, and the Jewish tree and the minister's tree will not be a part of it. These are God's new instructions to me, and I am going to obey his word, even if it cost me life."

Hitler was not pleased; however, he cannot over rule the will of Gunther's almighty God. All that he can do at this point is to order Gunther's death, a death that Gunther himself is ready for.

"You say that God himself gave you these instructions?" Hitler asked, just as Gunther pulled into the carport.

"Yes my Fuhrer, he told me himself. He entered my thoughts while I was driving home."

"How is it that you can hear God, and I was divinely placed on earth by him, and I have never heard him speak?" Hitler whined, beating both of his fists on his thighs.

"That question I cannot answer my Fuhrer," Gunther replied, opening the car door, and getting out.

"I'm not through talking to you Heisman; get your ass back in this car; that's an order!"

Gunther, for the first time, ignored Hitler, and went into the house to change his clothes. He had forty five minutes to get to the Mayor's house.

When he returned to the car twenty minutes later Hitler was gone.

On the way to the Mayor's house, he reflected back on his killing of the windshield washer.

He thought to himself, although it was extremely refreshing, the kill was foolish. He could have easily been caught or identified. The bullet casing was still in the street somewhere. Crime scene investigators would soon find out that the bullet came from a German Lugar; not the typical weapon used in street crimes. The information will be sent to Washington and analyzed by FBI crime lab technicians. Then that information will be sent to Jim Bruce in California. Jim will compare that information will the ballistic data he has already gathered. He will look at the possibility that the man or woman that he is desperately looking for is now killing people in New Orleans.

The only reason Gunther was not totally falling apart, was the fact that he wore gloves while loading the bullets into the gun.

However:

This was a major fuck up.

He can't be doing the same wild shit he did in California.

As he listened to the mayor give a toast, raising his glass to the many guests in the large dining room, his mind went back to California…

August 15th 2004

Gunther felt like a man on the run, although no one was chasing him. He had the entire west coast on lockdown. He had killed so many people that he lost count. People were afraid and confused.

A radio station in LA held a contest to come up with the catchiest name for the killer.

A seventeen-year-old girl from Pacific Palisades High School named Martha Westinghouse won the contest. Her winning entry was called, The Scorpion Killer.

The name went viral on the Internet. Beware of the Scorpion Killer, coming to a city near you.

Gunther did not like the name at all; however, there was nothing he could do about it. He certainly was not going to call in to the TV stations and complain about it. He was not into self-glorification; no self-promotion for him. All he wanted to do was kill as many people on the West Coast as he could before it was time to move on.

He was in a rush and felt like a nervous drug addict. His basic principles of the perfect solution were pushed to the side for now. It did not matter to him who he killed or what tree they grew from. God had him on rush mode, and he must do God's will.

"Hey fellas', where can I score some smack? I need ah' hit bad," Gunther asked a group of four young black thugs that were hanging on the corner of Sunset and Vine in Hollywood. It was two in the morning on a Tuesday; not much happening on the streets, although the clubs were still jumping.

"You do mean heroin, right?" one of thugs asked.

"Yeah man, that's what I'm looking for," replied Gunther looking around nervously.

"How much you are looking for?" another one asked.

Gunther pulled out a fat wad of one-hundred-dollar bills, and held it out for them to see, and answered, "About this much."

"We have to go get it; do you have a car?" the first one asked. He seemed to be the leader. He was the only one that had gold teeth in his mouth. His entire front row of teeth, both uppers and lowers, were glistening with gold.

"Yeah I got a car; follow me," Gunther replied, leading them down the street. He had rented a van earlier in the day.

Changing cars every other day was routine for him during those early and crazy times in California.

Law enforcement were scrambling around like ants; going on one lead after another. Last Friday he changed a rental Chevy station wagon for a rental Ford truck and went across the border into Tijuana Mexico.

He went into the first bar he came upon. The place had whores advertising themselves around the tables, walls, and the bars. He ordered a round of drinks for the people sitting around the bar. Most of the patrons were off duty military. Both the Marine Corp and Navy had bases nearby in San Diego. He looked up and saw a Marine coming back down stairs tucking his shirt back in his pants. The young man obviously had been knocking boots with the young woman following him down the stairs.

All the rooms used for sex were upstairs. You could pick out a girl while you were downstairs or you could go upstairs, and a whole lineup of pretty young whores would be waiting. They were all sitting in chairs around the walls. They kept space opened in front of the room doors. Those doors were always opening and closing.

Gunther finished his Pineapple juice, and set the glass down. He wasn't afraid of finger prints on the glass because he always wore black leather motorcycle gloves. That seemed to be the style on the West Coast anyway since there were so many motorcycle clubs. He wiped off the area on the glass where his lips had been. He learned on the Internet that law enforcement had gotten real good at getting information about a person by analyzing their saliva.

Gunther looked tough. He had let his beard grow long. His hair was covered with a scarf tied off at the back. He had on dark sun glasses, and wore a black leather jacket that had a picture of a screaming eagle on the back. He looked like a member of some biker gang from the U.S.

He got up, and pushed back a few whores that were trying to push up on him.

They were all trying to get him to spend his money with them. They were saying that the woman upstairs were no good…

"I'll make you come! You come in me! I swallow! You fuck my ass! Only twenty dollars!!"

Gunther walked passed them all, and went upstairs.

When he got to the top he saw eight girls. It was only about ten in the morning; at night there would be over thirty girls crowding in this same area.

"Early bird gets the worm," Gunther said to himself.

He held up a wad of money, and the girls came rushing to him like heat seeking missiles. He picked out four of them, and went into one of the rooms.

Ten minutes later he walked back out, and held up the wad of money again. The remaining four girls followed him into another room.

None of the remaining girls stopped to wander about the first group; they were blinded by the almighty U.S. dollar.

Gunther quietly walked back out into the street. Things were still rather peaceful and quiet. He got into his car, and headed back towards the border. When he got to the entrance to the U.S. there were a long line of cars trying to get into Mexico; however, the line of cars leaving Mexico was very short. He only had two cars in front of him. When his car approached the man in the sharp Navy uniform, the man asked Gunther, "Did you have a good time in Mexico?"

"Yes I did," replied Gunther.

"Did you bring anything illegal back with you?" the man asked.

"No I didn't," replied Gunther.

"Do you mind if we search your car?"

"Yes I do mind. Why do you want to fuck with me? I'm a tax paying American citizen. Just because I look the way I do, does not give you the right to profile me. I don't do drugs man."

"Yeah right pal. Pull the truck over to the right, and step out with your hands up."

Six border agents came over to the car after Gunther pulled the car over to the inspection area. Two of the agents searched Gunther; after find nothing on his person, they ordered him into a small building where they did a more detailed search after ordering him to strip naked.

While that was going on, four other agents went over his car like a colony of ants on a dead carcass. They pulled back the seats, searched under the seats, looked into the glove compartment and the arm rest compartment. They looked under the hood, under the car, behind the hub caps and in the trunk.

They couldn't come up with anything illegal.

"Sorry about that, we're just doing our jobs. There is competition to get drugs into the U.S. That competition has even led to a drug war. On behalf of the United States of America we sincerely wish to apologize for any inconvenience that you have experience re-entering the United States."

"Kiss my white ass!!" Gunther screamed, while turning, and walking back to the truck.

On the way back to LA he smiled. It had been a good morning. There were eight young women dead in two different room's right across the border.

In the first room Gunther followed the women in, and immediately pulled out a 38 caliber with the silencer already screwed on. He shot three women in the back of the head before the forth woman could turn around. When she did, he put a bullet in her forehead. There were no screams; it was over that quickly.

He sat on the bed for a while. Then Hitler appeared on the bed next to him. "That was good work Heisman," Hitler said, brushing his hair back with his right fingers.

"Thank you my Fuhrer," Gunther said proudly.

"What about the other four women outside?" Hitler asked.

"What about them?"

"I want them dead also," Hitler said, now standing up.

"But that's going to be extremely difficult to do. Those women sitting outside will be suspicious; they are going to wonder about what happened to the other women. How can I get them to follow me into another room so quickly when they just saw me go into this room with these women?" Gunther asked, totally confused.

Hitler stood up and shook his head in disgust. He threw up his hands in the air, then turned and looked Gunther directly in his eyes. He looked like a man that has run out of patience…

"Hold up your money again; they will be blinded by it. You've got to learn how to quickly think on your feet," he said, angrily.

He then faded away.

Gunther got up, walked out, and held up the fat wad of money. The women followed him into the next room like sheep following the Shepard.

Eight prostitutes were now pruned from the vast tree of prostitution.

The following Sunday Gunther rode across the border again. This time he drove a Volkswagen Beetle. He bypassed the clubs downtown, and went deeper into Tijuana. He drove until he came upon shanty homes, and small farms. He began knocking on doors, and killing everyone that was unlucky enough to be at home.

This time he used an M-16 combat rifle. He sat the selector switch to automatic. There were no searches from the border police going into Mexico; only coming from Mexico. And only then, when the driver looked suspicious.

He killed grandfathers, grandmothers, fathers, mothers, brothers, sisters, aunts, uncles and little children. He knocked on seven doors, and killed forty two people.

Just like he did three days earlier, he left the weapon behind. Local law enforcement will write it up as drug war killings. When drug Lords suspect someone of being an informant or snitch, they kill the person's entire family.

His mind snapped back to the here and now.

He turned where the leader of the thugs told him to turn. The three in the back seat were whispering. They knew what they were about to do; they had done it many times before. This was going to be easy. They were going to rob this dumb ass white man, take his car, and leave his broken body by the side of the road up in the Hollywood hills.

What they did not know was that this was no ordinary white man. This was no goofy drug crazed white man with a pocket full of Benjamin Franklins. This man was a homicidal maniac.

He was highly trained in martial arts, long range sniper killing and was an expert in close combat with knives, swords and axes. He was also particularly good with explosives. In other words, he was the total package. Some of this training was gained using the Internet. Most of the training was done by hiring personal black belt instructors of the martial arts, as well as expert Ninja swordsmen. He studied hard and became one of the deadliest men on the planet.

The next morning, the Los Angeles police department's homicide unit was in the Hollywood Hills. They were investigating the deaths of four young black males. They each had their heads removed from their bodies. The heads were laid out in a circle. Each head was placed facing another head as if the heads were in a group conversation.

Jim Bruce and his team arrived two hours after getting the phone call. He had to do a few things before he left Mexico. He was there trying to get some sort of lead in the Tijuana murders. He got a call on his cell phone from his second in command Mark Hinny back in the states before boarding the helicopter.

"Jim, Matt has all the details on the Hollywood Hills murders. If it's alright with you, I would like you to talk to him."

After Mark gave Matt the phone, Jim settled back in the passenger seat in the chopper and braced himself for some more terrible news.

"What have we got Matt?" Jim asked the lead investigator.

Matt Washington was a fifteen-year member of the LAPD homicide unit; before that, he spent six years in narcotics. He was a big burly man, well over three hundred pounds, but was light on his feet when in pursuit of a suspect.

He, as well as all the other homicide units throughout the West Coast gave Jim Bruce their full cooperation. Normally this good working relationship between local law enforcement and the F.B.I. was nowhere to be found. The locals do not like to be pushed to the side by the government. Investigations in the past between the two organizations were always strained to say the least. However, this case has put new life in the word cooperation. The locals needed help and they were grateful to get it.

"Four black males are dead, their heads cut off and placed like they are having a meeting or something," Matt said, shaking his head in disgust.

"Do you think the decapitations were the actual cause of death?" Jim asked, looking out the window admiring a flock of Geese flying in military formation. They looked like billiard balls that have just been racked up, and ready for play.

"Well, as you know, we don't have anything conclusive yet because the bodies have to be autopsied; however, it does look like death could have occurred as a result of several deadly wounds that we have found so far," the big man replied.

"All the bodies had stab wounds to the torso, back, and legs. The killer cut only the vital arteries; he really knew how to end a life," Matt said, rubbing his huge stomach.

"Looks like our guy went straight kamikaze on them; a sort of Bruce Lee with knives," Jim said, envisioning a martial arts expert going berserk on the four victims.

"It looks to me like the heads were chopped off rather cleanly," Matt said, kneeling to take a closer look at the heads.

"He must have used an ax or something. Whatever he used, he did not take but one swing at each head; because we can't find any signs of sawing," Matt added, looking even closer with his magnifying glass.

"Have your men found anything that we can use?" Jim asked, still staring out the window of the chopper.

"My guys have combed this area like a swarm of ants for the past seven hours. They have not found anything that we can use. All the samples found so far belongs to the victims. Do you think this is our guy, the scorpion killer?" Matt asked.

"I just don't know right now. I wandered about that in Tijuana; was this maniac our guy? He never leaves anything for us to link one murder to another. He does not seem to have a pattern in his killings. He uses different methods and weapons in the killings. He goes to different parts of the West Coast at random. Most of all, he seems not to want any fame;

now that's scary and rare." Jim replied, looking up to the sky to watch a formation of F-16 jets flying in the distance.

"The people from the LA examiner's office have been here and gone. My guys will continue combing the area until it gets dark. If it's alright with you, I will order the bodies to be moved downtown to be autopsied," Matt said, motioning to an ambulance that was parked downhill about fifty feet from the crime scene.

"Sure Matt, we need to allow the medical examiner to get his work done. I'll send in a specialized unit Quantico Virginia. They are from the behavioral analysis division. We're going to need all the help we can get on this one."

As the helicopter copper now touched down on the roof of FBI headquarters in sunny LA; Jim reflected upon his life up till now…

Jim Bruce was born in Columbia South Carolina December 19th, 1952. His Father Tom and his mother Helen had both been attorneys and senior partners in the very powerful law firm of Bruce, Walker, Morgan and Holmes before their retirement in 1990.

After graduating number three in his class at Dreher High School in Columbia in 1970, he entered the University of South Carolina in Columbia. He graduated in 1974 with a 3.6 GPA. His major field of study was history. He entered law school at the USC School of law in Columbia in 1975.

After graduating law school, he worked at his parent's law firm for three years; then applied, and was accepted into the FBI academy.

He rose through the ranks quickly; making field director in 1998. He went back to Quantico to study behavioral sciences for a year after the deadly 9/11 twin towers event in Midtown New York.

Since then he has been promoted to deputy director of the entire bureau; he oversees the FBI's operations on the West Coast of the United States. He is married to a lady from Athens Georgia named Martha; they have a son Charles, who is an assisted district attorney in Greenville South Carolina and a Daughter Cindy, who teaches first grade in Athens.

After picking up his team and getting them settled into their rooms at the Hilton in Englewood, he met them all in another room that would be used as a staging area for the manhunt, as well as a briefing room.

The team had five members including him. There were four males and one female. All were seasoned agents with at least ten years of work in the field. On top of that, for the past four years they trained other prospective agents at the academy in Quantico Virginia. They each were well educated with a concentration in the field of psychology. All had taught courses in behavioral sciences at the academy.

"Agents, I hope you all enjoyed your meal here at the hotel. I know you all are tired from the long flight. I won't keep you too long; I know it's late. I just have a few things to go over with you about tomorrow; then you will be able to get into your nice warm beds, and get some much-needed rest," Jim told the group before he uncovered a large map of California.

The man now known as the Scorpion Killer was already in bed. He had a luxurious suite on tenth floor of Caesar's Palace in Las Vegas Nevada.

While Jim Bruce and the entire state of California was on the lookout for him—even though they had no idea what he looked like—he decided to chill out in Vegas for a month. He was now a multimillionaire, and occasionally, he liked to spurge like any other red blooded American multimillionaire.

He needed a rest; he had been terribly busy the last couple of years murdering people. Taking someone's life can be very taxing on the mind as well as the body. After targeting a victim, there is a lot of maneuvering that must take place very quickly. You do not have time for long range planning. This kind of killing was not studied on the planning board as if you were a sniper studying a potential target.

Although his killings up to this point have been random, he did have something in mind that would take plenty of planning. Sometime in the near future, in a city to be determined later, Gunther was going to plant a series bombs.

He had not worked out the details yet. All he knew at this point was that these bombs were going to kill thousands of people. These bombs were going to be timed set to go off in two-minute intervals. He needed his intended victims to be in a large and confined area such as a football stadium.

He toyed with this idea several years ago; however, he quickly dismissed the idea because it seemed to conflict with his pruning solution doctrine. The doctrine's principal idea was to prune from trees; not just kill indiscriminately.

But one day while sitting on a bench in a small park in South Central LA, Adolf Hitler came to him. He saw him walking towards him in the distance. He walked by people—mostly black people—sitting on benches or on the grass with picnic baskets. He walked past children running around playing. As he got closer, Gunther could see a slight smile on the Fuhrer's face; that was good news.

"I have an idea," Hitler said, now standing directly in front of him.

Gunther said nothing. All he wanted to do was to sit and listen. Most of the time when Hitler paid a visit to him, he would be furious with him for doing something that he did not like. It was a nice change of scene to have his Fuhrer smiling at him, and presently talking calmly to him. So he said nothing, not wanting to spoil the moment.

"You could please me and God at the same time by pruning from many trees at once. I have been thinking over this perfect solution of yours. You have missed something very simple in this process. The entire population of America comes from one of thousands of trees. There would be no random killing in pruning thousands at one time. There would be no innocent person that would die for no reason. Every one of them would play a vital role in your solution. Do you understand what I am telling you Heisman?"

Gunther nodded his head up and down to show that he understood.

"Good, now this is what you are going to do. First, you have got to get it in your head that time is running out. You can't go on like this forever, sliding around like a slow-moving snail. You are going to get caught one day or even killed. Jim Bruce is going to someday pick up your scent. You are not killing fast enough. You should have killed thousands by now. I want you to start planting bombs. I want those bombs planted in stadiums, nuclear power plants and anywhere else that could yield thousands of deaths. It's time to step up to the plate, and get on with your God's work," he said, before fading away.

Gunther would start laying out the initial steps necessary for this task. It was going to take plenty of planning and patience. He had the skill for the job. All that was needed now were the targets.

Gunther reached up and cut off the light above his head and quickly drifted off to sleep. He planned to do a little gambling in the morning after breakfast. Then he planned on spending some time in the pool, and maybe shake a tail feather in a few night clubs later into the night.

Jim Bruce rose early the next morning. He gave one more short briefing to his team before they set out on their separate ways.

Joan Forest, the lone woman on the team was assigned to head up the San Diego task force. She was an unmarried woman of thirty-six. She was slim in statue, and very pretty; blessed with naturally blond hair, and an eye-catching bombshell of a body. Nevertheless, anyone that knows her will tell you that she was all FBI.

Dave meadows a father of four, and one of the few high level African Americans in the bureau, was assigned to head up the Sacramento task force. He was well built, just as fit as he was when he was an all-ACC football tailback at Maryland 92-96.

John Price was a single man of fifty, and also African American. He was close to retirement age and considered it an honor to finally get a command. He came up the hard way; cleaning floors and toilets at the bureau headquarters in Washington after graduating high school in 1979. It took him eight years to get his degree in criminal justice at Howard University going to class in the evenings when he got off work. After he finally received his degree, he was accepted into the FBI academy.

He got to head up the growing task force in Mexico. There he had to deal with two major problems: First of all there was a serious drug war going on between the cartels, and it was spilling over into the United States. Second, there was the problem of the Scorpion Killer that routinely crosses the border to slaughter people at will.

Finally, there was Peter Manningham, a married father of twin girls ages nine. At thirty years of age he was the youngest member of the team. He was an honor graduate of MIT. Before joining the FBI, he considered going to grad school at Stanford on a full grant from NASA. His specialty was mathematics and physics. He applied to the FBI after his grandmother was carjacked and killed in Memphis Tennessee one week after his graduation from MIT. The carjacker was never caught. Peter was assigned to head up the Inglewood task force.

Jim was now relaxing on his flight to Washington. He had to immediately head to the FBI headquarters to meet with the director. The next morning, after his meeting with Jim, the director is to have breakfast with the President at the White House. The President wants to stay on top of the Scorpion killer situation.

Gunther also got up early the next morning. He was now eating breakfast in the buffet at Caesar's Palace in Las Vegas. He had just taken a sip of his coffee when a beautiful red head woman wearing a very short mini skirt asked him if she could join him. Gunther looked around nervously at all the available the empty tables and wondered why she wanted to sit at his table instead.

"Sure, you are welcome to join me," he said, forcing a smile.

As he got up from the table and pulled the chair out for the women to sit, it dawned on him why the women wanted to sit with him. It was the same reason that women—and some men—wanted to be near him; he was extremely handsome.

Most people will immediately drop all their defenses when they see him. Although they were adults, for their own safety, they really needed to start going by the children's golden rule: Never talk to strangers.

"My name is Gunther Heisman, and you are?"

"Mary Foster," replied the women.

"Are you in town for a convention?" the women asked, eating a piece of her crispy bacon.

"No, I'm just here for relaxation, and maybe a little gambling," he replied, taking in a forkful of his pancakes.

"This defiantly is the right place for relaxation and gambling. However, unless you are planning on staying in the pool area or in your room, it's going to be hard to relax in this city. It's just too much to see and do. People like to say that New York is the city that never sleeps; that's not true; at some point during a 24 hour period, New York goes to sleep. On the other hand, Las Vegas never sleeps; four in the morning is just like four in the afternoon," she said, now spooning some eggs.

"You know, I've seen over a hundred men dressed as Elvis Presley walking around; what's up with that?" he asked, taking a bite of his smoked sausage.

"In the next four days, over two thousand Elvis impersonators will be in town for the international Elvis Presley week. There's going to be concerts, contests, demonstrations, and all things Elvis. The King is a legend in this town", she said proudly.

"So, are you here on business or pleasure?" Gunther asked, now sipping his coffee.

"This is my home, born and raised. Right now, I am a showgirl here at Caesars. The reason why I am up so early this morning on a Friday is we have a mandatory practice. Tony Bennett is the headliner starting Sunday night; he has a three-week run; management has been really cracking the whip getting us ready."

No one uttered a word for over five minutes. Mary just kept a girlish gaze into Gunther's beautiful blue eyes. She was thinking about what it could be like waking up every morning in bed with him. She had heard of the term: Love at first sight; however, she did not believe in it, until that moment. She wanted to get down on her knees, and propose marriage to him.

Gunther had a smile on his face that seemed frozen in time. It was a warm and inviting smile. At the moment he was thinking about a young woman in San Diego that he strangled to death with piano wire. He dropped her body in a trash dumpster in a dark alley a few steps from where he killed her. Her head was almost separated from her body.

Mary snapped out of her love trance and broke the ice.

"We have been practicing for three straight weeks, and that's after we get through with our regular routine backing up Usher, who has been headlining this past week," she said, stretching her arms in the air trying to loosen up.

"Looks like you are going to be very busy this weekend," Gunther said, relieved that she would be too busy to suggest getting together.

"Hey, tell you what, we got Usher for one more night. His show ends about one in the morning. A few of the girls along with their dates will be going over to the Mint; they have a wonderful after-hours Dee Jay named Kid Funk. You'll have a good time, and I will get to show you off; my girl pals will be so jealous!!" she said, laughing hysterically.

"OK, I'll meet you and your friends at the Roman bar at about two," he said reluctantly.

"Fantastic! Two in the morning is great; that will give us enough time to shower and change. See you then handsome," she said, spooning the last of her eggs, and getting up from the table.

He watched her head out from the restaurant; all eyes were on her. She was indeed beautiful. However, Gunther did not have any feelings toward her. All she was to him was a potential branch that needs pruning. He did not come to this city to kill; however, if the opportunity presents itself, he will not hesitate to cut her throat.

He made up his mind. He will meet her, and her friends.

After he finished his breakfast, he went back upstairs, and changed into his swimming trunks. A few minutes later he was swimming in Caesars's magnificent swimming pool.

He, for the first time since he arrived in Vegas, felt truly relaxed. Other swimmers were also relaxing and having a good time. Only a very few people were eyeballing him. He wasn't the only good-looking man at the pool.

Not only were there plenty of handsome men there from out of town, the pool boys bringing the drinks were fine specimens themselves, walking around in their period Greek and Roman togas.

The women bringing the customers their drinks looked like goddesses from MT Olympus. Everyone was enjoying this fine autumn morning. The sun was breaking through, and a slight wind was blowing; this was paradise.

That evening after a couple of hours at the blackjack table, he jumped in his rental car and headed for downtown Vegas. This is the area where the Frontier, Horseshoe, Mint, Showboat, and Freemont hotel and casinos were located.

He parked a few blocks down from the casinos and went into the Lucky Lady pawn shop. This is the place where gamblers that were having hard luck on the tables go to refuel. They pawn everything from wedding rings, watches, tools and anything else they could lift and carry in the place. Some would pawn their own spouse if the shop would oblige them.

Gunther walked out of the shop with a pick and shovel. He had some grueling work to do.

Four hours later, just when the sun was ready to start vanishing for the night; he was through with his work.

He put the shovel and pick back into the truck of his car and changed out of his dirty clothes. Before getting into the car, he walked back to get another look at his work. He had just dug two graves. The graves were located about a hundred yards in the desert off Bolder Hwy. They were dug about twenty yards from each other. He didn't know if the graves would be needed. After all, killing was not really what this trip was all about; however, it pays to be prepared.

On the way back he thought about Mary and her friends. Although he dug the graves to occupy one person per grave, he saw no problem in putting two to a grave; especially if all the girls were thin like Mary. Most likely they would be thin; he had never heard of a heavyweight Vegas showgirl.

He would play it by ear and see what happens. He was not going to push the issue. He would go out with the girls to the club, and just might have some fun for a change.

He turned on the radio. It was a thirty-minute drive back, so he thought he may as well relax with a little music.

As he was pushing the buttons trying to find some nice music, a news broadcast caught his ear.

"…This is what we know so far: On August, 23, 2005 a tropical depression formed over the South Eastern area of the Bahamas. The next day it was upgraded to storm status, and given the name Katrina. The next day, the storm was upgraded to Hurricane status after entering the Gulf of Mexico. On August 27 the storm reached category three hurricane status. The next day the storm doubled in size, reaching category five with winds at 175 mph. Mayor Ray Nagin ordered the first ever mandatory evacuation of the city of New Orleans. Monday, August 29 the storm slammed into Buras-Triumph, Louisiana…"

Gunther changed the station, he was still trying to find some jazz…

Finally, Grover Washington Jr. was playing one of his hits on the saxophone. Sitting back now listening to Grover's rendition of Marvin Gaye's 'Mercy mercy me', Gunther was able to relax, and think about getting together with Mary and her friends in a few hours.

Mary would have no idea that her date with him would be his very first date.

Gunther did not have the slightest idea as to what to do in the company of a woman as far as dating was concerned. He has never danced with or kissed a woman. Never has he given flowers to a woman or whispered sweet words into a woman's ear. He has been to nightclubs before in California; however, he was there only to seek out someone to murder.

Because he learned early on that his hero Adolf Hitler stayed away from women, he also stayed away from women. Even growing up in Iowa, he played games with boys only. His behavior did not set off any alarms in his tight knit religious community. His parents were proud of the fact that their son kept his eyes in the bible instead of on the girls. They just had no idea that he learned from reading Hitler, that being a true Arian, he was superior to women; and should not mix his Arian blood with any women unless she was sent to him by God, and with one hundred percent pure Arian blood in her veins.

He became very serious on being a pure-blooded Arian.

So far he had not found any woman that has met God's qualifications for him. Hitler finally found his true Arian woman in his niece Ava Braun; maybe one day he will find his; however, Mary was not the one.

The Ramsey Lewis Trio came through next on the radio. They played a tune by the 70's funk group 'War'. The name of the tune was, 'Slipping into Darkness'.

As he drove down the strip in Vegas heading to his hotel, his mind turned to New Orleans and Katrina. He tried to envision the shock, confusion and desperation taking place in the city called, 'The Big Easy'.

He had never been to the city; however, he has come close to it several times while traveling to the east coast. New Orleans has never been on his to do list of places he wanted to visit, simply because he read that it was a party city. People come to New Orleans to party and have a good time. He saw nothing wrong with that other than it would be distracting to his objectives. Whenever he would visit a city, his objective would always be to stay focused on the task of removing people from the roles of the living. He always thought that if he were to go to New Orleans, he would find himself in the middle of some party, and he would lose sight of what God wants him to do.

He made up his mind to pray about it when he got to his room. It was now ten thirty; he had plenty of time before his meeting with Mary.

He pulled up to the parking valet attendant just as Nat King Cole was ending his song, 'Unforgettable' on the radio.

When his got to his room, he immediately dropped to his knees, folded his fingers together, put his elbows on the bed and started to pray.

He prayed for continued guidance. The gulf coast was experiencing the worst natural disaster in American history. Katrina turned out to be a real live monster; more violent than any monster that any science fiction writer can pen. This was going to be a life changer for anyone living in that region of the country. What Gunther wanted to know from God is this, how will it change his life?

He started praying and looking for answers at 11:15pm. It was now 12:05am, and he was finally through. He had his answer.

As he rose from the bed to undress for the shower, he looked across the room, and there sat Adolf Hitler on the small bedroom sofa. He was wearing a brown suit and tie. On top of his head was a matching brown fedora.

No one spoke while he continued to undress. He left the room and headed for the shower. While he soaped up in the shower, his mind slowly drifted back to Mary. The more he thought about her, the more eager he was to see her again. Was she the one after all?

Drying off now in the bedroom, Gunther looked over to the sofa; Adolf Hitler was still sitting in the same spot. Gunther tried to go on with his dressing, totally ignoring the presence of the Fuhrer.

It was now 1:00am; he was in danger of missing his meeting with Mary that was set for 1:15. He was almost ready…Now a quick hairbrush…Splash on some cologne…He was acting like a high school kid on prom night…Wait ah' minute…For him, this was prom night.

He reflected to his High School Prom:

His graduating class had ten students: Four girls with dates for the prom. Six boys; one boy took his sister to the prom. One boy named Joshua, who was a bully at school, came to the prom alone. Gunther took a girl to the prom named Sarah. She was six feet and four inches in height. She played center on the three-on-three half court High School basketball team. She was a very pretty girl that stood over the six foot two Gunther.

Gunther was persuaded to go to the prom with Sarah by his mother. She could not go to her own prom, because her father had forbidden it. Now she would go as a chaperone and watch her son enjoy his prom. Gunther was pleasant to Sarah during the prom; even bringing her punch several times. However, he did not ask her to dance. When Sarah did get a chance to dance, she danced with one of the other boys.

Meanwhile, Joshua bullied people at the prom, the same way he did at school. Joshua was five foot ten inches tall. However, he was built like the Hulk. He loved to lift weights in the school weight room, when ever he could slip away from his chores on his family farm. Everyone in his family was a little afraid of him, even his own father.

During the prom, he pushed boys to the side, and danced with their dates, even when the girls did not want to dance with him. They had no choice! He just grabbed them by their waists and pulled their slim bodies close to him. A few of the boys complained to the principle who was in attendance; however, the principle did nothing to stop the bullying on the dance floor.

Gunther stood next to the refreshment table, and silently watched Joshua move from one girl to the next girl: pushing their dates to the side. Every so often, Joshua looked over at Gunther. Since Gunther was not dancing with a girl, Joshua had no way to humiliate him.

He walked over to Gunther and looked deeply in his eyes. Then he looked around to make sure no one was listening.

"Fix me a bowl of punch fagot," he whispered to Gunther.

"Do you want ice cubes in it?" Gunther replied.

"No ice…"

Gunther dipped the large spoon in the punch bowl, then handed Joshua a cup of punch…no ice.

"You know what fagot…You are prettier than any girl here…Do you know that?"

"I didn't realize that Joshua. Thanks for letting me know."

"Are you gay?"

"I don't know."

"Do you like girls?"

"Not particularly, I just don't know."

"You like guys?"

"Not particularly."

"Want to hold my cock?" Joshua asked, while rubbing himself between his legs.

"No, I don't want to do that," Gunther replied, looking down at his shoes. "Well, you're going to. Now I want you to walk out the back door of the gym, and wait for me outside... You got that fagot?"

"Yes, I do" Gunther replied, slowly walking back towards the back of the gym.

Joshua slowly drank some of his punch and looked around to see who else he can humiliate. He needed to kill a little time before following Gunther outside. Now slowly walking through the crowd of students dancing, his eyes fell on a nerd named Harry that was dancing by himself. He walked over and kicked the boy in his butt, sending him to the floor. Some students laughed; others looked at the boy with horror. However, no one came to assist the boy off the floor. Harry slowly got up, put his glasses back on and slowly walked towards the principle, who was standing near the stage with his wife.

The students then returned to dancing. Joshua smiled as he watched the nerd slowly get up off the floor. He then slowly did a silly dance by himself... slowly moving toward the back of the gym. When he got to the back door, he put his back to the wall, and stood there for about five minutes. Now that no eyes were on him, he slipped out the back door.

Although it was now dark outside, he could clearly see Gunther waiting for him in front of the nearest cornfield, about fifty yards away. He started breathing harder as he walked closer and closer to Gunther. He stopped about six feet from Gunther. He suddenly began to feel uneasy... Gunther, to him, looked like a statue or a person made of stone. Although there was a slight smile on Gunther's face... Still, Joshua did not like the feeling that he was getting. However, lust took over, and he walked toward Gunther, unzipping his pants. Just when he was about to grab Gunther by his head to pull him down; Gunther stepped back into the cornfield without turning around. Joshua looked around to make sure no one was watching... He then stepped into the rows of corn stalks.

For the next three days and nights, a missing person amber alert was posted on all the media outlets. All the local barns, homes and cornfields were searched. Gunther also joined in on the search. School was canceled in Plains, so that all students can join in on the search.

On the fourth day Joshua was found standing naked behind the local Church. He had lost his ability to speak. And he seemed to still be in shock!! He never spoke again.

What in the world happened to him in that corn field? Only Gunther knows. And he never told anyone.

Now back to Las Vegas…

Gunther snapped out of his trance on his past life.

He now had fifteen minutes left to get downstairs, jump in his rental car, and drive to downtown Vegas to meet his date. He had to make it. Never has he felt this way—never thought he would ever rush heart pumping toward a women. This strange new feeling was somewhat mystifying; but also welcomed.

Just as he reached for the door knob to leave the room, Hitler said something to him that made him stop in his tracks.

"You fuckin' piece of shit!! How dare you ignore my presence? I am the Supreme leader of Germany!! I am a God on earth you golden haired maggot!! Get your ass back over here and sit down!!"

Gunther went over to the edge of the bed and sat down. Hitler got up from the sofa, and walked over to the bed, and sat down next to him.

"Why are you all of ah' sudden smitten over this women; you've just met the wench," Hitler said now folding his arms.

"I can't understand it myself. I've never felt this way before. However, I know she is not the one for me. I just want to try to get to know her, that's all," Gunther replied, his head now sinking down almost to his thighs. After a few seconds he raised his head back up, and continued:

"All I want to do is experience something new. I want to hold a woman's hand, and ask her if she wants to dance. What I really want to do is kiss a woman on the lips; and maybe slide my tongue in her mouth. When I watch real kissing on TV, it makes me very curious indeed.

"Let me save you the time and trouble," Hitler said, now standing up and facing Gunther.

"First of all allow me to apologize for calling you those awful names; I did not mean a word of it; I was just furious with you for not acknowledging my presence. As you well know, that is a show of disrespect to me; and that my friend could be interpreted as treason. Treason is punishable by death; do you understand my reaction?"

"Yes my Fuhrer, it will never happen again," responded Gunther, now a little more relaxed.

"Dating a woman is boring. Kissing a woman is disgusting. Holding a woman's hand is no different than holding your grandmother's hand; I see no difference there. So please get all of this foolishness out of your mind!!

"Why can't I at least experience these things for myself?" Gunther asked, now almost crying.

"First of all, regardless of my profanity laden outburst earlier, you are my best symbol of Arian superiority. You are a genius in finance; the money you have made in investments are mind boggling; and you did it all from your computer. You are the most handsome man on the planet. Women and men alike climb over one another just to be near you. If you wanted to, you could make a serious run for the White house. You could run as a Democrat or as a Republican; it really would not matter. You would get the money and backing you need from either party."

"Let's think about that for a moment...President Gunther Heisman! It has a nice ring to it, don't you think?" Hitler asked, extending his arms out to the side, and looking up to the ceiling.

"You could really take your program you call the pruning Solution to another level. Congress would tie your hands a bit; but you could get around that with a little thing called executive privilege."

Hitler was excited now; moving rapidly back and forth across the room.

"Do you know the things you could do with executive privilege?" he asked, stopping in front of Gunther, and looking him straight in the eyes. He was in a state of sheer frenzy at this point. It was obvious that this revelation had just come to him. He started out wanting to explain to Gunther that Mary was not the right women for him; however, at this point he was off and running in a whole new direction. Adolf Hitler was now displaying his true inner madness.

"Yes my Fuhrer, I know that the President has vast leeway with this power," Gunther replied.

He had thought in past years about maybe running for President at some point; however, he always put the thought out of his mind. Hitler's rant was giving him fuel to seriously think about the possibility of actually running and winning the Presidency of the United States of America.

"After 9/11, the country has developed into a nation of fear and suspicion; you could play on that fear. National security could be your umbrella that you could stand under when using executive privilege. If you do become president,

you will only get one term. America will not vote you in for a second term after you do the things that I dictate you to do. You may even have articles of impeachment drawn upon you after you have been in office for a year or two; however, in that short period of time, you could totally do plenty of damage in this country."

He waved his right hand close to Gunther's face to make sure he was paying attention; and not just sleeping with his eyes opened; which he was not. He was listening to every word coming out of Hitler's mouth. Satisfied that Gunther was paying attention, he continued with his madness.

"When you strike the blow, it must be hard and quick. The nation will just be getting settled and comfortable with their new president when you make the announcement on national television that the United States has just invaded Israel and also because of national security reasons, all Jewish citizens in the United States are to be rounded up and put in camps. The forced camps right here in the United States will be nothing new to the country. America rounded up all the Japanese Americans, and put them in camps after going to war against Japan. It will be the same situation."

Hitler then walked over to the couch, and sat down. He knew that Gunther would have reservations about a future attack on Israel if he were to somehow one day find himself as the leader of the free world. He relaxed himself in order to address any and all concerns that Gunther would have.

"Alright, let's get real here. This country has a deep love for Israel. We as a country have a written agreement to always protect Israel. Every president that has taken the oath of office in my lifetime, and many before my lifetime, have reaffirmed that commitment to the security of Israel. How in the world am I to justify an attack on our best friend in the Middle East?" he asked, now beginning to sound nervous and confused.

"You don't have to justify anything; you just do it! You are going to be the commander and chief of all the armed forces in the United States. When you give an order, it must be followed. Soldiers will always do as they are ordered."

After about thirty seconds of silence, Hitler stood back up, and started walking back and forth again.

"It will be about six months after the invasion before congress gets over the shock of what has taken place. Questions will arise almost immediately from the media as to why the invasion took place. You can answer their

questions if you like or you can simply ignore them. You can always make up reasons. Whatever reason you give, you will be attempting to sell the idea to the American people that Israel was not the friend to them it claimed to be. You could list a few made up instances of passing off sensitive information to America's enemies in the Middle East in exchange for better relations with their neighbors. After all, Israel is surrounded by countries that would love to destroy them. It's only a matter of time before they give in, and start working for the people that hate them. It's all about survival."

Hitler brought his hands together, and began to pray in silence. During the next ten minutes, the room was quiet. Gunther for maybe the first time in his life, kept his thoughts on the words of Hitler; no matter how crazy he sounded. When listening to other people that talked to him, his mind always wandered on past killing or planed killings; not this time.

After ten minutes Hitler stood up, brought his hands up to his chest, and continued his ravings. He began right where he left off before.

"You could say just about anything you want. Most likely it won't change public opinion; but who cares? It won't take but maybe two weeks to destroy Israel; then you can work on executing the ones you have in the labor camps. Like I stated earlier, congress will start making its move on you in about six months after the invasion. It will take another six or seven months to bring about the Articles of Impeachment. During that time you could be doing other things."

"Other things like what?" Gunther asked, suddenly looking very presidential.

"For one thing you could take those pathetic sub humans that are on death row out of their misery. You do this by executive privilege. For national security reasons, you will order that the appeal process will no longer exist. All death row inmates will be put to death immediately. It would be in the country's national security to rid the country of the threat of any future escape by any these criminals while they wait fifteen years for their appeal process to finalize. Any future prisoner sentenced to death would be put to death immediately. By executive order, there will be no more life sentences. Death sentences will replace all life sentences. By executive order, all parole boards throughout the nation will be dissolved. If a person receives a fifteen year sentence, they will serve the entire fifteen years. Fuck the American Civil Liberties Union and Fuck the Supreme Court; you will be the President

of The United States. You can do whatever the fuck you want to do with executive privilege. If congress or the Supreme Court determines that any of your actions were illegal, fuck it, it will already be done."

He walked slowly around the room. Then he turned his face towards Gunther's face. His eyes grew larger, and extended out of the sockets.

Then the eyes returned to its normal size. He then continued his speech:

"Also you could issue an executive order giving doctors the right to assist in suicides. You should get support for this order. The only group out there that would be against it would be the religious right, and fuck them too! There is one more thing you should do while I'm on the subject of your potential presidency; you should make it an automatic death sentence for any woman that gives birth to a child if they are poor and cannot afford to give a child what it needs in life. If a poor women gets pregnant they must get an abortion. You should also get support for this order. Again the religious right will scream fowl; however, the country as a whole is growing tired of poor women having five, six or seven kids, and can't afford them. There will be many other things you could do in the short time that you will be president; I will be there to advise and assist. Is there any other concerns before I move on?" Hitler asked, now stationary in front of Gunther.

"No my fuhrer, you have made yourself very clear," Gunther replied.

"Good, now let me explain something else to you. If you are going to make a run at the presidency one day you need to do two things in the coming years. First, you need to start getting into and winning some local elections. It matters not how handsome you are, how well you speak in debates, how much money you have made or how many powerful friends you have. You just can't pop up out of the blue, and expect the American people to send you to the White House without any political experience. You have to work your way to the top; just like I did. Secondly, you need a wife. There has never been a President of the United States that was single; and there never will be. That's where I come in. I will let you know when it's time to get serious with a certain women. Keep your mind on the business of pruning as you call it; and let me worry about the women in your life. When the time is right, I will send her to you. Do you understand me?"

"Yes I fully understand. I will never let my emotions overtake my objectives again," Gunther said, and he meant every word.

"Good," Hitler said, now returning to the couch.

"I prayed to God for guidance about the Katrina situation," Gunther asked, now taking off his clothes to get ready for bed.

"Did God give you the guidance that you seek?"

"Not yet," he replied, pulling the covers back on the bed.

"Give it time Heisman. God moves in his own time. I overheard an old nigger talking in Munich one day. He was talking to another old nigger. I was standing behind them waiting on the train. I was very young then, but already I hated niggers. I hated them long before I hated the Jew. I wanted to push those two old coons unto the train tracks just before the engine rushed by. I would love to have seen their faces just before the engine car ran over them. I did not do it because that would have caused me to be imprisoned. Niggers in Europe were treated much better than they were treated in America. They could live where they want, marry who they want, go to nightclubs and restaurants. Niggers had rights in Europe, but had no rights in America, the so-called land of the free, and home of the brave."

Gunther got into bed. He started to wander where Hitler was going with this latest revelation. What did two old black people having a conversation, while waiting on a train in Germany have to do with his wanting guidance from God?

"Anyway, I listened to their conversation instead of pushing them in front of the oncoming train. They were talking about God, and God's response to our prayers. One of the coons told the other: 'God may not come when you want him, but he's right on time'. That made good sense to me then, and it makes sense now. God will give you answers when he feels as though you are ready for the answers. God will give you blessings when you are ready to receive them. For example; people may think they want God to give them things in life; however, if God gives people gifts that they are not really ready to receive, it could be the worst thing that could happen to them."

"Thank you my fuhrer. If it's alright I will try to get some sleep now," Gunther said, closing his eyes.

"You sleep now Heisman; I'll be here when you wake in the morning," Hitler said, while walking over to the couch, and sat down on it.

After a few minutes Gunther was sound to sleep.

The next morning Gunther awoke to find Hitler still sitting on the couch watching him.

He started to ignore his presence, but he remembered what happened the last time he tried that.

"Good morning my fuhrer," he said, heading to the shower.

"Good morning to you Heisman," Hitler replied.

While he lathered up in the shower, he reflected back to what Hitler had told him yesterday about him being presidential material. He was flattered that he felt that way about him; although a few of the things he had in mind for him was out of the question. If he were to become president, he was not going to attack Israel or put American Jews in labor camps; that was out of the question. The other things he had in mind for him to do were reasonable—to a point.

"When do you check out of this place?" Hitler asked him after he returned to the room from showering.

"This is my last day here; I check out in the morning. I have business to attend to in Fresno tomorrow night."

"What kind of business?"

"I have to reconstruct and embalm a little boy that was killed in an auto accident. He was torn to pieces. His face I'm told…is missing. The funeral director in charge called me yesterday, and requested my services. I will start on what's left of him tomorrow night," Gunther replied, putting on his pants.

"Why do you bother with this funeral home non-sense? You are a very rich man; why bother with dead bodies?" Hitler asked, still sitting in the same spot.

"I do it because I'm good at it, and I enjoy doing it. People depend on me to make their deceased loved ones presentable for public viewing. But most of all, I do it because my father trained me himself," Gunther replied, now putting on his shoes. He was almost ready to head out for breakfast.

"You dug two graves in the desert; did you do that for nothing or are you planning to make use of them?"

"I don't know yet. I'm still a little mixed up. I dug the graves for the purpose of killing two, maybe three or even four people. For a while I even thought of killing Mary and her friends. But then I got that feeling of wanting to be with the woman…Then after your talk last night…I felt ashamed. I'm just confused; I can't think about that right now. I just might not kill anyone here in Vegas."

"Did God give you any messages in your sleep," Hitler asked, getting up to look out the window. The strip was alive with people; they were moving about like ants; getting an early start to their day. Las Vegas was indeed the most exciting city in the world. Hitler looked down at them with contempt.

"No, I slept like a baby; I don't even remember what I dreamed about."

"Like I said last night, God takes his own sweet time. Now I want you to listen to me for a few minutes; then you can get to that breakfast buffet that you like so much. This is the direction that I want you to follow. I want you to get to New Orleans as fast as you can. When you wrap up your duties in Fresno, I want you to head out immediately. This will be a golden opportunity for you to make a name for yourself. You have the money, connections and the will to help in rebuilding certain areas of the city; especially in the 9th ward that suffered the most damage, and loss of lives. Don't worry about the French Quarter and the surrounding areas on either side of Canal Street. They did not suffer that much damage; plus those businesses are mostly white owned; the state and federal government will give them what they need. The Superdome will be repaired to look better than ever. Money will rain down on it; however, the poor 9th ward will never be rebuilt. Like I stated earlier, niggers in Europe are treated much better than niggers in America".

He walked across to the other side of the room; then he turned around to face Gunther. Now folding his arms across his chest, he looked up to the ceiling.

"So far there are 1,836 confirmed dead and thousands more missing. The final death toll will be much higher; most of the missing will never be found. As the water recedes, the missing bodies will be washed out to sea. The hardest hit is the lower ninth ward, East New Orleans, Chalmette and St. Bernard Parish. Concentrate on these areas. You are not going to be able to help everyone; however, you will be able to help many. This type of national recognition for you will be the first step in your journey to the White House. Remember, the Great Wall of China could not be built without the laying of the first stone," Hitler said, now fading away in a mist.

Gunther made his way to the buffet line. He scooped up some eggs and grits on his plate; then he added a piece of smoked sausage along with toast, coffee and orange juice.

Sitting at a small two seat table alone, he mentally planned out his day. Since this will be his last day in Vegas; he wanted to get the most out of it.

First he planned on going to the pool area. He loved Caesar's pool because it made you feel like you were back in the Roman days of old. He had never felt so relaxed in his life.

After the pool, he was planning on catching the early 2:00pm Penn and Teller show. And then after that he wanted to play some Texas Holdem' poker at the Horseshoe. Then he wanted to top the evening off with the 8:30pm Wayne Newton show. If he could manage to get in all of that, it will indeed be good day in Vegas.

Back in LA Jim Bruce was sitting alone in a bar on the Santa Monica pier. His team leaders that were spread out along the West Coast were keeping him busy with phone calls. Murders had been the topic of the discussions. The murder rate had suddenly jumped to an all-time high during the past week. He managed to get to the scene of most of the crimes. People were in a state of panic. The media was really playing the Scorpion Killer card. The director and other senior heads of the FBI increased the pressure on Jim. They wanted the Scorpion Killer, and they wanted him now; dead or alive. The Scorpion Killer was now number one on the FBI's most wanted list.

After looking over most of the recent crime scenes, and getting the full reports from the team leaders; Jim came to the conclusion that the Scorpion Killer had not committed these new crimes. He did not tell anyone of his theory because he knew that they did not want to hear that.

Although he had nothing conclusive to go on, he knew something about the Scorpion killer. He knew that the killer was a person that people felt comfortable to be around; based on the women that they have found along the beach and in the water. There were never any signs of struggle. The women obviously were thrilled to be with him. Then they were suddenly killed. There were never any sex involved; no semen or vaginal penetration was ever found on the women.

As far as the women murders were concerned, they were dealing with a man that was pleasant to look at; even handsome. He blended in very well with the beach goers; however, this man has the body and the face to stand out even among all the rest of the good looking men on the beach. He was looking for a real live Mr. America; most likely with blond hair and blue eyes.

These recent murders were nothing like the Scorpion's murders. The Scorpion's kills were quick and to the point. The murders in the movie theaters were a perfect example of a stone cold killer; with nothing on his mind but to *end a life. An ice pick through the brain is pretty much the work of a natural born killer.*

The scorpion killer has never killed a person then gone through the victim's pockets looking for money. This killer has never invaded a home for the purpose of robbery. This killer has invaded homes throughout the West Coast and Mexico; however, the only purpose the killer had in the home invasions was to kill every breathing thing in the home; including the pets.

He got a call from Matt Washington from the LAPD. It was 11:30pm and he was still on the job. It's times like this that Jim knew why policemen around the country lose their wives in divorce. It's a tough way to make a living. Some investigators sleep on the job for two or three nights in a row investigating tough cases.

"What's up Matt?" Jim asked, raising his finger up to the bartender for another Scotch on the rocks.

"We got the report back from the coroner's office about the bodies that were found up in the Hollywood Hills."

"You mean they finished the autopsies this quick? It's only been two weeks, and we're talking four bodies," Jim said, raising his eye brows in amazement.

"I stayed on top of this case; I got them to skip over the other bodies that they had in the cooler, and jump on boys," he said, yawning into the phone. It was obvious that he really needed some shut eye.

"Nice going Matt; I really appreciate it. What's in the report?"

"Jim you're not going to believe what I'm going to tell you; but here it is pal: Our four boys had their heads cut off before the bodies hit the ground."

"Repeat that over to me Matt. I think the scotch I'm drinking is causing me to receive garbled messages," Jim said, now setting his drink on the table and lighting a cigarette.

"Tell me that again Matt, and this time tell it to me slowly," Jim said, now heading to the door. It was a little noisy in the bar; the outside was much quieter.

"Are you ready Jim?" Matt asked.

"Go ahead Matt, I'm in a much less noisy place right now," Jim replied, leaning up against his car that was parked out front.

"Alright, here goes, nice and slow. The autopsy report states that the four guys were decapitated a few seconds before their bodies hit the ground," Matt said.

No one spoke for over twenty seconds; then Matt broke the ice:

"You still there Jim," Matt asked, thinking that maybe Jim had hung up on him.

"That's fuckin' impossible man! That's almost going against the laws of physics. A body cannot stand up with its head missing. How in the fuck is that possible?"

"I told you that you were not going to believe it man; I mean this is some strange shit we have here."

"This has to be some kind of mistake. How did they come to that conclusion?" Jim asked, knowing that Matt would not have the answer.

"Jim, let me tell you something, you may or may not already know this: Those doctors over at the medical examinations department really know their business. When they give their autopsy report, they are 100% sure that the contents of the report are correct. Now as for how they came to the conclusion that they did, I really can't tell you that; I'm not a doctor. All I know is, those guys are smart, really smart; and they have the equipment and instruments to determine the facts in the case. How did they determine that the heads were cut off a few seconds before the bodies hit the ground? That's where loss of blood, blood flow, direction of blood flow, the time of blood flow vs. blood and blunt force trauma from the other wounds...I don't fuckin' know. But you can bet your bottom dollar that those nerds know," Matt said, stopping to take a sip of his black coffee.

"Matt, thank you. You are the one that's smart," Jim said, stomping out his cigarette butt on the pavement.

"Jim there's one other thing they mentioned: They are pretty damn sure that all the heads were cut off after their bodies suffered severe damage from stabs and cuts. The stabs and cuts were the fatal blows. The chopping off of the heads were done just for fun, I imagine. They called in some super nerds from Cal tech to run some mathematical programs. They gave the students all the data that they had on the crime scene. The nerds took the data, ran the programs and came up with their findings. These students all had masters' degrees, and are working on their PHDs in either mathematics or physics. They were not told beforehand that the medical examiner had already determined that the heads were cut off before the bodies hit the ground or that the stab and cut wounds were the true cause of the deaths. They were called in to only give their assessments. The student's reports all stated that all

the heads were removed before any of the bodies hit the ground, however the stabs and cuts to the body were the true cause of the deaths."

"That means that we are dealing with some sort of crazed ninja warrior; Bruce Lee with a sword," Jim said, now going back into the bar to pay his tab. "Looks like it," Matt said, trying to stay awake.

"Matt, I need you to do something for me; it's important."

"Sure Jim, what do you need?"

"I need you to go home, and get some sleep; will you do that for me?" Jim asked while paying his tab.

"Yeah, I guess I'm no good to you or anyone else in the shape I'm in. I'll get back with you in the morning."

"Drive carefully my friend; and thanks for the good work," Jim said, heading out the door again.

On the drive back to his hotel, Jim wandered what the Scorpion killer is doing at this moment. He hoped that he was somewhere sleeping.

Back in Vegas, Wayne Newton ended his last set at 11:30. He had put on a great show. Gunther truly enjoyed himself. It was the first time he had ever seen a live show in Vegas; although the city was nothing new to him.

He drove in three years ago to attend an undertaker's convention. He was all business during that trip. He didn't gamble or take in any shows. However, he did manage to find the time to murder three prostitutes in their hotel rooms.

Contrary to what many people believe; prostitution is illegal in Las Vegas, however; it still goes on. There are street walkers, nightclub solicitors, back page phone book hookers and high end expensive hookers that have their own rooms in luxury hotels on the weekends. Gunther killed one high maintenance prostitute on Friday, one Saturday and one Sunday; and left them all in their high class rooms with their throats cut. There was not much publicity in the papers about the murders; it would be bad for business. After all, these murders took place in just one weekend on the strip; no need to get potential visitors spooked about three hookers getting killed in Vegas. Hookers are killed every day, all over the country.

The power people in Vegas gambled that by keeping the coverage to a minimum, things would quickly get back to normal. The gamble paid off...

Gunther drove slowly along the strip. He was heading to his hotel, and looking forward to another good night's rest. Tomorrow morning he would be checking out, and heading to Fresno.

He passed by groups of people having the time of their lives in the most exciting city on the planet.

"I want you to ask those two drunken Elvis's up ahead if they need a ride," Hitler said, from the back seat.

"I need to get some rest. I have a long drive in the morning," Gunther replied.

"You need to do what the fuck I tell you to do!!" Hitler screamed.

Gunther slowly pulled over. The Elvis impersonators were indeed very much drunk. One almost fell to the pavement. They were trying to hold each other up; however, they were not doing a job of it.

They were both dressed to look like the ShowTime Elvis right before his death. They wore matching white jump suits with capes on the back. Both of them had what looked to be Elvis wigs on their heads, and dark sunglasses.

"Hey, you guys need ah' ride. You don't wanna' get yourselves locked up in Vegas," Gunther said, looking through his rear view mirror for any signs of onlookers or cops. The coast was clear.

"Sure man; you're ah' life saver," one of the men said, reaching for the back seat door handle.

One of the Elvis's was white, and one was oriental. The white Elvis was much drunker that the oriental Elvis. The oriental Elvis pushed the white Elvis in the back seat, and after pushing him over to the other side, he got in himself.

The white Elvis started singing 'Jail House Rock' as soon as he got settled. He didn't sound all that bad either. Gunther found himself taping on the steering to give the singer some sort of background beat.

"What hotel are you guys staying in?" Gunther asked.

"MGM Grand," the oriental Elvis replied.

"Fuck the hotel, I want some pussy!" white Elvis screamed, and then started singing, 'Don't Be Cruel', another classic from the King.

"You guys look like you need to get to your rooms and sleep it off, "Gunther said, smiling.

"My man rick here has got a real good point; a shot of pussy would do us both some good," Oriental Elvis replied, grinning.

"You guys are not gonna' get me locked up. Where are you gonna' find some pussy at? These street walkers are mostly cops in disguise. You get your asses locked up here, and it will be three or four days before you get bonded

out," Gunther said, *trying to give the guys some good advice; although he wasn't quite sure about everything he was telling them. He was trying to scare them more than anything.*

"I heard they got pussy ranches outside of Clark County where prostitution is legal," Oriental Elvis said.

"I don't know about that man; you can't believe everything you hear," Gunther said, *now getting a little bit pissed.*

"Love me tender, love me sweet..." white Elvis was at it again.

"Take these two to the desert; that way you can put those two graves you dug to good use," Hitler said, *from the front seat.*

"...oh my daring, I love you, and I always will..."

Gunther stopped the car in front of the MGM.

"You know your friend Rick here is a pretty good singer. He sounds just like Elvis," Gunther said, *looking back at white Elvis break into, 'You ain't nothin' but ah' hound dog..."*

"He's real good. As a matter of fact you are looking at the first place winner of the Elvis singing contest; he beat out over a hundred guys trying to win; he is just that good. He won it two nights ago at the Mint," Oriental Elvis said, *while punching his buddy on the shoulder. White Elvis just kept right on singing.*

"What the fuck are you doing Heisman? Let's get these two to the desert now!!" Hitler screamed.

Gunther wished that the two could see and hear Hitler; then they would gladly run to their rooms.

"You never told me your name," Gunther said, *trying to ignore Hitler.*

"Stan Vu; I'm Chinese American," Stan said, *pumping his fist in the air.*

"Where are you guys from? And what do you two do for a living?"

"We're from Seattle Washington, and we both are programmers for Microsoft," Stan said, *looking over at Rick who was now dozing off to sleep.*

"You guys do this often? I mean dress up like Elvis?"

"Man yes; we are Elvis freaks. We do birthday parties, and the whole nine yards back home. We usually go to Graceland in Memphis every year on his birthday, but when we heard about the Elvis convention here in Vegas we decided to come here instead."

"What's your name?" Stan asked.

"The name's Heisman...Gunther Heisman."

"That's fuckin' brilliant! Just go ahead and tell them your real name,"
Hitler shouted.

"Heisman, is that German?" Stan asked, leaning over, and shaking his
friend awake.

"Yes, my roots are German. Hey you guys should get on to your rooms;
I've got to hit the sack myself; busy day tomorrow."

"Do me this favor Gunther; I really want to get me some Vegas pussy
before we leave. I'll even pay for your girl; how about it my man?"

"Take these guys to the desert or I swear to God I'll make you pay. I know
deep down inside you want me to order your death. I'm not going to do that;
what I will do is make your life a living hell. I will be at your side twenty four
hours a day. You won't be able to function at normal daily activities. I know
you like doing other things when you're not killing people. Those things will
stop. No more music on the radio while you're driving; no more quiet dinners;
no more making millions on the Internet…Get my fuckin' drift pal?" Hitler
shouted, foaming at the mouth.

"I guess I could use a little Vegas snatch myself; especially if you're
buying," Gunther said, smiling at Rick snoring instead of singing.

"Alright, that's what the fuck I'm talking about!!" shouted Stan.

On the slow drive down the strip, Gunther started thinking about the
family dog while growing up in Plains. The dog was a Poodle named Lady.
She was a joy to the entire family.

Lady liked going on long walks with whichever family member felt like
walking that day. She was tiny, and cute.

One day Gunther started out walking with his fishing rod stationed on
his shoulder, and had a small can of worms sticking out of the pocket of his bib
overalls. He was heading down to the local pond to see if the fish were biting.

He was then twelve years old. He had been steady fishing since he was
eight. Lady was jumping around at his feet, happy to be going on the walk.
Every once in a while she would stop, and do dog things…things like sniffing
rocks, hiking up one leg to urinate or sometimes she would hunch up her
back, and release a tiny ball of shit.

About fifty yards from the pond, Gunther stopped walking and looked
up to the morning sky. The sun was nowhere to be found. It was a chilly
beautiful morning in September. And so he just stood at attention, looking
up at the light blue sky.

After about two minutes of standing still, as if he were a statue, he looked down at Lady whining at his feet. Just like a small child, she wanted to be picked up.

Gunther reached down, and picked her up. Lady was overjoyed. She started licking at his face.

Gunther grabbed her throat, and started applying vice like pressure. Lady tried to cry out; however, her voice was cut off. She wiggled and jerked, then she started shitting and pissing at the same time.

Gunther placed Lady's limp lifeless body under some rocks that lay under a small hill next to the mouth of the pond. He then walked over to the narrow part of the pond, and cast out his hook, with a nice fat worm impaled into a sharp hook.

He fished for two hours, and reeled in three Catfish...

Even as a young boy of twelve, he was a sick fuck...

Gunther turned on to Boulder Hwy.

After about ten minutes of silence, he looked back at the two from his rear view; they were both sleep. Hitler had long gone. He turned on the radio, and found a soul music station that played the oldies. Jerry Butler was singing, 'Moody Women'.

The desert air has a different kind of smell to it.

Even the sky looked different when seeing it from the desert.

The desert was cool at night; even bone chilling cold on some nights.

In the midday the can get so hot, it could cause a lost person to go insane.

After another ten minutes, Gunther knew that his spot would be coming up soon.

Smokey Robinson was singing his classic, 'Tracks of My Tears' on the radio.

After another ten minutes, Gunther shouted, "Hey, any of you guys have ta' take ah' piss? I know I do."

"Yeah man, let me out cause' I'm just a hunka hunka burnin' love, white Elvis proclaimed.

"Me too man, I need to take a leak. How far are we from pussy?" Stan asked, taking his shades off, and rubbing his eyes.

"If its two things in the world that I know you Asian boys love: it's fucking and gambling," Gunther said, while pulling over to the spot where the graves were dug. He then made a right turn, and drove about fifty yards

on a sandy road that was most likely used many times in the past during the early gangster years in Vegas. If only this desert could talk, the murders committed here, the bodies that were dumped in shallow graves. Dead men can't testify. In the 1950's and 60's the gangster's car tires rolled over the road numerous times, making a dirt driveway.

These newest graves were dug about twenty yards to the left of where the car stopped.

"Don't forget about math and science; we love that shit too," Stan said, putting his shades in his pocket.

"I didn't mean any harm; I was just trying to make light of the moment that's all. I know Asians are smart; the Ivy League schools are trying to cut down on the Asian enrollment before they completely take over their schools. I for one know how smart the Asian people are, and how much they like to study and stay focused," Gunther said, getting out of the car.

"You were also right the first time. We Asians also like to study and stay focused on the art of fucking; gambling is something we do until we run up on some pussy," Stan said, laughing and helping his friend out of the car.

Gunther kept the head lights on. The two Elvis's walked about ten yards in front of the car, and started pissing.

White Elvis started singing again.

Gunther walked up behind them, and pointed his trusty Luger at the back of Stan's head. He pulled the trigger. The bullet went through the chamber, through the silencer at the end, and finally into Stan's brain. It exited through his forehead, taking much of it away.

Oriental Elvis dropped to the ground. The Elvis wig flew off his head, exposing a very short crew-cut.

White Elvis was still singing one of Elvis's gospel songs: 'Precious Lord, take my hand'

He looks down at his buddy and smiles.

– "Looks like Stan is drunker than I am"—

'Precious Lord, take my hand, lead me on.'

He finished pissing, and turned around. When he saw the gun pointed at him he said, "Looks like we should have gone on to our rooms."

"Looks that way," Gunther replied, still pointing the pistol.

"You know, I really didn't feel right getting in your car; I tried to block the feeling out by singing."

"I wish you guys had gotten out at your hotel; I really do," Gunther said, slowly putting pressure on the trigger.

"Do you mind if I sing one last Gospel song? It was one of Elvis's favorites, and maybe it could help me get to Heaven," he said, trying to hold back tears.

"The Lord did tell the thief on the cross: 'this day, you will be with me in paradise'; so go ahead, get yourself right with God," replied Gunther, now backing up to turn off the headlights and still pointing the pistol at him.

The moon gave out a beautiful illumination; it filled the desert with a strange kind of off blue light. Gunther could still clearly see the man, and could even see his tears that were now coming slowly down his face.

What he was not prepared to hear was the most beautiful gospel singing that he had ever heard in his life. No one on earth could sing this song like Elvis; no one except this man that was dressed up like the King himself.

What he heard made him cry; it made him lower his weapon. It made him cry out to the Lord, and ask for his own forgiveness...

What he heard made him curse Hitler who was standing behind him, and leaning on the car, watching...

The man dressed up as Elvis, who now in the illumination of light looked almost exactly like Elvis, clinched his two fists, placed them across his chest, and started singing, 'How Great Thou Art':

"O Lord my God,
When I in awesome wonder
Consider all
The world thy Hand hath made,
I see the stars,
I hear the rolling thunder,
Thy pow'r thoughout
The universe displayed
Then sings my soul,
My savior God, to thee,
How great thou art!
How great thou art!
Then sings my soul,
My Savior God, to thee,
How great thou art!
How great thou art!

The man who, in Gunther's eyes, had truly become Elvis Presley in the final moments of his life said these words while looking up to the night sky: "I'm ready to be with the Lord."

Gunther raised the piston once more and shot him in the forehead.

The man dropped down on both knees, however, incredibly, he was still alive. Blood flowed down from the hole in his forehead. The bullet was lodged in his brain; it didn't explode out the back as what usually happens. The man seemed to be alert, and very much aware of his surroundings.

"This ain't Heaven," the man said, turning his head slowly from side to side.

Gunther started crying again, and walked over to the man, and said, "No my friend, this is not heaven. But I promise you, you're gonna' see Jesus real soon."

He placed the point of the barrel up against the man's temple, and pulled the trigger again. This time the bullet tore through the man's brain again, and exited out the other side of his head.

He reached down to pull off his Elvis wig...

He grabbed a handful of hair, and pulled...

The hair on White Elvis was real; he didn't need a wig at all.

Walking back to the car to get the shovel and change into his work boots and overhauls, he passed by Hitler still leaning on the front of the car with his back to the hood.

"Are you happy now?" he snapped at Hitler.

"Just bury those two so we can get the fuck out of here," Hitler said, walking towards the bodies.

After placing the bodies in their separate graves, he got on with the business of covering the graves with dirt.

He learned over the years observing his own grave diggers doing their work after a funeral, that replacing the dirt is much faster than digging it out. It didn't take him but two hours to fill both graves. He then covered them with brush and other debris that was available nearby.

On the drive back to his hotel, he reflected back on the two Elvis's. He didn't get a chance to learn anything about them, other than they were coworkers and good friends; that did everything together; even died together.

He didn't know if either of them was married or not. They both seemed to be fun to be around. If they had wives and children, it must have been a happy home that they came back to everyday after work; it's obvious that they were not the sort of people that took their work home with them.

When they returned home most likely it was 'party time' Elvis style.

"...Whatever you do, stay off of my blue swede shoes..."

New Year's Eve Thursday December 31 2009
Bourbon Street
New Orleans Louisiana

It was 10:35pm, and Bourbon Street was cooking. There were wall to wall people slowly moving in all directions along the street. Some wore costumes such as clowns, ballerinas, squash buckling pirates, and voodoo priests. One lady was dressed as England's Queen Elizabeth II. She looked stunning wearing a long white jewel incrusted gown, a long red cape (two girls held up the back of the cape as she walked), and a beautiful fake diamond and ruby incrusted tiara. She slowly waved at passersby. (She mostly gave the people the back of her hand in that special royal monarchy kind of wave). People parted a path for her; a few bowed or curtsied in a comical show of respect.

"Long live the Queen!!" some of the people shouted.

Moving towards her from the opposite direction was another world celebrity; worthy of praise and admiration. The people parted a path, so the two could meet.

"Make way for the Holy See!!" someone shouted.

The queen stopped, and stretched out her arms to receive a man that looked like he was the reincarnation of Pope John Paul II in full regalia. He looked almost exactly like the late Pontiff.

After the two world celebrities ended their embraced, they went together into Pat O'Brian's, and got wasted.

By the time 11:30pm rolled around people were getting arrested for solicitation, drunk and disorderly, fighting and selling drugs.

A woman on the balcony was warned not to expose her boobs again. She flashed them again. She shouted at the two cops looking up to her: "Fuck you!!"

She was arrested.

The scene started looking like Mardi Gras without the parade. It was wild.

Now entering Bourbon Street from the Canal Street entrance was Gunther Heisman and Adolf Hitler. They both wore masks on their faces and New Year's party hats on their heads. Other than the masks and party hats, they had on their usual attire; which were very much out of place in this environment.

Gunther was dressed as if he was attending a board of director's meeting of some sort; dark blue business suit, light blue shirt and a bright yellow tie. He also had on a pair of black Stacy Adams shoes.

Hitler had on his typical brown corduroy suit that he often wore when entertaining friends in his sanctuary called 'The Birds Nest' high up in the Swiss Alps. He had on a white shirt, brown tie; and also had on a pair of brown loafers.

They entered the noisy, music filled street very slowly; taking in all the sights and sounds around them.

They both stopped to observe two black boys that looked to be about ten years of age tap dancing for tips. A small crowd had gathered around the boys. People were clapping, and showing the boys support. After they finished their set, most of the people around them put money into a bucket for the boys. Gunther bent down, and put in a five dollar bill.

"They were pretty good weren't they" Gunther asked Hitler as they moved on down the block.

"Darkies are always good at dancing and sport; those two most likely will grow up to be gang bangers," Hitler replied.

"One of them could very well grow up to be president," Gunther said, growing ever so tired of Hitler's racist views.

"Let's talk about something else; how do you think your Solution is panning out?" Hitler asked, leading Gunther into a gay bar called, 'Our Place'.

"It's almost midnight; let's not talk shop for the rest of the year; if that's alright with you," Gunther said, finding a seat at the bar. Hitler chose to stand.

Gunther often wondered if Hitler was a spirit or some kind of demon. He observed him standing like some sort of statue. He did not have to move over to allow people to pass by; people simply walked through him. As the years have gone by he had become less afraid of Hitler. He did not think Hitler could physically harm him because he was a spirit. If he tried to hit him or shoot him his fist or his bullets would simply go through his body like air. The only thing that still made him a little bit afraid was his commanding presence. If Hitler would ever order him to put a gun to his head and commit suicide, right now he believe that he would do it. After all, he was, in his heart, Gestapo.

"We've got about a minute left in this year, and then we can get down to the business of killing Jews," Hitler said, while a young gay man in full drag walked straight through him.

"Are you going to join the countdown?" he asked Hitler.

"Fuck no!" Hitler shouted, putting his hands behind his back, and looking around at all the gays in the bar. He would love to round all of them up and gas them to death.

"Orange juice on the rocks," Gunther told the bartender. The bartender was a very good-looking black woman, who looked to be about sixty years of age. She had soft looking brown skin. She wore a white wig, and was dressed as an angel; complete with wings and a halo.

Everyone held up their drinks to the ceiling. Hitler stood on the bar extending his arm out in a Third Riche salute to himself.

"10…9…8…7…6…5…4…3…2…1…Happy New Year!!!"

After the bartender shouted out: "Happy New Year!!" she looked over at Gunther, who was still slowly drinking his orange juice. He did not seem to be in a festive mood. So, she waked back over to him.

"Hey handsome, why the sad face?" she said, while filling up his glass again with orange juice.

"I'm not sad at all. I'm happy and focused on the Lord," he replied while turning up his glass again, and drinking most of his juice.

"I'm focused on the Lord myself, however, I celebrate the coming of the New Year" the woman replied while pouring a straight vodka for a young man dressed as little orphan Annie.

"What do you do for a living?" Gunther asked.

"I a nurse, but I'm retiring in six months. What about you? What do you do?"

"I kill people, and even bury some of them. My occupation is funeral home director."

"Did you say you kill people?" The woman asked, as she stood directly in front of Gunther.

"Yes, I said that; however, I was only kidding."

"Normal people don't kid around like that."

"What if it's true?"

"What is what is true?"

"I really do kill people; I might kill a few people tonight."

"What is your name Mr.?"

"Undertaker is my name; killing is my game," he shouted for all to hear. However, all the party people could care less about a guy shouting nonsense at the bar.

"You need Jesus…Something is very wrong with you," the woman said while toping of a beer glass for a young man dressed like Little Red Riding Hood.

"What do you think is wrong with me?"

"You're bat shit crazy…that is what's wrong with you," she shouted back at him.

"I think you are getting crazy mixed with genius my dear," he said, while walking away from the woman, and moving the crowd. His death is still a mystery to me. I just can not understand how a person that works out running and doing wind sprints, lifting weights, doing push ups, and pull ups; just suddenly dies!! I just don't get it…I never will. I will always love my cousin Butch. Besides being a successful business man, he was the most brilliant artist that I have ever known. He could draw, and paint like the great Pablo Picasso!! All of a sudden one day, he just burned all of his art work, and retired from being an artist. I was crushed when he did that!! He told me that he did it because he wanted to put his full attention on his import clothing and shoe business.

Everyone hugged and kissed. Hitler looked down and observed two men dressed as Batman and Robin French kissing. He pulled out his revolver, and fired several shots at the pair. Just as Gunther suspected, the bullets just passed right through the men. They kept right on kissing. Gunther smiled at Hitler, and then held up his cup to him, and said, "Happy New Year my Fuhrer."

Hitler jumped down from the bar, walked over to Gunther, and said, "We have to talk."

"Let's go outside for a while," Gunther said, getting up from his stool, and heading for the door.

When he reached the sidewalk, he bent down, and sat on the curb. Hitler sat down beside him. Gunther was surprised to see that the Supreme German Chancellor was willing to sit down on a filthy street curb; however, there he was relaxing in a spot where drunken tourists most likely had pissed on before being taken to jail on indecent exposure charges.

Hitler's lack of invincibility was beginning to be exposed. He knew that Gunther was growing more independent of him every day. He saw the look on his face when he failed to kill the two men kissing. He now knew that Gunther had absolutely nothing to fear from him.

He took off his mask and party hat and threw them both into the crowded street. Both the objects sailed through the people like magic, and landed softly in the middle of the street.

"Look Heisman, I know that I have been hard on you lately; it's only because I care for you so much. You are a fine man; a strong, smart Arian symbol of German superiority. Under my direction, I have seen you grow from a curious young boy to a confidant, and courageous man," he said, while brushing his hair to the side with his fingers.

"I want you to one day become President of this country. You have everything it takes for the office. I know that you think that because you have never attended college, you have no chance of winning; that is not true. You have a great chance. America is giving you that chance. All it takes for you to be eligible for office is to be at least 35 years of age; and to have been born on American soil; you meet both requirements."

"I have no intension of running for president or any other political office, and that's final," Gunther said, taking off his mask and party hat, and setting them down beside him.

Hitler was lightly shocked at Gunther's response, however; he tried to save face, and remain in control of the conversation.

"That's fine. You don't have to go into politics; that was just one of the many paths that you could take," Hitler responded, turning his head away from Gunther, and observing the Queen coming back down the street. She had the Pope on her arms; and they both were drunk. They were being closely followed by two undercover policemen.

When they approached the entrance to the gay club, the Queen put the pope down, and turned to Gunther and said, in a soft male voice, "Handsome one, come with me at once; I am in need of your services."

"No my Queen, I am fine just where I am," replied Gunther, turning up the last of his juice.

He knew that the Queen was a man. However, she was so beautiful.

The Pope looked at Gunther and said in a slurred speech, "Bless you my golden haired one," then staggered on in to the club behind the Queen.

Gunther then looked at Hitler intensely; he said nothing for about a minute.

"What's wrong Heisman? Why are you staring at me," Hitler said, breaking the ice.

Gunther replied, "I have been wondering about you lately; wondering if you were a ghost or some kind of spirit. I have come to the conclusion that you are neither ghost nor spirit. You are nothing at all. You are just an imaginary image that I have in my mind. I love Adolf Hitler; however, you are not him. I want to start the New Year off without you; I can take it from here. Bye bye birdy."

"Do you know who the fuck you are talking to?" Hitler shouted.

"Yes, I know very well who I'm talking to; I'm talking to no one. I'm talking to myself. People are walking by looking at me as if I am crazy. They see a man sitting on a curb arguing with no one. So let me continue my dismissal of you before I was so rudely interrupted. Be gone with you forever. Do not come to my mind or conscious ever again."

Hitler slowly vanished from view. His mask and party hat that were lying in the street also vanished.

Gunther then put his own mask and party hat back on, and walked back into the gay club. A few minutes later, he was on the dance floor with Tinkerbelle, a very pretty young man wearing a skin tight fairly costume, complete with wings and all. They were dancing to Michael Jackson's hit 'Billy Jean'.

The year was now 2010, and Gunther Heisman is going to be doing things his way. He was going to take his Solution to new heights.

Jim Bruce woke up early. He was now operating out of a suite at the New Orleans Hilton Hotel on Canal Street. His entire team had now moved to New Orleans with him. Each member of his team had their own rooms here at the hotel. Jim's suite was used as the unit command center. There were computers, and video equipment all over the place.

Jim had recently been promoted to Director of the FBI. He had reached the top of the mountain. Years of training, and dedication to the task of bringing in America's most wanted criminals had paid off. He now called all the shots. He had a blank checkbook; nothing was out of his reach. He could go anywhere in the world, and take any number of persons with him in his pursuit of criminals.

He has never spent much time in his office in Washington since his promotion. Instead, he has been relentlessly in pursuit of the Scorpion Killer. He was now convinced that this killer was operating in New Orleans.

Things started coming together after Katrina. He and his team were still on the West coast chasing a ghost. The Scorpion Killer had stopped killing. At least Jim knew the killer had stopped. The rest of the country thought the killer was still wreaking havoc because killings were still taking place. As a matter of fact, murders in California were increasing at an alarming rate because of gang warfare and Crack Cocaine. However; Jim knew that the spike in murders had nothing to do with his killer. He didn't have proof; he just knew it. Almost all the bodies discovered in the next few years were blamed on the Scorpion Killer. The media kept the fires burning.

Although Jim was working the West Coast, he still got data on events that were taking place in the rest of the country.

Then he started getting data about missing people. This data showed a pattern over the past two years 128 people had traveled to New Orleans from all over the United States, and never returned home. They just flat out disappeared. Of the 128 people 17 of them were from other countries.

Also 11 people living in the city were murdered for no apparent reason. Two bodies were found sitting on a bench in Jackson Square with their throats cut. Six were found in three different movie theaters with ice pick fatal wounds to the back of the head; and three was found on back streets, shot at close range in the face. One of those shooting victims was shot while trying to make a few dollars cleaning car windows in the Street.

Although there were many more murders in the City of New Orleans, as a result of gangs, drugs, domestic violence and prostitution; Jim had a six sense when it came to separating common crimes from serial killer crimes.

There was still no panic in New Orleans yet. This city was too drenched in music, parties; parades and tradition to worry about violent deaths. After all, death is often celebrated in second line jazz funerals. Coffins often danced in the air.

Jim looked at his four member team, and smiled. He was proud of them. They were as patient and relentless as he was.

Jim was now receiving information from Washington. The fax machine made its usual whining sound as it slowly spit out a sheet of paper with a picture on it. The picture was a profile of the Scorpion Killer, based on the limited amount of information the FBI had on him.

"Guys, this is what we think the killer looks like. The profilers in Washington have spent the last few months analyzing data, and this is what they came up with. The profile will most likely change as the investigation moves forward. This is the best they could come up with at this time."

The picture showed a face of a narrow faced white man with glasses. The face was that of a girlish looking man with black hair and brown eyes.

Gunther started his day off by getting rid of anything that reminded him of Adolf Hitler. He took down the Hitler portrait, and destroyed it. All the books he had on Hitler were burned. The Nazi uniform he had in his closet was also burned. When all of that was done, he showered, and headed out the door for breakfast.

This morning he decided to have breakfast at La French, an upscale eatery on Canal Street.

As he sat at his table eating French Waffles, eggs and Canadian bacon, he started thinking about his new plan of action.

His pruning solution will be altered a little bit. He felt as though to have a solution, you first needed a problem. He was the problem, and the solution will be his death.

No longer will he hide behind some kind of Nazi philosophy. He was going totally solo with his new direction.

He now discovered what he really was. He was a natural born killer. He kills because he enjoys it. The wooden chair in his killing room was only another outlet for his enjoyment. The enjoyment he gets from bounding a person up and killing them with a sledge hammer is his version of sex. The real reason that he has never had a woman was not because he was trying to be like Hitler; it was because he could never enjoy a women. Women to him were always nothing but a distraction.

Even as a child he would turn away from a girl that was trying to kiss him. Instead he would run away, and trap some fury animal, and torture it…then he would get a small erection.

He did not need some imaginary person in his head to order his death; he would do it himself, on his own, when the time was right. The world will be much better off without him in it; he thought.

However, he planned on having a little bit of fun before he puts a fatal bullet into his brain. He planned on turning this city upside down. He was going to be another Katrina.

He wanted to increase the number of people he killed; the wooden chair was nice, but it only served the purpose of giving him a sexual pleasure.

When he got home, the cleaning lady was hard at work. Also the cook was there preparing his weekend meals. He greeted them both, and went into his office. He sat there staring at his computer for over ten minutes.

The cook knocked on the office door.

"Come in," he said, snapping out of his trance.

"I got a nice hot cup of coffee for you sir," Betty Mitchell said cheerfully.

Betty came from a long line of black cooks and housekeepers; going all the way back to the days of slavery.

"Thanks Betty, that's just what I need," replied Gunther, moving a few papers out of the way.

"I also brought you some of my raspberry muffins that you like so much," she said, setting the tray down beside the computer.

"Let's get married Betty," he said, smiling, while picking up one of the muffins.

Betty laughed and said, "That sounds good to me; only one problem, I'm already married."

"Just say the word, and I'll get rid of him," he said, smiling and eating.

After Betty left the room, he finished his coffee, and turned on the computer. After a few minutes he found the site that he was searching for: HOW TO MAKE BOMBS...BOMB MAKING 101...MAKE BOMBS AT HOME...BOMB MAKING FOR DUMMYS...BOMB MAKING MADE EASY

Jim Bruce was sitting alone on a bench looking out at the busy Mississippi River. Tug boats was pushing cargo, oil tanker were on their way to sea, and cruise ships were taking vacationers to exotic destinations.

Jim wished he could be on one of those cruise ships with his wife. He needed a vacation. He had built up over ten years of vacation time. Beginning in the fall of 1999 he was assigned to head up the Illegal immigration situation along the Mexico and Texas borders. After the twin towers were attacked in New York on 9/11, he was called back to Washington to work with homeland security. Then in 2003 he was sent to California after it was discovered that a serial killer was on the loose.

After Katrina in 2007 he was asked if he wanted to come to New Orleans to head up an investigation looking into the possibility of home grown terrorism in breaching the levies. He turned that offer down; he was now committed in stopping the Scorpion killer no matter how long it would take.

He knew that the killer was here in New Orleans; and he somehow knew that the killer knew he was also here.

He was tired. Frustration was a constant in his life. It was a wonder that his wife has not left him yet.

He heard laughter behind him.

Children were playing in the court yard in Jackson Square. As he turned around to look at the girls playing with their dolls, and the boys running around playing cowboys and Indians, he thought about his own children.

He had not been much of a father to his two children; Tom who is now a third year law student at Duke University School of Law, and

Becky a second year medical student at the University of Georgia School of Medicine.

He and his wife Marcy gave their children all the material things they need in life growing up, however; it was Marcy that gave them the quality time they needed from a parent.

He did make it home for all holidays, and most weekends, however; that did not make up for all the time he spent away from his family.

He missed both of his kid's first steps, and he was not there to put their tooth under the pillow for the tooth fairy. Although he didn't watch them breaking in their tricycles or the training wheels on their bikes as they got bigger; he was at home to train them both when they wanted to try to ride without the training wheels. That was one good memory; watching each of them ride for the first time without the training wheels.

He only got to watch his son play high school football seven times, because most of the time he got home to late on Friday nights.

He never got the chance to escort his daughter to the annual father daughter dance. His father would always have to step in and take her. The dance would always fall on a Saturday that he was on an extended assignment.

His career had taken away a large chunk of his family time. He thought about making a career change in the near future. If and when he did finally catch of kill the Scorpion Killer he was going to retire from the Bureau; maybe write a book about his time chasing the killer, and get a job teaching law. That way he can at least be home with his wife. He would also be available to his children, who would always be in need of fatherly advice from time to time.

He turned his head back to the river, and wondered what his killer was up to?

Gunther drove slowly towards east New Orleans listening to his Frank Sinatra CD. With him in the car were two women he had picked up at a bar near the Superdome. The white women called herself 'Candy' and the black women called herself 'Cookie'. They were both fairly good looking women. Candy was tall with long red hair and green eyes. Cookie was short; with long black braids; she also had a very large ass to go along with a slim waist, with beautiful brown eyes.

He met them while sitting at the bar drinking his very first Martini. They sat on either side of him, and struck up a conversation. It didn't take long for him to realize that they were hookers.

The conversation was light at the beginning; then it drifted on to what they could do for him in bed; for a price. He bought them drinks, and they started feeling comfortable with him.

After about an hour of chit chat, the conversation turned to drugs, heavy drugs. Gunther told them that he knew nothing about drugs, and that he had never even tried pot. They kept on talking about it until Gunther began to show some interest. He asked them what kind of drugs to they do, and they both told them that they were heroin addicts. Gunther's curiosity took over. He agreed to purchase the heroin for them in exchange for allowing him to watch. The women gladly agreed, and off they went.

"So you're a watcher?" Candy asked, lighting a cigarette.

"Not exactly, I just never saw anyone doing heroin, that's all. As a matter of fact, I've never seen anyone doing any kind of drugs," he replied.

The women told him to stop in front of a large plantation era looking house on Esplanade. He handed the black woman two thousand dollars cash. She went up the stairs, and rang the doorbell. After a few seconds, an elderly looking black woman dressed in a maid's uniform opened the door, and invited the woman in. When ten minutes had passed, the woman returned, and climbed back in the back seat, and said cheerfully, "We got Peter Pan from Afghanistan; let's roll motherfuckers, let's roll!"

They then headed towards St. Charles Avenue.

Sinatra was singing, *"...it's up to you New York, New York..."*

The white women started rubbing the tracks on her arms in anticipation.

"Hey man, thanks for the trust. I could have taken your money, and split. How did you know that I was an honest woman?" Cookie asked.

"It would have made no difference to me if you had run off with the money; I'm loaded. Two thousand to me is like nothing," he replied.

"Well thanks anyway. I might be an addict, but I don't take anything that doesn't belong to me. I've always been trust worthy. If I give you my word, you can take it to the bank, it's that good," she said, settling back and relaxing.

After traveling on St. Charles for about five miles, she told him to make a left on Pine, then a right on Dominican Street. She then told him to stop at the last house on the right. They were now very close to Leake Avenue which runs parallel to the Mississippi River.

The house was a plain brick home; nothing fancy about it that stood out. They had passed several homes that looked much better from the outside at least.

Candy got out, walked to the front door, and knocked.

"There are two black guys that live here. They're brothers, and they are some treacherous pipe hitting dope heads. And they will kill ah' motherfucker for little or nothing. Whatever you do, don't act like you're scared; they can smell fear."

Cookie didn't know it; Gunther was a walking, talking, ass kicking machine; as deadly as real Scorpion.

"Don't worry, I won't let nothing happen to you; I promise," Cookie said, looking out the window as Candy went inside. She then rubbed his right shoulder in order to comfort him. She was sure that he was nervous and a little frightened inside. *Bless her heart*

"I'm not worried; I feel safe with you," Gunther said, smiling.

"We like to come here when we got some serious dope to do. It's quiet, and you don't have to worry about people coming and going; they don't play that shit. Everything is going to be alright," she said, still looking at the front porch for Candy.

Candy finally came out, and waved for Gunther to drive around to the back of the house. He backed the car up, and pulled into the driveway; then drove to the back of the house.

They got out, and walked to the back door. Candy was waiting for them with the door opened. When they walked in, Candy bolted up the door, and turned several locks.

Gunther was standing in the kitchen looking around when two hard core looking black men walked in from the living room. They were both tall and muscular. They looked to be twins; both had gray eyes and hard stone looking faces. The men looked like they have had a rough life; which they did.

The tallest one that looked to be around six five was named Tony, and the shorter one was named Mitch. They both had done hard time for murder, kidnapping, rape and drug dealing. Both looked to be around forty years old; however, over twenty of those years were spent in Angola State Penitentiary. Tony had served twenty one years, and Mitch did a twenty three year stretch.

"What's your name white boy?" Mitch asked, stepping up to Gunther, nose touching nose."

"Gunther is my name," he said, not flinching at all.

"What's this shit Candy said about you watching? You gonna' watch while I fuck her too?" Tony asked, moving in on him from behind.

"Hey guys, settle the fuck down; Gunther is alright. He bought us plenty dope, and if he wants to sit and watch, that's just fine with me. Let's just get high alright?" Cookie said, pulling the two men back off Gunther.

Everyone moved on into the next room; which was the living room. The place was spotless; that was not typical for the average bachelor pad. Everyone took off their jackets and sweaters, and laid them across a straight chair next to the door; then the four of them sat down on the long couch behind the coffee table. Gunther remained standing for the time being. The coffee table was almost as long as the couch.

"You guys have a nice clean place here," Gunther said, taking a seat in the single chair across from the four of them, and facing the front of the table. There really wasn't enough room on the couch for five people to sit anyway.

"When you're doing time, you learn to keep your living space clean or you will go fuckin' stir crazy. I can't stand roaches, bugs or flies. If you keep a nasty ass place, you're gonna' get germs; I can't stand that shit," Tony replied.

"I can't either. I know bitches that have kids, and their place stinks like hell.

They got dirty dishes in the sink, and the bathroom looks like a pig sty. They have their kids running around with shit in their diapers all day long," Cookie said, pulling out the plastic bag that contained the dope.

"Our kitchen and bathroom stays fuckin' clean," Mitch said, getting up and going into one of the two bedrooms.

Tony got up also and went into the kitchen.

When they returned they had everything on the table that was needed to shoot dope. They had clean needles, rubber straps to go tightly around the arm. They also put on the table; spoons, water to heat the dope, and four cigarette lighters. They were all set.

Everyone silently got to work…

Candy was the first to tie off her arm, and stick the needle in. Cookie was next, and then came Mitch and Tony.

When Tony slowly pushed in the knob on his needle, he started shaking. Gunther got concerned.

"Is he going to be alright?" Gunther said, standing up.

"He's fine," Mitch said, pulling his own needle out after he got all the dope in.

"It's just that this dope is so fuckin' good. Good dope like this makes him shake like Jell-O," he said, closing his eyes and smiling.

Gunther sat back down to enjoy the show.

"Cookie, this motherfuckin' dope is off the chain," Candy slurred, her tongue hanging from the side her mouth.

"Come here, and give mama some ah' dat' white boy dick!" Cookie shouted, pulling up her skirt and opening up her legs.

"Get yo' ass over here, and service me motherfucker!" she shouted again. Her head was now twisting toward one shoulder, and then to the next shoulder like she was watching a tennis match.

Gunther just smiled, and made no move toward Cookie, who now had her fingers inside her pink panties.

Candy stood up on one leg. She brought up her other leg with her knee almost chest high; then she stretched her arms out to the sides, and curled her palms out like the Karate Kid. And she stayed that way for five minutes without falling down. Heroin can make a person do strange things with their body.

Mitch got up, and started staring at the ceiling. He stood that way for ten minutes.

Tony was still shaking. Cookie was still masturbating. Gunther was still just enjoying the show.

Forty minutes later when everyone was back in their original positions, Cookie said, "Gunther, if you're not gonna' fuck me, at least give me another hit; I can't do it myself; I'm too fuckin high."

Gunther being an extremely fast learner got up to get started. He had payed close attention to the process of shooting up dope earlier. Every step the four made was observed by him, and recorded in his machine like mind.

He first dipped the spoon into the bag of heroin, and scooped up about a third spoon full—which was more than needed—and placed it back on the table. Then he added a little bit of water to the power. After that he heated the bottom of the spoon until the substance came to a boil, and then he stirred it.

This does not turn clear like mixing cocaine powder; this will have a light brown color after heating and mixing.

He then balled up a small piece of cotton, and placed it in the mixture to absorb it. The only thing left to do is draw it up into the needle, which he did.

This was going to be a very potent shot. Cookie had drawn up 40cc on her first hit, this was going to be an 80, however; he correctly calculated that it would not cause her to over dose.

He tied off the left arm of Cookie; an arm that already looked like a train track. He tied it off about four inches above the elbow, and started looking for a good vein. After smacking the area several times with his four fingers, he found a good vein. He then stuck the needle in, and slowly pushed in…

When he got to 40cc, he stopped to check out her eyes. She was in another world; however, she was in no great danger. Her body seemed to turn into a bowl of slow, sweet, fluid molasses. She was as high as a Georgia Pine. *And that's high*

"Gunther baby, I love you," she slurred.

"I love you too Cookie Wookie," Gunther said, relieved that everything was going well.

"Gimme' da' rest of that shit hunny bunny," she pleaded.

"Here it comes Cookie Wookie," he replied, slowly pushing the knob down.

"Fuck ah' duck' fuck ah' duck fuck ah' duck fuck ah' duck…" was the only thing she was able to say, as she drifted off to planets unknown.

He pulled the needle back out and put pressure on the stick zone until the opening closed.

He liked Cookie. As he looked at her slowly moving her head from side to side, he was happy to see her finally getting the kind of high she had always dreamed about. In the streets she had to turn a trick in order to get twenty dollars to buy one hit. Then it was back to the street again.

She was smiling now; smiling at someone in her mind. Gunther thought that it might even be God that she was smiling at.

He sat back down and looked at the other three people. They all had their arms stuck out before him. They were ready for their second feeding. They reminded him of bird chicks in the nest; with their baby beaks opened wide, crying for a piece of worm. The mother bird comes in with a worm and separates the worm into smaller pieces. Then she puts one piece into each opened beak.

He looked at his three bird chicks. They all are aware that the forth chick has been feed; now they were all jockeying into position to be next. He is the mother bird, and the mother bird has a decision to make; which chick is to be feed next?

He decides that the only civil thing to do is move on down the line from left the left of Cookie, to right. That means that Mitch would be next. Candy would be after Mitch, and Tony would be after Candy.

Just like the bird chicks, Candy and tony would cry. They had beaks opened wide…

After giving everyone their second feeding, Gunther sat back down to relax.

He looked at his watch; it was now 5:15pm; he needed to get away from here at some point. He had to conduct a funeral tomorrow morning at 11:30am, and needed to wrap up a few details tonight before going to bed.

He walked over to the neatly arraigned bookshelf located at the other end of the room, and fingered through a few book titles. He was very impressed with the selections that were available to read: Steinbeck, Melville, Hemingway, Steven King, and Edger Allen Poe…

He picked out 'For whom the Bell Tolls' by Ernest Hemingway, and returned to his chair.

Jim Bruce was lying across the bed in his hotel room. It had been a long day, and it wasn't over yet. His team was scheduled to arrive at his suite at 6:30pm for one last briefing before calling it a day.

He wasn't getting anywhere with the case. He was starting to second guess his hunch that his killer was in New Orleans. On top of everything else, the United States Attorney General Mike Holmes was putting pressure on him to return to Washington. He told him that it was out of character to have a sitting director of the FBI not to be at his desk in the Hoover building. He went so far as to suggest that if he wanted to remain on the road like a lower grade federal agent, he was willing to reduce him back to that level.

He got up, and walked over to the mini-bar to get a scotch. Just as he was pouring to contents into his glass, the phone rang.

"Hey boss, what's cooking?"

It was Louis Walker, assistance director of the FBI, and one of his loyal confidantes.

"Same old thing Lou, what's up?"

"You remember the slaughter in that Tijuana bar where those eight whores met their end?"

"How can I forget? That shit was brutal," Jim replied turning up his glass to his lips.

"Well we finally got ah' break. One of the patrons of the bar agreed to give us a description of a man seen walking away from the scene. He got a real good look at him because the man had to walk down the stairs, and pass a lot of people before he got to the door."

"What led to him coming forward now, assuming that the patron was a man; was he?"

"Yes he was a man. As you well know it is very difficult to get any information out of people in Mexico for fear of their lives. These drug cartels and gangs are no joke. They not only cut off the heads of people that talk to police; they cut off the heads of their family members as well. So yes it was very difficult to get anyone to come forward; but our guys were relentless in their efforts. Plus a little money added to the equation helped out as well. Someone finally came forward with information;

however, he had hand stuck out first. He was paid one thousand American dollars for the description. I'm going to fax you a composite of what our witness gave to the sketch artist."

"Thanks Lou, I owe you one," Jim said, walking over to the fax machine in the living room.

Gunther was a ravenous reader. He was on page 122 before Candy brought him back to reality. He had always heard that Hemingway was a brilliant writer; now he found that out for himself.

He looked at his watch; it was now 7:46pm.

Candy was crying for more dope. She along with Mitch had urinated on themselves, and didn't give ah' rat's ass who knew it. Gunther came to the conclusion that both of them—as well as the others—had lost the ability to move about on their own.

"Gimme' ah shot Gunther dear," Candy pleaded.

He picked up the bag for inspection. The group had really put a huge dent in the contents. Over half the bag was now gone. At the rate they were going, they had at best two more shots each.

One chick crying in the nest caused the remaining three chicks to open their beaks. Now once again Gunther was looking at four babies crying to be fed.

He decided to feed the females first. This move was out of order according to the way they were seated. It really was to go from left to right in that order. However; he was the mother bird, and the mother bird had the authority to feed the chicks in any order it wanted to.

"Ladies first," he said reaching for the rubber to tie off candies arm. While he was mixing up the spoon, he looked up and there were eight wide opened eyeballs looking at him. Behind each set of eyeballs were four people that had turned into wild ravenous animals.

Candy was first to get fed, followed by Cookie, then Mitch, and bringing up the rear would be a very angry Tony.

After everyone had their third shot, he returned to his seat, and resumed reading where he left off.

When he got to page 200 he checked the time; which was 8:35pm. He looked at the group on the couch.

They were all in another world. Cookie was fucking an invisible man, and he evidently was giving it to her pretty good. Candy was staring at the ceiling with her tongue hanging out from her mouth. Mitch seemed to be acting out a scene in the 'Matrix'. Tony was talking to his dead grandmother.

Gunther folded the page where he left off, and headed to the back door. He put the book in the truck of the car, and picked up an ax. This was no ordinary ax. This ax looked like one of the ax's you saw in one of those 1940's movies. It looked like one of those axes that a French executioner would use before they came up with the Guillotine.

This ax had a short handle; maybe about three feet in length. The blade was long and wide. The razer sharped edge curved into a slight half-moon. The reason why this ax was so extremely sharpened, was because of the many nights when Gunther had nothing in particular to do, he would get this ax and a good honing stone, and slowly sharpen it for hours as he watched television.

Quietly he closed the trunk of the car, looked around and stepped back into house. When he got to the living room, he sat the ax on the floor. He then reached into his back pocket, and retrieved a pair of tight fitting leather gloves, and put them on. Then he went over to the table, and carefully picked it up, and moved it to the back of the room. He tip toed back to the ax, and picked it back up.

He now stood in front of Tony, who kept saying, *"Granny, I'm so sorry..."*

None of the four were aware that Gunther was standing in front of them with an ax so sharp that it could cut a mosquito in half in mid-flight. They were all unaware that they were spending the last few moments of their drug addicted lives.

Gunther got into a good solid stance; just like a baseball player getting ready to take a swing at a fastball.

The blade whistled through the air, and cut through Tony's neck like a hot knife through butter. The head easily flew off; landing on Candy's lap. Blood shot up as if it was lava shooting up from a volcano.

The flying head snapped Candy back into some sort of reality. She looked down at the head on her lap, and tried to scream; however, she could not. Then she looked up, and saw Gunther raising the ax. She put her arms across the front of her face in an x shape.

Gunther swung the ax down hard, and took off her arms; just above the elbow. The two arms fell at her feet. She held up her two stubs; this time she did let out a scream.

Mitch was still in Matrix mode. The blood that splattered on him and the scream from Candy did not pull him away from his slow moving motions with his arms. He looked like a person practicing the ancient Chinese martial art form called Ti Chi in slow motion.

He turned from Candy that had stopped screaming; and was now just staring at her two bloody stubs in disbelief.

He stood now directly in front of Mitch, and raised the ax high above his head. He came down hard with the ax, and split the man's head right down the middle. The head was separated evenly. The blade had made its way down to the neck area.

The blade was stuck into the top of the spine. He could not get it out. After tugging and pulling on the handle for about ten seconds, he put his foot into the man's chest to get more leverage. He pulled hard…

Finally the blade was freed.

Cookie was now looking at him. They looked into each other's eyes for almost a half a minute.

He then turned his attention back to Candy.

"I don't want my head cut off," Candy said, in almost a whisper.

"Well then, I'll just have to make sure you bleed out," he said, pointing at her thighs.

"What about here?" he asked, still pointing at her slim thighs.

She nodded her head up and down instead of saying the word, *yes.*

Gunther raised the ax, and came down hard about four inches above her right knee, and cut off her leg. The woman did not scream this time; she only made a grunting sound. He then raised the ax again, and cut off her left leg in just about the same spot as the right one.

This time she shouted, "Oh my God! Why? Why? You sick fuck!"

He bent down over at the waist to watch the life drain out of her. It took only five minutes for her to pass out; and seven more minutes for her to die. He then checked her pulse; just to make sure she was dead. Then he turned to Cookie.

He turned himself into a switch hitter, bringing the ax back to his left side, and getting into a batter's stance.

"Wait motherfucker!" Cookie shouted.

"Wait for what?" Gunther replied, still in his south paw batter's stance; looking for that good pitch.

"Just fuckin' wait that's all," she said in a much lower voice.

"I hope you're not gonna' try to block me with your arms like Candy did," he said drawing the blade back even further.

"No you freak, I ain't gonna' go out like no punk; I just want you to wait awhile, that's all," she said defiantly.

He swung the ax from left to right. Cookie's head flew off, and landed in Mitch's lap. The head landed perfectly upright with the front of her face facing Gunther. Her eyes were still open, and staring at him. He reached down, and closed them.

He looked at his watch. It was now 9:15pm.

"Almost past my bedtime," he said to himself in a low voice.

He wiped down everything that he might have touched before he put on the gloves. He was extremely patient with this task.

He took one more look at the gruesome spectacle he left on the couch, and then he slowly walked out the back door; wiping the door handle on both sides as he left. He put the bloody ax and gloves back in the truck.

On the way home he put on a Bill Wither's CD:

"…Grandma's hands, clapped in church on Sunday morning…"

When he pulled into the driveway, he didn't go straight into the house. He sat out in the car, and listened to the entire CD: *'Bill Withers Live'*.

It was 11:15pm Friday Jan 2. Jim Bruce was in bed, however, he could not sleep. He tried everything from sleeping pills to counting sheep; nothing worked. The meeting was over by 8:30, and he had been trying to get to sleep ever since.

At 11:52pm he gave up, and tossed the covers off. He reached over, and cut on the night lamp. Lying still in the bed, his thoughts went to the drawing sent to him by the number two FBI man Washington.

He got up, and walked toward the kitchen, cutting on lights as he slowly walked. He picked up the picture on the table, and sat down on the couch.

The drawing was that of a man that looked to be in his late thirties. He had short blond hair and blue eyes. The man was definatly easy on the eyes. He can see now why he was able to get up close and personal with so many women in California. He is the kind of man that you would let in your home or in your life. He would be successful as a salesman. If this guy was trying to sell you a vacuum cleaner or some insurance, you may not buy on the spot, however; you're not going to close the door in his face either.

Jim was slipping. He forgot to send the picture out to the area's law enforcement centers. When he got his copy; he seemed to be hypnotized by the killer's beauty. He had never seen a man this good looking. Looking at the picture caused him to go into a trance.

He made copies of the drawing for his team, and faxed a copy to all the law enforcement agencies in the city. He also included instructions on another sheet of paper that ordered them to keep this information in house. He did not want the media to find out anything about this investigation. It might not be the best thing to do at this point, however; he felt as though he had to play the cards that were dealt to him.

The only straw he had to grab was his belief that the killer had no knowledge that he was right on his heels. If the media found out that he was in the city, he would have a panic situation on his hands. The killer might even decide to leave.

What he needed now was more time. How was he going to get the Attorney General to go along with his hunch? What he was doing now was not sound police work. Hunches were not facts. His boss was not going to play this game much longer. He wasn't the kind of guy that likes to waste tax payer's money; and that's the feeling that the Attorney General was getting lately; his FBI director was wasting the people's money.

He needed a break, and he needed it fast. If he could just show his boss a little something…

He got the break he needed the next morning.

A man called the local police station to report a horrifying scene he had found inside one of his rental homes.

He always collected his rent on the last day of every month. His tenets on Dominican Street had always paid their rent on time; so it was very much out of character for the two brothers that rented this home to be a couple of days late.

Early this morning the landlord, named Norman Leflore, went to the home, and knocked on the front door. After about a minute of knocking, Leflore went around back, and knocked on the back door. Still no one answered after repeated knocking. He looked behind him, and saw that he brother's motorcycles were still parked under the wooden shed.

Suspecting that something was very wrong, he stuck his key into the key hole, opened the door, and looked inside...

When he saw what looked to be the bloody footprints leading out from the living room, he quickly closed the door, and called the police.

Gunther received the call from the local police around 9:45am. He was at the crime scene at 10:10am.

When he arrived, there were police and forensics experts all over the place. News people from several local newspapers were outside. Luckily there were no television cameras on the scene.

Jim quickly took over. He ordered everyone out of the house except the crime scene investigators. He looked over the bodies, and quickly walked back outside to face the media.

Just as he began to talk to the newspaper people, the local Television truck pulled up. A Female news reporter and a camera man jumped out, and ran up close to the house.

Jim waited until the woman and the camera man got close before he began his briefing.

Right before he started to speak, he hesitated. He held up his pointer finger to let the crowd know that they needed to wait a moment.

He then went over to Parish Chief of Police George Foster, and started a private conversation with him. Chief Foster was a slim dark skinned black man originally from Mobile Alabama; he came to New Orleans twenty years ago, and rose through the ranks from walking the beat to the position of top cop.

Although he had no college in his back ground, he was very smart; and like Jim, had a six sense when it came to picking up the scent of a suspect.

"Good morning," Chief Foster said to the crowd.

A few in the crowd returned his greeting.

"I'm Parish Police Chief George Foster. I am going to give you what I know at this time. This morning four bodies were found dead in this house behind me."

All at once his voice was drowned out by newspaper personnel asking a ton of questions at the same time. They all wanted to know the cause of the deaths.

The only one not screaming out questions was the woman from the television station.

"We cannot at this time determine the cause of the deaths. Further details will be provided to you after autopsies are completed on the bodies. This should take about two weeks' time. At this time I will be taking a few questions," he said, pointing to a newsman in the back.

"Can you determine a motive yet?"

"No we have not. Our investigation has just begun."

"Do you think it might be drug related?" another in the front asked.

"We don't know yet; although we did find drugs in the house."

"What kind of drugs were found?" the female television reporter asked.

"High grade heroin," the chief replied.

"Were the victims shot?" the same woman asked.

"We are not at liberty to release that information at this time; I assure you all that we will be getting to the bottom of this case; and will fill you in on any new developments as we move through the evidence stage. Thank you very much," he said, walking away from the podium, and going back inside where Jim was located.

Jim took George into one of the bedrooms, and gave him all the back ground information he had on the Scorpion Killer.

He changed his mind about speaking to the media because someone would want to know why was the director of the FBI at a crime scene in New Orleans. It wouldn't take long for the media to figure out that he was in the city tracking the Scorpion Killer.

Later on that evening Jim sat relaxing on the couch in his suite. It had been a long eventful day. He woke up with nothing to go on, and now things were looking promising.

After he left the crime scene, he called his boss in Washington. He had already faxed the gruesome pictures of the victims, as well as the details of murders: There was no sign of forced entry. Based on the bloody footprints, the killer was acquainted with the victims. There was no sign of robbery or theft; all the victim's person effects such as wallets, purses, handbags, jewelry and money were not touched. Also a fairly good amount of heroin was found on the coffee table; street value around seven hundred dollars' worth. It was hard to tell how much was in the bag when the group started getting wasted; autopsy report will give a more precise number. Finally, he told his boss that the manner of execution was that of a madman on a mission.

The attorney General was pleased with his report. He gave permission for him to personally stay on this case until he got his killer. He gave him his full support.

It was now 6:00pm. He got up, and turned on the television. The local news anchor was giving the viewer the latest on the murders.

"...Now on the scene in East New Orleans is our own WKSN reporter Kathy Norman. Kathy what's the latest?"

"Sam, from what we have gathered so far, it's a horrific scene inside this house here on Dominican Street in the Eastern section of New Orleans. At least four bodies were discovered by the land lord early this morning. It is not confirmed that the land lord actually looked at the bodies, however; it is confirmed that he discovered blood on the floor, and had a feeling that something was terribly wrong inside."

"We have not found out how the victims died, however; neighbors heard gun shots late into the night. We will keep you updated on the latest as we learn more from the investigation. This is Kathy Norman reporting, WKSN New Orleans; back to you Sam."

Kathy Norman has been a reporter in New Orleans for eleven years. Before that she spent twelve years at a station in her hometown of Houston Texas. However, the bulk of her career was spent at a local television station in Gainesville Florida. She spent sixteen years working the streets of Gainesville doing everything from driving the camera truck, to running the camera and finally doing the reporting.

She got her break into television after graduating from the University Of Florida School of Journalism in 1971. She was a real go getter in school. She was on a full ride academic scholarship, and she had no intension of letting down the scholarship's benefactors. Her school work and internship was her primary focus; and those two priorities took up most of her time; at least on weekdays.

When she finished her classes for the day, she would always hightail it over to the local station, and do whatever they had her to do. By the time she graduated, she was already a seasoned reporter. Naturally she started work at the local station fulltime.

As the years flew by, she dove into her work even harder. She never married, although she often dated. There was never anyone that came along to sweep her off her feet.

After ten years of reporting in the streets of Gainesville, she was ready to move up the ladder. Just like any other person working at a television station, she wanted to anchor the news. She sat her eyes on the weekend anchor desk. However, the station didn't even give her a chance at the job. The more she begged, the more they pushed her away.

When she came home to Houston, she was met with the same road block; she could get no further than street reporter.

Finally she got an offer from WKSN New Orleans came along. Her old dean of the journalism school at the University of Florida was station chief there. He told her that she would have to do street reporting for a least a year; then she could start doing weekend anchor work part-time. She was elated.

After hitting the streets for six months the station chief—who was up till then her best friend—died from a heart attack.

And that was that.

Now she was a sixty two year old street reporter in New Orleans.

The reason why such a talented and dedicated newswoman never got a chance at the anchor desk was simple. She was unattractive.

To put it plainly: She was ugly. She had a few birth defects on her face. Her left eyeball was closer to the bridge of her nose than the right one. The nose was unusually small and pointy, and her cheek bones stood out noticeably.

However, what God didn't give her in the face; he made up for it in the body. She had the kind of body—as the great James Brown had sung about—that could make a cripple man walk and a blind man see again. She was tall for a woman; six feet and one inch; and had long curvy legs that went on forever. She had hips like 'Betty Boop' and tits like Dolly Parton. She was Miss America with a paper bag over her head.

Even at the age of sixty two, she had the same body that she had when she was twenty two. She never had a problem finding a date; just as long as she promised to put out afterwards. In college, men—both students and professors—were constantly nagging her for sex. So she took the steak dinners, trips to Miami Beach on weekends, late night movie dates and drinks at the bar; all on the weekends. Her week days were filled with study and work at the television station.

What the men did not know was, she was getting what she wanted on both ends. She wanted sex just as bad as they wanted sex. As a matter of fact, she was a nymphomaniac. She loved getting fucked, however; she played on the man's need to feel like he was buying her services with their gifts. And some of the men did buy sex from her. They didn't beat around the bush with dinners or trips; they pulled out the cash for that ass.

Even now at sixty two, she was getting more dick than a woman forty years her junior.

All her life she had her pick of men, however; she had never received a marriage proposal. All she got out of her sexual encounters with men were satisfaction and a wet ass.

Every once in a while throughout the years there would be a certain man that she would like to go to bed with. After throwing herself his way, she would on occasions get the man she wanted because her body was so irresistible, however; most of the time her face would turn them off. She would be rejected. Thus, although she was getting more dick than the law allowed, she was getting it from men that were chasing her luscious ass; and not from men that she really wanted for love and affection. That in a nutshell was the sad and pathetic life of Kathy Norman.

Life can sometimes be cruel; however, we all must play the cards that are dealt to us; and play them to the best of our abilities.

Sunday morning found Gunther in church as usual. This time he was at the Our Lady of Consolation Catholic Church of New Orleans during Sunday Mass.

Father Eugene Mellow was teaching the flock about Job:

"...Job was indeed a righteous and God fearing man. God had blessed Job with many riches. He had farm animals by the thousands. He had gold

and silver. He had many daughters, sons and a beautiful wife. He was the most wealthiest and blessed man in all the land.

However, my brothers and sisters, you can be tested. You can be hit where it hurts. You can lose your life's savings. Your 401K can be taken away. Sometimes, in your journey through life, you are going to have to take a stand for God, and his word. You are going to be faced with the ultimate test. Job was tested, and he passed his test with flying colors."

"Satan challenged God one day. He told him that if he takes away all that Job has, even his good health, he would surly curse him. God took him up on that challenge. He took his hand away from Job. Then as he lay on the ground, suffering with sores and boils all over his body, and his children all dead, and his farm, gold and riches gone; his wife came to him and said, 'Why don't you curse God and die'. He looked up at her, and said, 'Get away from me foolish woman'. For his continued faithfulness to him under the harshest of circumstance, God restored everything back to Job, including his children. He even gave him more riches than he had before. My brothers and sisters, do you know when God is putting you through a test. Will you curse him when you don't get that promotion at work? Will you curse him when someone steals your car? Will you curse him when your child starts doing drugs? Or will you say these words: 'Dear Lord, I know that you will not put any Burdon on me that I cannot bear. Let us pray..."

On the way home he stopped by the Salvation Army men's homeless shelter, and wrote them a check for ten thousand dollars. The sermon had got to him. He was indeed blessed like Job. He was a very rich man. Ten thousand was nothing to him. He should have written the check out for a million; next time he will, he thought to himself as he made his way to Bourbon Street.

At the same time Jim Bruce was in the shower. He had slept late, and woke up only an hour ago. His team had left his room at 12:30am; they were jacked up with optimism. They were sure now that the killer was in the city; thus they recommitted themselves to his capture; dead or alive.

He put on jeans and t-shirt this morning. He decided to take his mind off the case for a while, and catch up on some reading. There were a few books he had on his bucket list to get read.

Just as he opened the dresser draw where his three novels were, there was a knock on the door.

When he opened the door, there stood Kathy Norman.

She looked gorgeous from the neck down. She had on white tight fitting slacks, a black blouse and a black leather coat that was unbuttoned. Her long black hair was rolled up in a bun, and she wore no makeup as usual. She had given up on trying to make her face presentable.

"Hello, I'm Kathy Norman from WKSN TV. May I come in?" she said, walking right in without waiting for an answer.

Jim followed the woman into the living room, slightly amused at the intrusion.

"Can I take your coat and beret?" he asked, while guiding her over to the couch.

"Thanks, she replied, taking off her coat and black French leather beret, and handing in over to him. She then sat down on the couch, and crossed her long legs.

"Would you like something to drink? Coffee maybe?" he asked, turning on the coffee maker.

"Negative on the coffee; but I will have a beer if you don't mind," she replied, kicking off her shoes, and making herself right at home.

He brought her a Bud Light from the refrigerator and a glass from the counter. He noticed that she had undone the top two buttons on her blouse; he could clearly see her tits.

"You don't mind if I get comfortable do you," she said, pouring the beer into her glass.

"No I don't mind," he answered, smiling.

"Aren't you going to have a beer with me?" she said, smiling.

"No, it's a little too early in the day for me," he replied, sitting down in a cushion chair directly in front of her.

"I saw you at the crime scene before you disappeared into the house," she said, looking him directly in the eyes.

"I saw you too on the six o'clock news that evening," he replied, lighting a cigarette.

"I'm sorry, I should have asked first. Do you mind if I smoke?"

His eyes were now all over the woman.

"This is your suite; you can do as you please. I have no rights in your domain," she replied, licking her lips.

"If you don't mind my asking, what is the purpose of your visit? And how did you find out where I'm staying?"

He sat back in the chair, and waited patiently for his answer.

Kathy reached into her handbag, and took out her own cigarettes, and lit one. She then took another sip of beer before answering his questions.

"I'm going to answer your second question first. I've lived in this city a number of years; I get around. My job as a television reporter gives me access to information that the public cannot. Getting the information about your current place of residence was child's play. As for the purpose of my visit to you, I'll get right to the point."

She took another drag of her cigarette, uncrossed her legs, and began…

"I'm here to inform you that I know that the Scorpion Killer is in New Orleans. How do I know? I know because you're here in New Orleans. I am a creature of detail; and I like to put details together."

"How much do you know?" he said, putting out his cigarette.

"I know that you have been chasing this killer for quite some time now. I know that you are the first FBI director to work full time in the field, and not behind a desk in Washington. You are 53 years old, married with two grown and very successful children. You are in excellent physical shape, and I know that you're going to fuck me," she said, now getting up and walking towards the bedroom.

Jim had never cheated on his wife; and he had no intension of starting now. "Hey what in the hell do you think you're doing!" he shouted, following her to the bedroom.

She started slowly taking off her clothes.

"This is the deal. Either you get naked, and climb into bed with me or I walk out the door, and head straight the television station. I'm sure my boss would love to get the biggest story in New Orleans history outside of Katrina.

That's the kind of news that might get me an anchors job; even with my plain Jane looking fucked up face," she said, neatly folding her clothes on the chair.

When she turned her naked body around to face Jim, his jaw dropped. He was looking at perfection.

"Yes, I am a freak of nature aren't I?" she asked, rubbing her full breasts.

Jim fell into her arms, and kissed her hard. He then started taking off his own clothes. They fell into the bed, and made love. He pounded her hard; and felt like a young man of nineteen.

At two thirty Jim called down to the kitchen for food. They ate lobster, salad, baked potato, and had peach cobbler for desert. They showered together, and watched 'Forest Gump' on HBO. And then they made love into the night.

At ten thirty, she showered again, and told him that she would see him again Tuesday night. She had to attend a staff meeting after work the next day.

"Those meetings often lasted well past midnight," she said, grinning."

Jim walked her to the door. They kissed like school kids, and giggled.

It was an very nice January afternoon in New Orleans. The temperature was a balmy seventy six degrees. It was an absolutely gorgeous day.

Gunther was on a date; with himself. He was lying on a blanket in one of the most beautiful places in the city: Armstrong Park.

The park was located at 835 North Rampart Street; just a few blocks from the French Quarter in the Congo District.

The park is dedicated to the memory of its native son, the great 'Louis Armstrong', who was one of the best trumpeters the world has ever known.

The park had plenty of bridges, ponds, flowers, trees and spacious grassy areas for people to picnic, and enjoy each other. There were areas of quiet and peaceful serenity and areas where one could take in the music from singers and bands performing free concerts. The park had something for everyone's taste.

Gunther had brought fried chicken and potato salad for his picnic.

He was enjoying himself in a quiet area away from the music.

He wanted to plan his suicide in peace and tranquility. He knew that his time on earth was coming to a close.

Now pouring into his glass some very fine dinner wine, he put his mind back to enjoying the last of his meal. He looked up and saw a group of children kicking around a soccer ball.

The ball bounced on to his blanket; it almost knocked over his bottle of wine. Picking up the ball; he decided that he wanted to play also. The next thing he knew, he was the goalie in a rather good game of soccer. The United States is the only developed country in the world that calls the game: soccer; the rest of the world calls it football. That is not the only thing America does, that tells the world: "We do things our way." Another go at it alone stance is this: Every other developed country in the world uses the metric system of measurement except America.

The harder he played the game with the kids, the more he thought about the country that they were living in. He thought about why God had made him into a killing machine. It seemed to him that God had placed him in America to give it a gentle slap on the wrist. Just a just a small love slap, that's all. His actions will not change the way this country does business; however, it will give it a little wake up call.

The way he sees it, God has never been pleased with America. First of all, Europeans came, and almost wiped out the entire Native American population. They brought with them disease that did the most damage. Then they rained down genocide on the population until laws were passed to put the remaining Indian population on reservations. After that they brought millions of Africans to the country to work as slaves in the cotton fields.

After the Civil War, things changed very little for the Africans; they were now free to live as dogs.

America is now turning into two Americas; a super-rich America and a super- poor America. The so called middle class is rapidly disappearing. This country that calls itself the land of the free and the home of the brave is now showing its true colors:

…the land of guns, the land of churches, the land of gangs, the land of greedy Politian's, the land of lobbyists, the land of the banks, the land of the homeless, the land of the jobless, the land of the super-rich, the land of the drug craze, the land of the teen mothers, the land of religion, the land of prisons…

"Thank you for allowing me to serve you, and to do your will. You have made me a Scorpion. I will strike as many deadly blows as I can before you give me the order to make one final strike; that strike will be made on my own body. And then I will come to you, and stand by your side in heaven forever," he said looking up to the sky as the soccer ball shot by him for a score.

Tuesday night Kathy knocked on Jim's door at 9:15pm. He rushed to the door like a world class sprinter. She had been on his mind ever since she walked out the door Sunday night. He never imagined that he would ever feel as he did about a woman other than his wife. He was indeed smitten with the love bug.

After just one night, he was head over heels in love with this woman; a woman that was sixty two years old, with an odd looking very unattractive face.

As for Kathy, she felt—for the first time in her life—that at last she had met the man of her dreams. She was already thinking of the day that he would leave his wife, and move in with her. Looking far ahead into the future, she envisioned that one day they would move to Brazil; buy a farm, and live out the rest of their lives in that beautiful country.

The only time she had been outside of the country was when she worked at the station in Florida. Carnival was going on in Rio. The reporter that was assigned to go and report for three of the days came down with the flu the day before leaving. Kathy, being single and willing to go on a moment's notice was selected to go.

Not only did she take in the carnival, sending back an outstanding feature; she took in the country side of Rio, as well as San Palo. She fell in love with the country and the people; however, she was disappointed with the conditions of the poor living in shacks in the hills. She tried to broadcast the plight of the poor back to her station back in the States; however, her feed was blocked by the station. The same thing happened when she tried to broadcast local farmers burning the rain forest to make room for more farm land; that feed was also blocked. The only reason she could come up with as to why her stories were blocked was because Brazil is scheduled to host the 2016 Olympic summer games.

Putting aside a few of the negative things she saw in Brazil, she still wanted to retire there. Now she had the perfect man to retire with.

He was not ashamed to be seen with her in public. He had made reservations for them to dine at Pete Fountain's on Bourbon Street for this Thursday night. Friday night they are going to take in a concert put on by Bradford Marcellus on the campus of Tulane University.

Everything was falling into place. All that was needed now was money. If she was to take her man to Brazil in the near future to retire in paradise, they needed money; and lots of it.

Monday night lying in bed talking, Jim told her that he was planning on retiring right after he captures or kills the Scorpion Killer.

That statement got Kathy thinking. His monthly retirement check will not nearly be enough for what she had in mind; plus a large chunk of that would have to go to his wife after the divorce.

Her retirement check, along with Social Security will only be enough for one person to retire in a nice senior community in Florida. That will never do. First of all, Florida is not Brazil; and second of all, her man would not feel comfortable with the remainder of his retirement check going toward expenses living in a senior citizen retirement community.

What she needed was money; real money, and plenty of it.

Early Wednesday morning around 1:00am, she got the break she was looking for. On the way out the door—after another night of love making—in Jim's suite, she noticed the drawing of Gunther sent to Jim by his second in command in Washington.

She asked, "Would you be a dear, and make a copy of this drawing for me?"

He replied, "What do you need it for?"

"Just in case I see him," she said, kissing him again.

"Please, do not show this to anyone; I am trusting you on this. I am not ready to reveal information to the public; they will panic, and the investigation will be in jeopardy. On top of that, the killer might skip town. I need him to stay put, until I can put a net around him," he said while walking over to the copy machine.

Kathy smiled as she pulled into her apartment parking lot. She cut off the engine, and sat motionless. Reflecting now, she looked back on her tragic life.

"Kathy Kathy…Open the door sweet heart," her father begged.

"You better open that door! Open the fuckin' door bitch!!" he shouted louder.

His wife was at the Southern Baptist Convention in Dallas. She had been gone for three days. She had four more days to been there. Her husband being an oil company executive in Houston, had put her up in the Hilton Hotel, and gave her five thousand dollars to spend. On top of that he put ten thousand dollars more in her checking account, just to make sure she had enough for shopping. He had carefully made all the arraigments to make sure that he would not be disturbed. He wanted a full week of uninterrupted sex with his only child Kathy.

"Haven't daddy been good to you sugar?" he said, trying to break the door down with his shoulder.

He had been coming to her room every night after the maid and butler left for the night. She was sore and wore out.

She looked down to the opening at the bottom of the door; three one hundred dollar bills slid in to her side of the door. She picked up the money; then slowly opened the door.

"That's my sweet sugar pie," he whispered, leading her to the bed.

She was eighteen years old, and never had been on a date. She had never been invited to a party. She had no friends. She had no one to kiss her or tell her that they love her; no one but her father. He was the only one that held her close in the night, and whisper sweet poems in her ear.

He secretly took her to Mexico to have her tubes tied when she turned thirteen. After that was done, and he didn't have to worry about her getting pregnant, he had sex with her every chance he got.

After her High School graduation, her father wanted her to attend Rice University so he could still get to her on the weekends; however, he was furious when she accepted a soccer scholarship at the University of Florida. Although she would later in life work in Houston; she never sat foot back into the house she grew up in; nor had she seen her family again.

She hated her father for what he put her through, and she hated her mother for looking the other way. Her mother had grown accustomed to a certain lifestyle—which was a high society lifestyle—and was not going to lose that lifestyle just because her husband was screwing their daughter. She was ashamed of her looks anyway. She never took her shopping with her. Her daughter's face was hideous to her. The only place where she accompanied her daughter to was church services.

Yes Kathy was dealt some brutal cards in life; however, she now had true love in her life. And with the Scorpion Killer drawing, she now had found a way to get filthy rich. Brazil was now clearly within reach.

After her parents died, she investigated the possibility of some money being left to her. Unfortunately, the family lawyer informed he that her father had left his entire fortune to charity. That was just another blow to her pitiful life.

She finally got out of her car, and walked up the five steps that led her into her Esplanade Street apartment. Opening the refrigerator now, she searched for milk. Holding back tears, she filled her glass with fresh milk.

If there was ever a time when a person cried for joy and sadness at the same time, this was the moment.

She climbed into bed thinking of Jim.

Gunther was not in bed. He was on the hunt. It was two thirty in the morning, and he was relentlessly looking for someone to kill. Now driving down Canal Street toward the river front, he spots a policeman walking the beat. He stops at the corner of Canal and Decatur to light a cigarette.

He parked one block ahead and started walking back towards Decatur after he put out the remainder of his cigarette. He was desperate just like a person on drugs. The closer he got to the officer, the deeper his breathing became.

The officer stop walking when he got to his squad car. He leaned against the door of the car, and watched Gunther slowly walking in his direction.

Gunther stop about ten yards from the cop and pulled out his half empty pack of smokes. He put one between his lips and felt around his pockets as if looking for his lighter.

"You got ah' light?" he asked the cop, moving in closer.

"Sure, here you go," the cop replied, holding the lighter up to the waiting cigarette Gunther had in his lips.

"Thanks," Gunther said, after taking in a good draw and looking around.

"You're most welcomed," the cop replied, looking Gunther over.

"Are you having a busy night?" Gunther asked, reaching into his right coat pocket where his pistol was. He grabbed the handle, and took another look around. Things were quiet. No other person was in sight.

"No it's been a rather quiet night," the cop said, lighting one of his own cigarettes.

"Hey, I think I know you. Aren't you Mr. Gunther Heisman, the funeral home man?" the cop asked, smiling and glad to be meeting one of the city's most important people.

"That's me," Gunther replied, getting ready to pull out the pistol.

"Man it's great to—hold on…"

The cop opened the squad car door and picked up his receiver.

"…roger that, I'm rolling!!" He then got all the way in the car and got behind the wheel, and pealed rubber. He cut on his siren, and raced down Canal Street like he was in a race car.

That policeman will never know how close he came to getting killed. It just was not his time to meet his maker.

Gunther walked back to his car, and drove towards home. On the way he pulled over to talk to three white bikers that were parked on the side walk at the corner of Canal and Basin.

"Any of you guys know how to get to North Roman Street?" he asked getting out of his car, and walking towards the men.

"No man, we rode up from Tampa; we don't know shit about New Orleans," one of the bikers said. They were laughing; it was obvious that they were on some sort of drug.

Gunther pulled out his pistol, and shot all three men in the head. Over the years he had become really fast with his shooting; and also very accurate. All three men had bullets in and through their brains in less than two seconds. Gunther had already turned around towards his car before the last man fell.

It was now 3:30am; and Gunther was finally in bed. He drifted off to sleep quickly. He went to bed satisfied. The Scorpion had struck again; and he got a triple to boot. Tomorrow morning at nine he had to meet with a new potential employee.

Jim woke up at 7:00am. He showered and called downstairs for breakfast. A meeting was planned for 8:30 with his team. Then he needed to meet with police Chief Foster at 10:00. At some point during the day he needed to call his wife. He had not talked to her in three days.

He was at a cross road in his life. He was married to a good and decent woman. She has done a wonderful job as a wife and mother. There was no way he could find another woman as faithful as she was.

However, Kathy has just brought something fresh and new to the table. He felt like a young man just finding love when he was around her. She gave him a new kind of energy in his love life.

He is going to have a big decision to make after he catches his killer.

Kathy took a vacation day off. She wanted to devote the entire day on the computer. She knew the identity of the killer. The drawing is not a dead ringer; however, she was certain that the drawing was that of one Gunther Heisman.

She knew Gunther quite well; having served with him on several boards over the years, including this year's Mardi Gras planning board. She also knew that besides being the number one funeral home director in the state, he was also a multi-millionaire. And that was the part that interests her the most, his money.

So she patiently and relentlessly went to work on her home computer. She already knew the history of the Scorpion Killer. She pulled up his name in all the locations where the killings took place on the West Coast, Mexico, Vegas, Montana, and the Dakotas. She didn't get that much information; however, DMV did show that he had a California driver's license during the time of the Scorpion's killing spree in that state. When a rash of unexplained killings started in New Orleans, he had a Louisiana driver's license.

As a top news reporter, she had access to Federal, state and local police and DMV files. She had more contacts than any other newsperson in the state. Her digging was done with precision and discretion. No alarms were set off. No one had Gunther on their radar except her.

She stopped working at 4:30. She started to call Jim; however she did not because she knew that he would be very busy investigating the murders of the bikers.

She hated that she could not tell him about Gunther; it was best that he did not know at this time. She knew that the result of her not telling him most likely would result in more murders; however, at this point, she didn't give a rat's ass how many more people he killed; he was her ticket to Brazil.

She went to her bed room, and flopped down on the bed. She needed a nap before going to Gunther's house.

After she could not fall off to sleep, she decided to take a chance in getting Gunther on the phone. She didn't know his private number, so she called the funeral home number.

"Heisman funeral home, may I help you?"

"Yes, could I speak with Mr. Heisman?"

"This is Gunther Heisman; may I help you?"

"I need to talk with you privately."

"Who am I speaking with?"

"I cannot tell you that; however I really need to talk with you in person. Is it possible for me to come to your home tomorrow evening? It is extremely important, and I'm sure it will be beneficial to you as well."

"This is very unusual; I don't like doing business this way."

"Please Mr. Heisman; I'm sure you will understand why I couldn't give you my name after you see me. I won't take up much of your time; I have some very important information for you. Please sir, will you see me?"

"Alright, I'll give you a few minutes tomorrow evening, say around six?"

"That will be perfect. Thank you so much; I'll see you tomorrow at six."

"Do you know where I live?"

"Yes I do."

"Alright then; I'll see you at six."

They both hung up; and Kathy took a deep breath.

"It's now or never," she said, lying back down to try and catch a few winks. Back at police headquarters, Jim Bruce and Parish black Police Chief George Foster was engaged in a heated discussion. The senseless biker murders had sent law enforcement over the edge. The mayor had just jumped into Foster's uniform. He was threatening him with his job if he didn't come up with anything before the start of Mari Gras, which would kick off February 16th. That only gave him a little over a month. He like Jim was planning on retiring this summer.

They were in the Chief's office. Both men had already given out their assignments to their staff. They were now alone; and George was pissed.

"Jim I don't wanna' hear that shit! My fuckin' job is on the line here; I could lose my pension!!" he shouted, wiping sweat from his bald head with a towel.

"George listen to me, we can't release this picture to the public right now; it would put the case in jeopardy. We got him right where we want him; right here in New Orleans. If we spook him, and he runs, it could take years before he's caught."

"Look Jim, the mayor has crawled up my ass, and in my ass he's set up camp; I know him, he's fuckin' serious; and I know if I don't deliver on time, my ass will be kicked to the motherfuckin' curb. I want that crazy son of ah' bitch that's going around killing up people in my city dead! I want his ass lying on a slab in the morgue. Do you feel me?" the chief said, looking Jim directly in the eyes.

"I want him too George. You're not the only one feeling the heat. I've got an Attorney General in Washington that is threatening to kick me down five pay grades."

"Well at least you won't be kicked down to the fuckin' unemployment line," George said, getting up and walking to the coffee machine. He brought two cups of hot coffee back to his desk, and handed Jim one.

"George, listen to me. We are going to catch or kill this freak in a week; maybe two at the most, I can feel it," Jim said, taking a sip of his coffee.

"Feel this, I don't fuckin' believe you. This eye witness drawing of the killer is a gold mine, and you don't want to use it. This is my town, my investigation and my black ass that's on the line. The drawing will be released, and that's final," he said, reaching for the phone.

Jim grabbed his hand.

"Who are you trying to call," Jim asked, still pressing down on George's hand.

"Oh shit, I know you ain't grabbing my hand, and asking me who I'm gonna' call in my own fuckin' office. Who the fuck do you think you are asshole? You are in my office, and I'll call anybody that I feel like calling. You better check yourself; this ain't Washington, and you ain't my boss; so pull your dick beater back before you lose it!"

After he pulled his hand back, Jim settled back down in his seat. He already knew who George wanted to call; the Mayor.

"George…Alright, then call the Mayor if you want; but please grant me just a few seconds more. I just want to explain one other thing to you first," Jim said, looking up to the ceiling.

"Go ahead Jim, give me some more bullshit; then I'm going to cover my ass. The Mayor will be delighted to know that we have a drawing of the so- called Scorpion Killer. Maybe then he'll crawl halfway out of my ass," George said, sitting back in his chair, and folding his arms across his chest.

"Look George, you've got the right and the responsibility to take this to the Mayor; however, I truly think you will be making a mistake. There are hundreds of men in the city with blond hair and blue eyes. Do you want those men harassed and possibly harmed by vigilantly mobs? Of course you don't; you've got enough problems to deal with already. Give me a chance here George. I know this is your town, your investigation and your ass that's on the line. We are going to catch this guy. Just give me some time here; do it as a friend. I know I've only met you for a short period of time; but in that short time I've come to think of you as a friend. That's why I trusted you enough to show you the drawing," he said, settling back to hear the verdict. He had given all he had.

"Friend my ass! I only got two friends in this whole wide world that I can depend on; both of their names start with the letter P. One friend is named Paycheck and the other friend is named Pension; and I truly love both of them, and hold them both close to my heart. If you cause me to lose either of my friends, I'm going to personally shoot you in your motherfuckin' head; do you feel me?" George said, slapping both hands on the desk.

"I feel you man," Jim replied, feeling better about the situation.

"To keep me from shooting you, I'm giving your federal ass just one week. After that, I'm fully taking over. Then you can take your team and your equipment and get the hell out of my town. Do we have a deal?" he said, standing up and extending his hand.

"Yes we do have a deal," Jim Said, shaking the man's hand.

Kathy met up with her camera man at the scene of a gang related shooting in Jackson square. Two gang members were dead, and five were wounded in the shooting. She then went a house fire in the Ninth Ward that had burned during the night. Firemen worked through the night putting out the blaze so that other homes would not be damaged. By 9:00am the smoke had settled; nothing remained of the house except the ashes. The house had been abandoned, as well as most of the homes in that area in the aftermath of Katrina.

"…information that has come forward so far indicates that that the fire may have been set by homeless people trying to keep warm in the night. There is no way to know for sure until fire investigators get on the scene…"

She went to a staff meeting at 2:00pm, and then went to do a feature on Mardi Gras preparations in one of the large warehouses that parade workers used to store the floats, and work on costumes.

By 5:00pm she was in the shower getting ready for her meeting with Gunther.

While showering, she thought of Jim, and the night he had planned for them. She had lived in New Orleans for eleven years, and never had the chance to visit one of the many trendy places to dine. She had never been asked out on a date to a concert or just to relax and have dinner at a restaurant. Now she would get to do both; dinner and music at Pete Fountain's and a concert by Bradford Marcellus at the University of New Orleans. She was giddy with anticipation. She finally felt like a real woman. Jim was the right man for her; although she wished that she could have met him forty years ago.

"Better late than never," she said to herself, getting out of the shower.

She decided to take a cab so no one would see her car in the driveway. Also she dressed as if she was in her ninety's: Brown scarf to cover her jet black hair, dark sunglasses to cover her brown eyes, a long overcoat to cover her shapely body, low healed grannie shoes, and carried a large shoulder bag that old woman like to carry. She also walked with a cane to pull off the ultimate old lady look.

She had the cab driver to drive past Gunther's home; in was only 5:50; she didn't want to arrive too early. At 5:55 she had the driver to drop her off one block from the house. As she slowly walked towards Gunther house on her cane, she started thinking about the love making she would have with Jim when they return from dinner. Her plan was to really put it on him. This was the night she was going to ask him to leave his wife. She knew that the best time to make a man say *"oh yes yes yes…"* was right before he climaxed. And she truly believed Jim to be a man of his word.

At exactly 6:00pm she rang the doorbell. Gunther opened the door, and stepped on to the porch to take a look around. There were no people walking about and no car in front or in the driveway.

"Come on in," he said, stepping back in the hallway, and extending an inviting hand to his quest.

Kathy followed him into the living room, still walking on the cane. When they reached the living room she asked, "Are we alone?"

"Yes we are, my staff has gone for the day," he replied.

She took off her coat, scarf and sun glasses, and handed them to him.

"My my, aren't you a shapely one," Gunther said, gazing at her bombshell of a body.

"Thank you very much, it compliments my hideous face," she said, smiling. Her cocked eye and her good eye were locked in on Gunther's handsome face.

"Oh I would not say all that; you have a nice face; you should try a little make up that's all," he said taking her things to the closet.

"No thanks, I gave up make up a long time ago. I hear you can work wonders with a face; do you think you can do something with mine? Without me being dead of course?" she said, looking at him smiling; however, at the same time wondering if he could really do it.

"Anything is possible," he said, returning back to her, and looking at her face intensely.

"Have a seat my dear," he said still locked in on her protruding cheek bones and her cocked eyeball.

"Yes, I believe I could do it, although it has to be our little secret; you see I'm not a licensed plastic surgeon; however, I have the knowledge to reconstruct your face, and make you beautiful."

"Even my eye?" she asked.

"Yes my dear, even your eye," he replied.

She was so taken with his response that she almost forgot why she came to see him. She needed to get back to business. It was nice to know that her face could be completely reconstructed; however, this man was not going to do it; not after she tells him the reason behind her visit. She also figured that if he could do it, and not be a real plastic surgeon, then a real top notch plastic surgeon could surly do the job.

Why haven't I considered this before? Is my face so hideous that I didn't think it could be done? Was my reluctance due to the fact that this was going to be a very complicated surgery? This is no simple plastic surgery job. This involves removal of facial bones. This involves repositioning of the eye and tendons. I still have my skepticism.

No surgeon can make me beautiful. I just do not believe it.

I was just dealt some bad cards at birth, and there was nothing to do but play the cards I had. That's why I never considered surgery; because I knew it could never be done. If there was a chance that my face could be fixed, my parents had the money to have it done. They most likely looked into it, and were told that there was no hope for me.

That's why when my father first got me alone, he whispered into my ear as he pulled down my panties: "No one else wants you. I'm the only man you'll ever have. I'm the only man that will love you. I'm the only one that will be seen in public with you. You must accept this fact my dear. My good sweetie pie."

Thinking about her years of sexual abuse from her father had her in a trance. She just sat there on the couch like a mannequin in a store window. She was not aware that Gunther was trying to get her attention. She was back in Houston…

"Can I get you something to drink Kathy?" he said walking over to the bar.

Finally she snapped back into reality. She looked at him and smiled.

"So you know who I am?" she said, rubbing her bad eye.

"Yes I do; I enjoy your reporting. You are a true professional."

"Thanks, I'll have a vodka and orange juice if you don't mind."

"Coming right up; I think I'll have a little something myself," he said, setting out the glasses.

"You have a very lovely home," she said, looking around.

"Thank you my dear," he replied, mixing the drinks.

He walked back to the couch and handed her a drink, then set two napkins on the coffee table. He sat across from her in the single chair that matched the couch.

They drank in silence for a few moments, until Gunther broke the ice: "Well my dear, what brings you to my humble abode?"

She looked at him with a bit of reluctance. She didn't know if she had the heart to do this. She had never stole, robbed or extorted money or property from another person in her life. Because of her disfigured face, she always worked harder than anyone else. The journalist awards that she had received over the years were well earned. She did not receive them as a result of pity.

The higher ups realized that she was a rare find; a person that would go to any lengths to get a good story.

This situation was totally new to her; however, it was also totally necessary. She had been fucked over all her life. Men had fooled her to come to parties; when she got there, she was the only woman there. She could have left; they weren't going to rape her. Instead she stayed and let them take turns screwing her. It gave her just a little power over the men.

She could make them give her things…She could make them beg…

Now she was in another position of power. She needed to stay focused, and not show any weakness. *It's now or never time.*

She pulled out her copy of the drawing that was faxed to Jim, and handed it to Gunther.

"That looks a little bit like me," he said, studying the drawing at different angles. He held it close to his face, and then held it up towards the ceiling.

"It is you, and you are the Scorpion Killer," she said, drinking the last of her Vodka, and setting the glass on the table.

"Is that right?" he asked, returning the drawing back to her.

"I am one hundred percent certain of it. You are number one on America's Most Wanted List," she said, folding her arms across her huge firm breasts.

"Do you have any proof?"

"Plenty," she replied, pulling out her data that was gathered on her day off. She handed him the folder and said, "Do you mind if I fix myself another drink while you look over the files?"

"Go right ahead my dear; you should find everything you need behind the bar. The juice is in the cooler," he said, with his eyes still fixed on the paperwork.

As he silently read through the files, she slowly sipped her drink, and thought once again about Jim.

At the same moment Jim was wrapping up another day of surveillance around the French Quarter. He was looking for any man with blond hair that seemed out of place or acting strangely. At this point, it was all he could do. He planned to get with George tomorrow, and come up with another strategy. What he was thinking about doing may not be constitutional. He wanted to start questioning every man they see with blond hair. They wouldn't bring the men into the station—that may be grounds for a law suit—only talk to them on the street; if they are willing to answer a few questions. If any were not willing, they could go on their way. All it would amount to was a fishing expedition. Maybe someone will volunteer some crucial information; maybe someone will flip out and make a run for it. Many cases in the past have been broken just like that. Suspects get nervous, suspect runs. He would run it past George tomorrow.

Right then it was 6:45. He was walking through the door of his hotel suite. Kathy would be picking him up at 8:30 for dinner. He needed to put the Scorpion Killer out of his mind for the night, and keep his mind on Kathy.

Gunther read the entire folder. When he finished, he handed it back to Kathy, and said, "Good job."

"Thanks," she replied, looking relieved.

"Where do we go from here?" Gunther asked, leaning back in his chair.

"I want ten million dollars; that's where we go from here," she replied, looking into his eyes.

"That's a whole lot of money my dear. Just what do I get in return for such a large sum?" he asked, now bringing his fingers together under his chin.

"First of all, you get silence from me. If you ever get caught, it won't be because of me. I really could care less how many people you have killed or how many more you're going to kill. All I want is the money."

"What is to keep me from killing you right now, instead of paying you to keep quiet?" he asked.

"Good question. In my place of work, there is a very trusting friend of mine that has a copy of the files that you have just read. If I do not show up for work in the morning, she has been instructed to give those files to the police," she said, smiling.

"I see that you have covered all the bases. You are indeed a rare breed. It looks to me that my hands are tied."

"You could say that."

"How would you like payment?"

"A check will do fine. If I have any problems at the bank, I can always call you."

"That's right; as a matter of fact, I'll put my cell number on the check just in case you need to get in touch with me, and I'm out of the office. If you have any problems, I'll come right over. Most likely you will have some sort of delay; it's not every day that the bank receives a personal check in such a large amount. Excuse me, I'll be right back."

After he left the room to get his checkbook, she glanced at her watch; it was 7:15. She envisioned Jim in the shower. He had a wonderful body; hairy at the chest and very muscular. She liked grabbing his hips when he was inside her. His hips felt as hard as his penis.

Gunther returned, and sat down to writing out the check. When he finished, he handed it to her.

"Satisfied?" he asked.

"Yes, thank you very much. I never dreamed that I would ever possess this much money. Thank you again, and sorry that I had to get it in this manner," she said, almost crying with joy and sadness at the same time. This was the first time she had ever done something criminal; however, she knew it had to be done.

"That's alright my dear; a woman has to do what a woman has to do; it's your time to shine," he said, smiling and clapping his hands.

"Well, it's been nice doing business with you; however, I do have a dinner date tonight. I've got to get going," she said standing up.

"Now that the business has been taken care of, what about us having one more drink for the road? Then I'll call you a cab. You did arrive by cab didn't you?" he asked, still smiling.

"Yes I came by cab. I didn't want anyone to see my car in the driveway. And yes, one more drink won't hurt," she replied sitting back down.

"That was ingenious of you dressing up as an old woman; you were really detailed and convincing. You need to work here with me," he said, bringing the drinks back to the table.

"Thanks for the offer; however, working with you killing people is not my cup of tea," she said, now laughing.

"No I mean working here at the funeral home part time. I bet you could really bring in the business. I like smart people like you. Maybe I could learn something," he said, turning up his drink to his lips.

"Like I said before, no thanks; I plan on moving to Brazil with Jim," she said taking a few sips of her drink.

"Are you speaking of Jim the FBI man?" he asked, setting his glass on the table.

"Yes, that's the one," she replied, turning up the last of her drink.

"How did you know it was Jim, that I am going out with tonight?"

"Lucky guess…"

"I knew he was in the city. Somehow I just put two and two together," he said grinning.

"When are you planning on leaving?" he asked.

"Just as soon as we both retire, and that should be in about six or seven months; however, Jim has a real hard on about catching you. He plans to leave the FBI right after killing or capturing you. However, I have a gut feeling that you will never be caught," she said, laughing again.

"Well, you caught me didn't you?" he said, getting up to get her things from the closet.

"Since we're just talking here, I need to ask you something. Why do you kill people anyway?" she asked, starting to feel a little drowsy.

He put her things on the couch beside her, and sat back down. "I thought you had to leave?" he asked.

"I do have to leave; however, I want to know why you kill people. It shouldn't take that long; just please answer that one question so I can get gone."

After mixing her another drink, he sat down to give her the full story.

"Well it all started in my childhood; back in Plains Iowa…"

Jim was looking at himself in the mirror. He had on a two piece gray Brooks Brother's suit, with a black shirt and gray necktie. His black string laced shoes were Stacy Adams. He looked good, and he knew it. It was now 8:15pm.

Kathy was finally trying to come around after passing out for over two hours. The combination of the drug Gunther put in her last drink and the large overall amount of alcohol consumed by her, lead to a longer unconscious period than he was used to seeing in his female victims.

"Well well, sleeping beauty has finally awakened," Gunther said, walking towards her. He was wearing only his undershorts.

"You cockeyed whore; wake your ugly ass up!!" he shouted.

She looked around horrified. Her arms and legs were bound to a wooden chair. The chair reminded her of the electric chair.

She had once secured a press pass to observe an execution at Angola. It was horrible. Surly, she thought, this wasn't a real electric chair, was it? Was she now going to be electrocuted?

She was too devastated to know that she was naked.

"What the fuck?" she finally uttered, struggling at the straps.

"You're up shit's creek without a paddle my dear," Gunther said, sliding a chair in front of her, and sitting down.

"Please undo the straps and let me go. I promise, I won't say a word to no one about this," she said, still struggling.

"Oh, I know you won't say a word to anyone; because you're gonna' be fuckin' dead," replied Gunther, slapping her face.

"Remember what I told you about my friend at work? The police will know all about you if I don't show up for work. Let me go, and when I get to work, I'll get the files from her, and burn them; I promise," she pleaded.

"I knew as soon as you told me that story that you were bluffing, and I'm a hard man to bluff. I knew that there was no way in hell for you to trust something that explosive to a co-worker; no matter how close you were. Am I right?" he asked, smiling.

"I did give it to her, I swear I did!" she shouted.

"You're lying to me. Do you know how I know that you're lying?"

Kathy said nothing; she just looked at him in amazement. How did he know? She wondered the question to herself...

"It's because I'm a master at reading faces. That skill comes in handy when playing poker. Have you ever played poker my dear?"

"Please, I want to go home..."

"Have you ever played poker?"

"I'm so sorry that I tried to extort money from you. I'm way out of my league here. I've never done anything like that in my life. Please let me go home!" she pleaded again.

"The question before you is this; have you ever played poker?"

She looked at him hard. His behavior was not like a real person; he now looked and sounded more like a machine. She decided to get focused, and try to accommodate him. His question seemed off base considering her situation; however, she reluctantly answered him.

"Once or twice, I'm not sure," she replied, and starting to cry.

"In my lifetime of playing poker, I've lost a lot more money than I've won; mainly because I love playing the game so much that I hardly ever cash out with my winnings. I mostly play cash games when I go to Vegas; I've never played in a tournament. Anyway, during the games that I play in, I sometimes build up my stack of chips by calling people that try to bluff pots from me. As you should already know, bluffing is when you have a shitty hand, and you dump a bunch of money in the pot to try to take it. You want to scare whoever is in the pot to make them tuck their tail between their legs and fold their hands. Do you understand everything so far?"

Kathy wanted to scream. How in the hell could she wind up in this situation? She thought she had everything worked out. It wasn't supposed to be like this. She was supposed to be with Jim right about now.

Still sobbing, she said, "Yes, I understand."

"Fine, now we get to the good part of the story. You do like stories don't you? I mean, you put together stories all the time in your line of work; don't you?"

"I want to go home!! Please let me go!!" she screamed.

"Now now, be a good girl, and answer the question," he said, slapping her breasts repeatedly with his right hand. The two jugs bounced from side to side…

"Alright, alright, I like fuckin' stories!!" she shouted, lowering her head in pain and frustration.

"Hey, I got an idea. Fuck my poker story. If you like telling stories so much; what about telling me a story!!" Gunther shouted. He seemed excited at the prospect of listening to a good story. His mother used to tell him great bedtime stories.

"Please let me go. I'll do anything you want. I'll even come to work for you. Please let me go!" she pleaded, looking into his cold blue eyes for any sign of compassion.

"I want a fuckin' story bitch!!" he screamed, hitting her hard in the eye with his closed fist. The hit did not phase her one bit. She was now in another world.

"I can even help you kill people. I could be very useful to you. You need someone like me to be sort of an advance scout. Have you ever thought about killing hundreds of people at one time? With my press pass I could get into stadiums and arenas early, and show you the best spot to plant explosives. Hell, I'll even plant them for you, if you teach me how. I bet you already know everything about bomb making don't you? I'm sure a man of your vision has thought about bombing a whole fuckin' arena or taking down the Sears Tower in Chicago. What about the Capital building in Washington when both houses of Congress are in session? I have the credentials to get into any building in America, no problem. How does that sound? I know I can help you if you only give me a chance."

Kathy was speed talking. When Gunther hit her in her right eye, she did not even yell out. She was too busy wanting to quickly get her point across to him.

Again he hit her in the same eye with his closed fist. This time she did yell out. Her eye puffed out this time; and the color of it changed from ghostly white to sort of dark purple.

"Tell me a story bitch, and it had better be a good one," he commanded her.

"I am so sorry that I lied to you. Please forgive me," she begged.

"You are forgiven," he said, leaning back in his chair.

"Thank you sir, you are a kind and forgiving man. If you let me go, I will be forever grateful, and eternally in your debt," she said, crying again. Ever the optimist, she felt a slight ray of hope. If she kept agreeing with him, he might just set her free. She had no choice but to think positively.

Again he turned his full attention to her swollen eye, and hit the same eye with his closed fist. This time she screamed.

Gunther then picked up a pair of scissors that he had brought down with him. He then snipped at her nipples; trying to snip them off. She stopped screaming while twisting her upper body; which caused her two huge boobs to sway from the scissors. Every time her boobs swayed, he snipped at her nipples.

He could have grabbed hold of one of the boobs, and easily cut off a nipple if he wanted to. However, he enjoyed this game of *snip the moving nipple...*

After a while he threw the scissors to the floor, and stood up. He then closed his fist, and hit her flush in the mouth. She did not cry out. She just spit out her two front teeth, and groaned.

"Tell me a story," he said once more.

She spit out a little more blood, and said, "Otheh, I think thyou vill like thisth thory," she said try to make a smile with what was left of her face. Her lips were now grotesque, and swollen like two small balloons. One of her eyes was shut tight and had turned jet black. Still she tried to smile for him.

Gunther sat down on the floor, crossed his legs Indian style, and waited on the story just like a first grader would wait on a teacher to start *story time.*

"Dith thory ith one oth my fathorish thorishh..." she said, trying to use a tongue and a set of lips that were not cooperating with her. Her missing front teeth make her words start and end with a hissing sound.

The name of her story was called The Jungle Family. The story is set in the rain forest of Brazil. Gunther closed his eyes to get the full effect of the story.

She started off telling Gunther about the beauty of the rain forest. She talked of the strange animals and insects that live there. Some of the animals, insects and birds has never been discovered and cataloged, she told him.

There are numerus villages throughout the rain forest. There was one village that had a family of eight people. It consisted of a Father, a mother, three boys and three girls. One of the girls had a deformed face. She had a flat pig's nose, pointy ears like a goblin or a fairy and full beard like a man.

Because she was ten years old, and the youngest of the sisters; she was adored by her family and villagers. The villagers even came to her bringing gifts to please her with. They prayed to her for good luck and successful hunting. Before any couple got married; they came to her for her blessing.

This girl who her parents named Rain was already an expert hunter and fisherman. Those tasks were usually reserved for man and boys. However, her knowledge of those tasks was welcomed by her family and villagers. She often shared her prey with other villagers as if they were part of her immediate family.

One morning while quietly walking into the forest about three miles from her village; she came upon her favorite food: Spider Monkey. The monkey was about thirty feet up a tree eating fruit when the girl laid eyes it.

She slowly pulled an arrow from her pouch that she carried on her back. She then place the arrow in position, with the arrow on the bow, and slowly pulled back the string. She then released the arrow. It quickly traveled into the quiet air and struck the money in the arm. They arrow went all the way through, and stuck into the tree.

The monkey fell to the ground.

The girl grabbed the monkey by the neck, and opened a sack that she always carried to put prey into. Just before she attempted to put the monkey in the sack; it began to speak.

It begged the girl to not put it in the sack.

Little Rain had never heard any animal speak. She could hardly believe what she was now hearing.

The monkey told her if she would release it, it would make her beautiful by using its magic. Rain asked it if this was only a trick to gain its freedom. She told the monkey that as soon as she releases it, it would run up a tree again, and leave her crying. The monkey assured her that this was no trick. It told her that it had the power of magic, just like it had the power to speak like a human.

Rain thought about it a moment, then released the monkey. After all, she thought, there were plenty of monkeys in the forest, and she was going to shoot plenty of them with her trusty bow and arrow.

When the monkey was released, it ran about ten yards, and stopped. It then turned around and stood up. It then waved in front of its face, and told the girl to run to the river, and look at her reflection. She ran through the woods like a deer. When she reached the river, she dropped to her knees at the edge of the bank, and looked down at her reflection.

She cried out with joy!!

She was indeed beautiful. As a matter of fact she was the most beautiful girl in the village. She now knew that she would marry one day when she got older.

The young men in the village would battle each other for the honor of being her husband.

However when she returned to the village, her family did not know her. The entire village gathered around her to shout obscenities at her. They thought that she was a demon, because no human can be that beautiful. Her family asked her what she had done to their Rain. Her mother begged her to give her daughter back to her. Rain cried out to them that she was Rain.

The men in the village chased her out of the village. They shouted for her to never come back.

For the next six years, she wandered in the forest looking for the talking monkey. She wanted her deformed face back so she could return to her family. After the six years, she came to the conclusion that she would never find the talking monkey again. She found a deadly snake called the Black Mumba, and picked it up. Before the Mumba gave her the death bite; she cried out that she wished that she was never born.

"That was a great story!!" Gunther shouted out to Kathy.

"When did you learn the story?" he asked, while getting up from his Indian style sitting position on the floor.

"I thid noth learn ith. I madeth ith upfh asth I wenth athlong with theth ith" she replied, again trying to smile.

"You are a gifted story teller. There are not many people in the world that could make up a great story, and make it up as they go along with it."

"Ffthank you thirrth," she replied, calling him sir, and trying again to smile.

"Hey Kathy, guess who's portrait I had hanging on this wall. I only took it down a few weeks ago. I'll give you a hint; he almost took over the world," he asked, now walking around in goose step. "Alexander the Great?" she whimpered.

"No silly, Alexander the Great did take over the fuckin' world; now think, who did I have on the wall?"

"…I don't know; Jesus Christ maybe," she said, starting to cry again.

"Fuck no!! You are one dumb ugly bitch; do you know that?"

"Yes I know," she replied, now crying loudly.

"I had Adolf Hitler on the wall you cunt," he said running over to her, and hitting her square in the jaw with his closed fist. He knocked out two more teeth toward the right side of her mouth. She spit the teeth out before she screamed.

"Do you know he came to me again when you were unconscious? I told him before not to bother me again; however, there he was looking me in my face once again. What do you think of that happy horse shit?" he asked, now walking around faster in goose step circles.

Kathy was never much to look at; however, now she looked like something out of a horror movie. Her mouth was bloody, and her lips had swollen up like two balloons, and now her right jaw was puffed out.

She stopped screaming. Instead she was now just crying.

"He still has this thing about Jews. Now he wants me to blow up the Jewish school over in Dallas. They built a new school there; first grade through twelfth grade. He found out that I have studied all kinds of explosives. I am now an expert if I say so myself. I learned it all on the Internet. The things you can learn on the Internet will amaze you. I now know how the build a nuclear bomb. I thought only nuclear physicists knew how. All it takes is patients and focus; anybody could learn it; even your ugly ass," he said, punching her in her good eye.

Her good eye was now fully swollen. Now she looked like a monster.

"I told that motherfucker that I was not going to blow up a dammed thing. Blowing shit up is for cowards and dickheads; I only learned it just in case I really needed to use it for emergencies. The Jews don't bother know body. I can't understand why people want to fuck with them. I can't think of any group that's worth blowing up, can you?" he asked, seriously looking for an answer.

Kathy shook her battered head slowly to the left and then to the right to indicate that she agreed with him that no group is worth blowing up.

"When I kill people, it's kind of personal. I like to look at a person before I kill them. If I set off a bunch of bombs using a remote control—in which I am very capable of doing—I lose that sense of closeness; you know what I mean?" he asked, clinching his fist as if he is going to strike again.

Kathy quickly nodded her head up and down to indicate that she knew what he means.

He unclenched his fist and headed for the door. When he opened the door, he turned around to look at her for a few seconds before heading out, and shutting the door behind him.

It was now 1:15am Friday morning, and Jim was just getting into bed after a frantic search for Kathy. Although normally the wait is 24 hours before a person is declared missing, all hands were on deck after Kathy failed to show up at Jim's suite. He waited around until 8:30pm before trying to call her; he got no answer. Then he went to her apartment; although her car was in her space, she didn't answer the door. Jim had the feeling that something went terribly wrong, and he also felt like his killer was right in the middle of it.

Kathy lived in a large house that was divided into four apartments. He knocked on the door of the other three apartments. No one had seen her coming or going. He found the apartment manager who agreed to open the door for him. She was not there.

He then called Chief Foster, and his entire team. The chief put out a missing person's bulletin on the recommendation of Jim. He, after hearing Jim's account of their plans for the night, and the fact that he had given her a copy of the killer's drawing, agreed that most likely the Scorpion Killer had her. They could only hope and pray that they find her before it is too late; however, based on the killer's motive of operation, finding her alive would be a miracle.

After talking with the chief on the phone, he decided to stay in the neighborhood for a while and knock on some more doors. He went across the street, and got a huge break when he knocked on the door of the home directly across the street from Kathy's apartment. An old man that looked to be about ninety years old told him that he stepped on his porch to feed his cat around five or five thirty that evening. He said he looked out and saw an old lady walking with a cane coming out the right side door of the large house across the street. The right side door was the door that leads to Kathy's apartment. She said when the woman walked to the parking area, she open Kathy's car door and got in. The old woman waited until a taxi cab showed up before getting out of the car, and locking the door. Then the old man told her that the woman slowly got in the cab, and away they went.

Jim had something to go on now. It was obvious that Kathy had decided to dress up as an old woman. Why? He didn't know.

From that moment up until about 12:30am, he and his team along with the taxi cab dispatchers, were attempting to check the logs of every taxi driver in New Orleans to see which driver picked up an old woman at Kathy's apartment around five or five thirty. So far they had no luck. Everyone needed rest. They would start back early in the morning. More than half of the cab companies had already shut down for the night anyway.

At the very moment Jim was crawling into bed, Kathy was quietly sobbing, and still trying to understand how she could get herself in this kind of deep shit. All she had to do was to play the cards that were dealt to her; that should not have been hard to do; she had been doing that her entire life. She finally had a man that loved her; no matter that he was already married. She had a pretty good job, with retirement right around the corner; however, that wasn't good enough for her; she got greedy, and wanted Brazil too. She reached for the stars, and pulled back straws. She now recalled something Professor Mike Rogers once told her: *"Always remember these words Kathy: A bird in hand is much better than two in the bush."*

Professor Rogers was her English instructor in college. He was a black man who was 71 years of age, and had no intension of retiring until he turns 80. They became friends. He was like another father to her; a real father, not the molester she escaped from back home.

He tried to teach her about life, and the ups and downs that will occur on this journey called life. He told her to grab hold of any foot hole in her journey, and hold on tight; until she could grab another foot hole.

*"Make sure your first step is on solid foundation before lifting your other foot
for than second step."*

Now all she could do was sit in this chair pray for freedom. She felt
like she had a slight chance; after all, he had been gone for over thirty
minutes. It was just like she had always heard: *"The longer the jury takes
in the jury room, the better the chance for the defendant."*

All of a sudden the door burst open. Gunther quickly stepped in
wearing full raingear including rubber boots and rain hat. The rain hat
made him look like a Lobster Fisherman' with the front rim turned up,
and the back turned down. He also had on a pair of swimming goggles;
the kind that people wear when they're snorkeling.

In his hands was a chain saw.

"Oh God no," Kathy said in a low tone of voice.

Gunther adjusted the choke, and pulled on the starter rope. The
engine roared into life. *Vvvrrrvuuummm…*

He pushed the chock back in place, and revved up the motor for a few
seconds: *Vvvrrruuummm Vvvrrruuummm Vvvrrruuummm Vvvvrrruuummm*

Smoke shot out the exhaust, and filled almost half the room. He
held it up, and continued giving it gas.

Kathy's good eye was wide opened in terror…

He then walked over to her and placed the spinning teeth of the
brand new chainsaw to her left thigh. The sharp teeth quickly torn into
her flesh…

As the teeth made its way through tendons, veins, flesh and muscle;
Gunther's rain gear was getting splattered with blood and tissue. His
goggles were so covered with the substance that he was hardly able to see.

Kathy's swollen lips were opened wide; however, her screamed were
drowned out by the noise from the motor.

The spinning teeth moved in quickly into the bone. That's where
Gunther should have slowed down because the teeth were taking too
big of a bite too quickly; the teeth got jammed into the bone; and the
spinning stopped.

Because the noise from the motor had stopped, the only thing in
the room making any sounds came from a screaming Kathy. She sounded
like some sort of wild jungle animal; maybe a new and undiscovered
breed of tree dwelling animal, found only in the rainforest of Brazil. The

screams were very high pitched; she might have been a great soprano opera singer if she had gotten the training at a young age. She certainly had the lungs and the voice. Even her swollen eye was trying to once again open. If they were not in a soundproof room, her voice would have made its way to the street.

Gunther struggled with the saw trying to free the teeth from the bone. It was stuck in tight. He twisted, pulled, jerked and pulled again. Nothing seemed to work. Finally he stood back and kicked the motor. The entire saw brock free, taking with it a jagged piece of bone.

Although he had used the chainsaw to cutup the fat man into manageable pieces for the cremation oven; Gunther was still a long way from being an expert chainsaw user. Back home in Plains he had observed his father using one during the winter months. This type of saw came in handy for cutting firewood. He would often ask his father for permission to use it himself; however, his request was always turned down.

So like many things he learned in his adult life, he learned by trial and error. Now he knew that the best way to cut through hard objects with a chain saw was to take it slow and easy. Cutting wood or bone fast will often lead to getting the teeth jammed.

He walked over to the right and picked up the saw; careful not to slip on the slime and blood that had built up on the floor.

"Please Gunther, no more..." the woman screamed over and over.

He ignored her pleas; pulling the rope and starting the motor again.

"Vvvrrruuummm vvvrrruuummm vvvrrruuummm..."

He went back to work on the same bone that had given him so much trouble before. This time he took it slow and easy. The teeth went through like a hot knife going through butter. He worked his way through the bone as well as the flesh on the other side rather quickly.

He pushed the leg to the side. The foot was still bound by straps that were tight around her ankles; so the leg just fell to the side; however, it was completely separated from the body; and that's all that counts to him.

He cut the motor off; and walked over to the sink, where he took off his goggles, and gave it a good washing.

Kathy had stopped screaming. She was only moaning, and looking at her left leg leaning to the side. It would have fallen to the floor if not for the ankle straps.

After he cleaned the slime off his goggles, he returned to Kathy, and cut off her right leg, as well as both of her arms. As he did with her legs, he pushed both arms to the side; however they didn't go too far; the hands were also bound by straps. The elbow of both arms just pointed to opposite directions away from the body.

Kathy took a good long look at her current condition, and screamed one more time. This scream was not because of pain; this scream was because of frustration and disbelief. She knew that she was going to die. She was never going to see Jim again or live in Brazil. She thought to herself, *"This is real fucked up; what a way to leave this life. I don't deserve this shit."*

Gunther took off his raingear; being careful not to get his bare feet on the blood and pieces of flesh on the floor. He threw all the gear on the floor next to Kathy; including the boots and goggles.

He then sat down Indian style on the dried part of the floor close to the door. His back was to the wall, so that he could watch the last few minutes of Kathy's life slip away.

It took her about ten minutes to die. She exhaled one last long breath between her grotesque looking lips, and dropped her head.

Gunther sat still for another ten minutes before he got up and left the room.

The next day around 7:00pm Jim found his cab driver. After checking his log he lead police and FBI agents to Gunther's home; a home that was also his funeral home business.

The cleaning lady let them in; she didn't have the faintest idea as to what was going on. Jim showed her a court order giving them permission to search the house. Around 9:30pm they broke down the door to the killing room.

The police and agents were not prepared for the smell in the room or the horrific condition of Kathy's body. The bad smell did not come from decay; the woman was not dead long enough for that. The smell came from blood, tissue, and shit. She had let loose a gusher from her bowels after the first leg was being cut off.

Every one quickly left the room; they needed to get the proper breathing equipment to continue. They also needed to call in a medical examiner, forensic experts and crime scene investigators.

On the way back out the door, with a handkerchief covering his mouth, Jim picked an envelope that was left in a dry spot in the corner next to the door.

He read what was written on the outside of the envelope: *For FBI Director Jim Bruce.*

He went upstairs, and set down on the couch. He then pulled the letter out from the inside of the envelope, and began reading:

> *My name is Gunther Heisman. I am the man that you are looking for. I want to tell you that I deeply admire your determination and perseverance in seeking my capture.*
>
> *You have followed my trail for years throughout the West Coast and the Midwest. You have remained focused on your task.*
>
> *I am informing you now that you can now return to Washington. I will never again kill another human being. I will not go into detail about what lead to my decision; all I can say at this time is that my words are sincere and true.*
>
> *I know that you are hurting right now about the death of Kathy. Try to move past the hurt and anger; know that God—in his infinite wisdom—has a plan for all of us. God knows what's best for us.*
>
> *I am sorry that I never got the chance to meet you in person; maybe—if God is willing—we'll meet each other in the next life.*
>
> *Goodbye Jim Bruce and I pray that God will continue to watch over you and your family.*
>
> *Sincerely, Gunther Heisman*
>
> *PS: I hate that name the media tagged me with. However, I am sorry now that I killed that girl that came up with the name, The Scorpion killer. Three days later I was still mad at the girl. I wished that I could bring her back to life so that I could kill her all over*

again. However, I knew that bringing her back to life was impossible; so I killed her entire family: The father, mother, and two brothers, age fourteen and fifteen. I also kill her little sister that was twelve.

Her grandparents on the mother's side of the family were at the home also; trying to comfort the family on the death of the daughter that first came up with the name.

It killed them too.

I was a nasty human being. However, I am now fully on God's side. I asked him to forgive me. And he did. I asked him to watch over all of my victim's families and bless them in a mighty way. I know he will.

From that time on, things got back to normal; whatever normal means. Since Gunther's disappearance five years ago, there have been mass school shootings in public schools; mass shootings in San Bernardino; as well as mass shootings at Virginia Tech University. There has also been a shooting at a private Jewish school, a movie theater and on a military base. There also has been a mass shooting at a Christian place of worship recently. However, none of the above murders have been linked to any serial killer behavior.

Jim Bruce has retired from the FBI. He and his wife sold their property in South Carolina, and moved to Tampa Florida. They are now renting a nice condo in a quiet community overlooking the Bay. In his spare time when he is not fishing, he has starting writing a book on his years of chasing a ghost called the Scorpion Killer.

Gunther got a non-paying job at an all-male Christian run mission in Calcutta India. He lives in a small house on the grounds of the mission with four Benedictine monks. They wash and feed the boys every day, and give them schooling, as well as teaching them about the Lord. It is a challenging affair trying to teach children about the Christian way in a country that is mostly Hindu. Sometimes the mission's dormitory is vandalized, and the boys are threatened by outsiders. Some are even kidnaped, and held for ransom in an attempt to extort money from the mission. However, for the most part the mission remains a safe place for the boys to grow and learn about the ways of the Christians.

Gunther tends a garden at the mission, and he is praised for his knowledge about growing vegetables. He also supervises the growing of a much larger garden that feeds the entire mission. Also the mission has chickens, lambs and cows for milking. The boys at this mission are not vegetarians. They were mostly left on their own long before the Hindu practice of not eating meat took root. Now they enjoy their meals of chicken, lamb, and vegetables; however, the staff does not feed them meat from the cows; since cows are considered sacred throughout India. If outsiders get word that the staff was killing and eating cows; no more mission.

The mission has no Internet, phones, television or electricity for that matter. All cooking is done on wood stoves.

Gunther gave the mission a small donation when he arrived. They were able to build an extension to the mission as well as buy much needed supplies.

The donation was a very large one by mission standards; however, it was merely pocket change for Gunther.

Before he left New Orleans a day after his last murder; he stopped by his lawyer's office; there he made some financial stipulations: He sent his family back in Iowa five million dollars and the male orphanage in India three million dollars.

He also gave the female Christian orphanage in Varanasi three million dollars. He gave the rest totaling three hundred sixty million to the Red Cross. He kept nothing for himself.

The female orphanage in Varanasi sits very close to the massive Ganges River. It is run by a handful of female Baptist ministers. The male orphanage sits very close to the much smaller Hooghly River.

At last he had found his *Solution*. In order to come up with a solution, you first needed a problem. On his last day in America, he realized that he was the problem all the time. The solution—he envisioned—was to totally get right with God.

Sitting down in the washroom one afternoon reading the New York Times, he began to weep. The Times subscription was one of the few small pleasures that he allowed himself to have. The Times, along with the Smithsonian, and the National Geographic kept his mind sharp. He left enough money in the bank to get these Subscriptions for the next thirty years.

However, the reason for his weeping was because of the following: He read in the Times that a lone wolf white supremacist walked into Mother Emanuel AME Church in Charleston South Carolina, and set down on one of the benches. He was welcomed in by the friendly worshipers as they engaged in bible study.

After a few minutes of quietly sitting and observing the group, he got up, and shot all nine of the members to death. Among the dead was the Pastor of the church.

Gunther walked out of the washroom still crying. He did not want any of the children to see him crying; so he walked a few hundred yards down to the river, and sat down on the bank.

He wiped his eyes with a handkerchief, and stretched out on the grass, locking his fingers behind his head, and relaxed. He watched the slow moving river, and begun to pray for the families of the victims in the Charleston shootings.

After about an hour, he started to get up after remembering that he had more of the children's clothes to wash. However, he stopped before he got to his feet. What he saw on the river caused him to sit back down in shock.

Adolf Hitler was walking on the water, and he was walking straight towards him. He also looked to be very angry at him.

What did I do this time?

THE END

www.ingramcontent.com/pod-product-compliance
Lightning Source LLC
Chambersburg PA
CBHW051146120626
46547CB00012B/964

* 9 7 8 1 9 6 5 3 9 0 3 1 3 *